REVOLUTIONS IN MODERN
ENGLISH DRAMA

Katharine J. Worth

REVOLUTIONS IN MODERN ENGLISH DRAMA

LONDON
G. Bell & Sons

FOR MY MOTHER

For kindly granting permission to include extracts from their plays in this book, the author wishes to thank the following playwrights, their agents and publishers: John Arden: *Armstrong's Last Good Night*, and *Serjeant Musgrave's Dance* (Methuen & Co. Ltd); Edward Bond: *The Pope's Wedding, Early Morning* and *Lear*; Samuel French Ltd: John Van Druten's *After All*; The Society of Authors as the Literary Representative of the Estate of James Joyce: *Exiles*; The Literary Executor of W. Somerset Maugham and Wm. Heinemann Ltd: *Sheppey*; David Mercer: *Flint* (Methuen & Co. Ltd); Joe Orton: *Funeral Games* and *What the Butler Saw*; John Osborne and Margery Vosper Ltd: *West of Suez* and *Inadmissible Evidence*; Alun Owen: *Progress to the Park*; Harold Pinter: *The Home Coming, The Collection* and *Old Times* (Methuen & Co. Ltd); Alan Plater: *Close the Coalhouse Door* (Methuen & Co. Ltd); David Storey and Jonathan Cape Ltd: *The Contractor*; Arnold Wesker & Jonathan Cape Ltd: *Roots, Chicken Soup with Barley* and *I'm Talking about Jerusalem*; Charles Wood: *Dingo* and *H* (Methuen & Co. Ltd).

First published in 1973 by G. Bell & Sons, Ltd.,
York House, 6 Portugal Street, London W.C.2.

ISBN 0 7135 1666 6

Printed in Great Britain by
The Aberdeen University Press, Aberdeen

Contents

List of Illustrations

Introduction

The English theatre in 1972 looks as though it might be about to move out of the orbit of realism which has held it throughout the century and into another for which there is as yet no name. Doubts arise of course in the moment of making a statement like this. People have been saying something of the kind ever since realism came in; since 1945 they have been saying it with increasing confidence, about Fry, about Eliot, about Osborne and Pinter and Arden. One of the main arguments of this book is indeed that the newness of postwar and especially of post-1956 playwrights has been overstressed, that much of this drama does not make a violent break with the realist tradition, as words like 'revolution' which have been used of it often suggest, but that it is, rather, a late – and possibly last – flowering of that tradition. The revolutions of my title are the Yeatsian kind, the turns of the wheel that bring up the past continually in new forms.

To be advancing such an argument is certainly a reason for caution in making the kind of prediction I began with. But the prediction is related to the argument; in observing the tenacity of a tradition, the way it can survive in all sorts of unlikely variations, one is bound to be struck by those forms which can't easily be taken as variations and wonder whether they are not a radically different growth out of which a counter tradition is forming. Some recent plays, those of Edward Bond and Heathcote Williams for instance, separate themselves in that way: in looking at them I shall be tracing a different line from the line of Pinter, Osborne and Wesker, though whether it will prove to be the line of the future only the future can tell.

What I understand by the term 'realism' will best explain itself, I hope, through my discussion of particular playwrights. I should perhaps make it clear at the start, however, that I am using it in its widest possible sense, to take in at one end the meticulously 'accurate' slice of life play and at the other the play which only just keeps within the bounds of ordinary social probability and indeed gets its special effect from striking a precarious balance between probability and fantasy, public and private experience, the worlds of daylight and dream. The illusion of actuality is an especially fragile, evanescent thing. The bounds of what is socially probable are always changing and what seems natural to one generation may seem anything but that to another, as the changing reactions to Noel Coward over the last fifty years rather amusingly illustrate: his plays struck many of his first critics as quite offensively realistic; then they came to seem the last word in mannered artifice; now again, they are starting to show their natural side, at least to an admirer such as Albee who praises the dialogue as 'very, very lifelike'.

The instability of the illusion allows a good deal of scope to play-wrights involved with it: experiment can go a remarkably long way without wrecking the necessary impression of social credibility. Even a play like Eliot's *The Family Reunion*, in spite of its verse, its chorus, its apparitions, aims at a surface impression of social actuality, and a great deal of the most interesting experiment of the twenties and thirties was conducted, as Eliot's increasingly was, with the idea of realism in mind.

Taken in this wide sense, realism has been an immensely fruitful force in the English theatre. I want to trace some of the typical forms that have come out of it in the post-1918 theatre, and the efforts that have been made to extend its limits by writers as different as Eliot and Priestley in the interwar period and along many different lines by present-day playwrights, most dazzlingly by Pinter. In discussing Pinter I shall have in mind particularly his relation to earlier writers like Noel Coward and to the English Chekhovian movement; his extension of the subtext by filmic techniques is of special interest here.

The connection between dramatic form and staging methods – especially as it strikes the playwrights themselves – is part of my subject. Attitudes towards the physical layout of the theatre can be very revealing – Pinter's preference for the proscenium stage, for instance, his love of curtains and privacy, or Osborne's divided sympathies, or Arden's feeling for an open stage. The movement away from the proscenium that has been going on steadily during the last decade has been by and large a movement away from realism towards the more aggressively theatrical drama which is now be-ginning to look like the nucleus of the next tradition.

The lines divide rather as Peter Brook saw them doing in 1964 when he embarked on his first full-scale experiment in Theatre of Cruelty techniques: his programme set out two lists of contrasting words – plot, character, message against collage, revelation, happening, and so on. One might add to his second list – music, dance, farce, looking out to the audience: above all, flexibility, an easy movement from one style to another: these are important features of today's experimental drama.

For some of the pioneers of the new, freewheeling, very physical theatre that is coming in, the proscenium stage is the symbol of a literal, Freudian tradition they find terribly oppressive. Like Alwin Nikolais, who inveighs against 'the asbestos drop confining the passion of the theatre to the nineteenth century' they see the last hundred years as a weight that has to be shaken off before the theatre can be freely creative.

And yet one of the most striking aspects of today's experimental drama is its fascination with the nineteenth century, with Victorian subjects and settings and especially with the techniques of the Victorian popular theatre: music hall, farce, pantomime and melodrama; not the later 'literary' melodrama but the true musical kind in which instrumental music and singing as well as extravagant spectacular effects were vital dramatic elements. This 'Victorianism' as it is found in writers like Arden, Charles Wood, Edward Bond, is something I want to pay special attention to in discussing their work.

It seems to me the new drama separates rather naturally into two main kinds: a warm, outward-looking 'people's theatre' of epic and melodrama, and a cool, inward-looking one of black farce and Grand Guignol, a 'mystery' theatre. They touch at many points though, and both have connections with the most radical anti-realistic drama of the interwar period, the drama of O'Casey and Auden and Isherwood. This I want to look at, for its own sake, and because it is such important pioneering work. O'Casey's late plays, in particular, anticipate some of the most fruitful developments in today's theatre.

Those early experiments were terribly hampered by the inflexibility of theatre building and the theatre system in the twenties and thirties. Today's playwrights are more fortunate. There is a great – and growing – variety of theatre buildings and a willingness to mix styles and experiment that goes right through the system from the big subsidized companies to the club/fringe theatres which have proliferated and thrust down some sturdy roots in the last decade.

At the centre of experiment now as in 1956 is the Royal Court Theatre, whose sedately conventional appearance so belies the revolutionary nature of its contribution to English drama. The Court does sometimes look back; it is loyal to its playwrights and puts on revivals of their earlier work from time to time (as it has done recently for Arden's *Live Like Pigs*). But it is essentially the most forward-looking of theatres, continually launching new experiments and helping to establish new playwrights. The most compelling original of our younger playwrights, Edward Bond, gravitated naturally to the Court – 'There was some relevance here that was lacking in other theatres' – and indeed feels that no other English theatre would have produced his plays. The Court gives hospitality to travelling groups like The People Show which have moved right outside the traditional theatre context, and in its small supplementary studio, Theatre Upstairs, produces plays in styles still more revolutionary than Bond's; one of these, Heathcote Williams' *AC/DC* I want to take as an illustration of the *avant garde* drama at its most bizarre and disturbing.

The postwar policy[1] of Government subsidies for theatres like the Court as well as the big national companies has been a crucial aid and stimulus to more adventurous approaches. Both the big companies, The National Theatre and the Royal Shakespeare Company, although sometimes criticized for not being adventurous enough, have made influential contributions to the evolution of a more flexible drama. There is always an experimental element in their repertoires, unexpected combinations – Brecht cheek-by-jowl with Noel Coward at the Old Vic, *A Midsummer Night's Dream* with *Old Times* at the Aldwych – and occasional productions (chiefly at the National) of audaciously experimental new plays: Charles Wood's '*H*' was one such. They too have their small subsidiary theatres – the Young Vic, the Place – where young companies perform to predominantly youthful audiences and flexibility is very much the keynote: Beckett and Genet as well as Molière in free adaptation take easily to the stage of the Young Vic with its stimulating openness and friendly closeness to its audience.

Openness and flexibility are qualities that have been increasingly sought in English theatre buildings since a stir was made in the early postwar years by the thrust stage at Chichester and the all-in-one

---

[1] For an incisive account of this policy and of the general economic and political situation in the English theatre from 1945–62, see W. A. Armstrong's 'The Playwright and his Theatre' in *Experimental Drama*, ed Armstrong, 1963.

auditorium at the Mermaid. It is becoming the norm for new theatres to have thrust or open stages and to incorporate a small studio where experiment can be free (to the point of financial failure, if need be). So it is, for instance, at the Crucible, Sheffield and will be at the National Theatre now being constructed on London's South Bank. Along with this architectural openness there often goes the idea of social openness, the idea of a theatre as a friendly place, catering in various ways (with restaurants, film shows and so on) for the community round about as well as for audiences. The Mermaid has been a very attractive model here. Appropriately it has been one of the few English theatres to offer a stage to the experimental later plays of O'Casey: there seems an interesting relationship there between style of theatre and style of play.

The doyen of this relaxed, friendly community drama is Joan Littlewood. It was ironic that when the Stratford Theatre Royal reopened recently, it stood out, as Frank Marcus put it, 'like a Martello tower on a deserted beach'[1] in a neighbourhood flattened for redevelopment. One can only hope that this is not an ill omen, that the theatre will eventually be part of the community's life in something like the way Joan Littlewood dreams of and that her inspiration will flow again into the English theatre at large.

Her often expressed wish to make drama a collaborative process involving the audience very directly seems to have already seeded itself. New spatial relationships between actors and audiences and new kinds of audience involvement are being sought in many different types of theatre, from Arnold Wesker's huge Round House, where recently the Théâtre du Soleil production of *1789* was set out in fairground booths before a mobile audience, to the small lunchtime theatres that are springing up all over London. Here audience and actors are very much in one room together (often the back room of a pub): the aim is to let the performance grow naturally in a casual context of eating and drinking. John Arden's short play, *Squire Jonathan*, was produced in that way and some of the younger playwrights, John Grillo, for instance, have become specialists in this new type of interlude drama.

A great variety of approaches is found in the club/fringe theatres which range from 'established' subsidized companies such as Charles Marowitz's at the Open Space Theatre to completely mobile groups

---

[1] In his review of *The Londoners* (musical version of *Sparrers Can't Sing*), the Theatre Workshop retrospective with which the Theatre Royal opened. *Sunday Telegraph*, 2 April 1972.

like The People Show, The Freehold, The Portable Theatre.[1] The phenomenal growth of these small experimental theatre groups in the last few years is one more demonstration of the new flexibility in theatres and the theatre system out of which a remarkably flexible drama is emerging.

The intense theatricality of this drama creates problems for the critic and I have been very conscious of these in writing of some recent plays. It is true that all drama needs to be envisaged in stage terms before it can be properly appreciated and that realism presents problems of its own in this respect: my discussion of Joyce's *Exiles* really turns on this point. But with total theatre techniques the problem becomes a very acute one and it does seem that criticism is going to need new apparatus – video tapes built into texts, perhaps – if it is to function usefully in the conditions we seem to be moving into. Fortunately there are signs that the problem is being recognized. More recordings of productions and rehearsals are being made on film and tape, both commercially and by academic bodies such as University Audio Visual Centres. The British Universities Film Council has now embarked on a much needed programme of cataloguing and co-ordinating some of these activities.

I think I hardly need to say that I haven't been attempting to draw a detailed map of the drama of the period. So much will be apparent from the omission of names – Christopher Fry, John Whiting, Howard Brenton (of the younger generation) are among them – which would certainly have to be included in any study that aimed at comprehensiveness. Neither have I set out to give a complete account of any one playwright, though I have tried to indicate the range and diversity of any writer I have discussed at length.

My aim has been to bring out significant contours in the theatrical landscape of the post-1918 period; to trace lines of continuity and development and lines of striking change. I have shaded in where the scene strikes me as especially interesting, sometimes round authors (Pinter, Osborne, Eliot, Bond), sometimes round a particular production (Pinter's production of Joyce's *Exiles*, the Royal Shakespeare Company's production of *The Silver Tassie*).

Of course maps of this kind are bound to be fluid and tentative,

[1] Useful accounts of club/fringe theatres now functioning are given in *Gambit* vol 4, no 16 and *Theatre Quarterly* 1, 1971. Both accounts stress the importance of improvisation to most of these groups. The People Show, for instance, have discarded the idea of rehearsing 'since the thing ceases to exist without an audience. The most vital material of The People Show's work is the audience'.

especially in relation to the most recent drama. There are large tracts in the earlier period too where little critical exploring has been done; one becomes aware of the need for some solid filling-in round the playwrights of the twenties and thirties – Noel Coward and Somerset Maugham, for instance – and for more light on general topics such as the relationship between the novel and the drama at that time.

I hope this study may prompt further exploration along some of the lines I have been following. And I hope that I have been able to render some of the essential quality of the scene and of the deep changes that seem to be coming about in it.

Forms of Realism: Playwrights of the interwar period

Realism was a 'strong' form in the interwar period in the sense of having an enormous attractive power, 'weak' in the sense that its range was so narrow and so many of the plays in the mode had a tentative, muffled quality: interesting potentialities that haven't been quite realized can often be discerned.

To take first the attractive power. Some of the most convincing testimony to this comes from the playwrights who resented and tried to ignore or defy the pull of the realistic convention but found themselves yielding to it all the same. Somerset Maugham was one of these. In his preface to the collected edition of his plays he complained bitterly about the bad effect realism was having on the theatre of his time, especially, as he saw it, on the more vigorous forms of comedy. Farce had practically disappeared – critics could no longer enjoy horse-play – and everything was judged by the criterion of 'cocktail bar' probability. He was also irked by the prevailing restrictions on dialogue, the fashion, as he puts it, for the 'baldness of contemporary speech'. He wanted freedom to use a more mannered and fluent speech, or even just the speech of 'people who express themselves in an educated manner' and actually risked this – it was felt to be a risk – in one of his plays, *The Sacred Flame*. The result was disaster: the play was criticized (Maugham partly agreed) as too literary, and in his later works he 'reverted to the naturalistic dialogue that seems to comply with the requirements of the present day'.[1]

---

[1] Somerset Maugham, Preface to *Collected Plays*, 1931, vol 5.

Not to comply with these 'requirements' often meant that a play-wright didn't get played. The most vigorous and cutting criticism of realism in the period came from O'Casey: 'Why, even the sawdust characters of the Moor, Petroushka, and the Ballerina are a more just image of human nature than the characters in the matter-of-fact, exact-imitation-of-life plays that flit about on the English stage.'[1]

He persisted in his own style, the freewheeling, musical style he had struck out during his years in England. The result was to prove him right in his view that the English critics were too attached to realism to be responsive to new styles: 'Matter-of-fact plays, true-to-life arrange-ment, and real, live characters are the three gods the critics adore.'[2] He received little understanding or critical support, certainly not enough to help to ensure proper professional performance in London for his later work; a sad situation which his wife, Eileen O'Casey, comments on ruefully in her biography, *Sean*.[3]

O'Casey was exceptional in his total rejection of realism and his total commitment to the other tradition of melodrama and farce. Far more of the experimental drama of the period was conducted within the framework of realism and depended upon its conventions quite as much as the simplest 'slice of life' play. J. B. Priestley's experiments are mostly of this kind. He says as much in the course of objecting to being classed as a naturalist rather than an experimental playwright. Instead of breaking right away from naturalism, he explains, he usually worked out from it, because 'The theatrical tradition of our time is a naturalistic tradition, and so I have had in the main to come to terms with it'. His wording 'come to terms with it' doesn't quite represent, I think, the degree of commitment to realism that can be sensed in his experimental plays. In *Dangerous Corner* (1932) and *Time and the Conways* (1937), for instance, far from threatening or leading away from the realistic illusion, the experimental element strengthens it by adding piquancy; the innovations have the effect of highlighting those features of the plays which relate them most firmly to the central tradition of English realism.

The experimental feature of both plays is their dislocated time scheme. In *Dangerous Corner*, as Priestley says, time divides to allow 'two alternative series of events'. The dividing point or dangerous

---

[1] Sean O'Casey, *The Flying Wasp*, 1937, pp. 121–2.

[2] *The Flying Wasp*, p. III.

[3] Eileen O'Casey, *Sean*, 1971. See for instance, her comments on the productions of *Oak Leaves and Lavender*, p 198 and *Purple Dust*, p 215.

corner is the moment in conversation when a casual remark could set off a sequence of unsavoury revelations about the members of a close-knit family group. Priestley ingeniously shows what might have happened and then switches back to the point of departure to show the other possibility of its not happening: this time the conversation safely rounds the dangerous corner. In the first series a lurid collection of skeletons pop out of their cupboards. The disillusioned husband enumerates them: 'My brother was an obscene lunatic. . . . And my wife doted on him and pestered him. One of my partners is a liar and a cheat and a thief. The other – God knows what he is – some sort of hysterical young pervert. . . .' In the second series none of this comes out, the family continue to seem to the eye of the friendly observer in the play a charming, cosy little group, of 'nice' people.

By another ingenious stroke, the events are dovetailed with the similar events in a radio play the characters are listening to. Called *The Sleeping Dog*, it ends with the suicide of a husband who 'insisted on disturbing the truth': the same thing happens with the husband in the first series of the 'real' play, the series that didn't come about. This is obviously a structure with Pirandellian possibilities, but significantly it comes out as something much nearer to Ibsen. It's a poor man's or thriller version of a typical Ibsenite process, an investigation into the secret life under respectable surfaces, the bringing into the light of what has been kept in the dark. It's on the characters' refusal to be disturbed, their complacent assertion of 'cosiness' and the disturbing social implications of this attitude that the dramatic emphasis finally falls. As an investigation of middle class respectability, a 'probing' play, *Dangerous Corner* belongs to one of the most popular types of English realism, a type ranging from unambitious who-dunnits such as Anthony Armstrong's and Agatha Christie's to subtle psychological explorations like Joyce's *Exiles*.

In *Time and the Conways*, again, an unrealistic effect – the disruption of the chronology at the end of Act I – is turned to a realistic effect. The flow of time is broken to allow a glimpse into the further future of the Conway family, after which the normal sequence is resumed and the third act is played in the shadow of the special knowledge the audience have about what lies ahead. As in *Dangerous Corner* the contrast between the two sequences of time is a broad, exaggerated one between jolly cosiness and black disillusionment. Pretty well everything goes wrong for the Conway family in the real future, in contrast with the hopeful future they are seen planning before and after we know what is coming. Priestley introduces what might be considered a note of anti-realism by allowing two characters, Kay and Alan, intimations of immortality. Act 2 is supposedly being seen by Kay, out of phase, as an 'observer' in the serial time envisaged by J. W. Dunne. However, although Priestley has much to say outside the play in prefaces and elsewhere about his interest in Dunne's theory of time, within the play it doesn't really amount to much, not enough at any rate to upset the realistic mode. Kay and Alan can be taken simply as two unusually intuitive characters who get clearer intimations of the future than the rest of the family and are interested in rationalizing their intuitions. The rationalizing consists mainly in Alan explaining to Kay in the second 'far future' act: '... it's hard to explain ... suddenly like this ... there's a book I'll lend you – read it in the train. But the point is, now, at this moment, or any moment, we're only a cross-section of our real selves. . . .'

The most substantial and serious effect of the time dislocation is an effect that Priestley often aims at in his conventionally constructed plays, in *The Linden Tree* (1948) for instance. What comes over most strongly is the pathos of ordinary people's humdrum lives wasting away in the relentless hand of time. This is the note sounded throughout *Time and the Conways*: the sadness of good or at least hopeful times passing and time 'ticking our lives away ... wrecking ... and ruining everything ... for ever ...'.

It is also the characteristic note of that most popular type of English realism, to which, it seems to me, both the 'experimental' *Time and the Conways* and the straightforwardly realistic *The Linden Tree* belong: the family drama and the drama of ordinary people's day-to-day domestic or working life.

Both Priestley, and in his different way Maugham, are deeply at home in this mode, however resentfully they may sometimes express their feeling about its dominance. But even writers who weren't so at ease in the mode, who really preferred other forms like the well-made play or the history play, were drawn into the irresistible orbit. 'Drawn' seems to be the word in the case of Rattigan, for instance. He talks amusingly in the preface to the collected edition of his plays[1] of his 'unregenerate' days when he would automatically have thought-up 'tragic' endings for two of his plays, *The Browning Version* (1948) and *The Deep Blue Sea* (1952), and how he resisted the temptation

---

[1] T. Rattigan, Preface to *Collected Plays*, 1953, vol 2.

with 'much sacrifice and self-abnegation', settling for realistically inconclusive endings, with the future left uncertain, instead of the unregenerate alternatives 'death from heart trouble in the one, a second and successful suicide in the other'. It was ironical, as he says, but perhaps understandable, that some critics reacted unfavourably: they would have preferred the leopard with his spots on. The ghost of that alternative ending à la Dame aux Camélias rather haunts *The Deep Blue Sea*. Rattigan's natural style made it difficult for him not to raise expectations of pat dénouements: it could even be said that the 'anti-climax' of *The Browning Version* when Crocker-Harris finally turns on the patronizing headmaster is just as pat a dénouement as the death from heart failure would have been. But however one rates its success, it's clear in this and in other plays like *The Deep Blue Sea* that a real effort at realism is being made. And it's being made against the writer's natural inclinations in response to the same powerful pressure that Maugham and Priestley felt working upon them.

Even history plays start pretending hard to be 'real' in the period. Gordon Daviot's Richard II talks things over with his wife; Reginald Berkeley's Florence Nightingale confides in her favourite doctor in a modern idiom that invites us to think of them – in typical realistic fashion – as people like us, or not so very different. Heroic figures are firmly placed in a domestic context, cut to the measurements of the 'matter-of-fact drama'. They get a touch of the Lytton Strachey treatment. When Strachey saw the production of Berkeley's *The Lady with a Lamp* in 1931, he recognized it, he said, as coming straight out of *Eminent Victorians*. Something similar to the Strachey deflating method goes on in the history plays of Shaw and Bridie, but the comparison with them only brings out more sharply the peculiar nature of what the realists were doing. Neither Shaw nor Bridie allow us to forget the incongruity of the manners and vocabulary they give to their Napoleons or Jonahs. They exploit it for comic or satiric purposes, as when St Joan is seen as the first Protestant, or Britannicus makes jokes that could only be appreciated by modern Englishmen. Jokes of that kind are a way of talking out to the audience, and the writers of 'realistic' history plays never do this. They are committed to the pretence that the play has no audience, is not a play at all but history as it happened, the real thing.

This wish for the real thing, the wish to see ordinary life on the stage is the great, potent drive behind realism. Other factors enter too, though, and one of them, the influence of the novel, I'd like to look at now. It relates to what I'm going on to discuss, the limitations of the realistic drama in the period.

There is strong pressure from the novel to make the drama as much like itself as possible. Many of the leading novelists of the time were also its leading playwrights, a fact which stands out sharply in the recently completed volume 4 (1900–50) of the *New Cambridge Bibliography of English Literature*. The editor, I. R. Willison, draws attention to the striking versatility which results in some curious spaces in the drama section: Galsworthy, Maugham, Priestley, all have to be sought for among the novelists. And altogether about a fifth of the playwrights dealt with in the volume have been reckoned as primarily novelists.

This remarkably free movement between the genres can be at least partly accounted for by the importance of the discussion element in realistic drama. No radical change of attitude was required of a novelist writing for a theatre which set so high a value on quiet talk as a means of holding an audience and so relatively little on peculiarly theatrical means such as silent scenic effects, music, song, breaks in the illusion. Many playwrights came into the theatre by way of adaptations of their own novels as Priestley did via his *The Good Companions*. He was aided by Edward Knoblock,[1] specialist in this kind of adaptation, whose collaboration with Arnold Bennett on plays and on stage versions of his novels is one of the interesting phenomena in the stage history of the period that would be well worth a detailed study. Whether an 'idea' would go better into novel or play form was a question writers commonly asked themselves. It was the question Ezra Pound considered when Joyce sent him the manuscript of *Exiles*: 'It is not so good as a novel; nevertheless it is quite good enough. . . . I see no way in which the play could be improved by doing it as a novel. It could not, in fact, be anything but a play.'[2] For Somerset Maugham the choice of medium was apparently the easiest, most casual thing in the world. Commenting on the stage versions of his short stories he says: 'The fact that so many of them have been turned into plays, successful or otherwise, seems to show that they might just as easily have come to me as plays in the first case. I think there are very few ideas that can be treated only in one way.'[3]

If novelists like Maugham and Priestley found a theatre well condi-

[1] His adaptations included works from Vicki Baum, Mrs Gaskell, A. J. Cronin, V. Sackville West, Beverley Nichols.
[2] Letter of 6 Sept 1915 in *Pound/Joyce*, ed F. Read, 1968.
[3] *Collected Plays*, 1931, vol 6.

tioned to receive them – Ibsen and Shaw had made prolonged discussion of events seem the natural theatrical mode – they themselves
strengthened its novelistic tendencies. What would in their novels
presumably have been authorial exposition emerges in their plays as
commentary by the characters on themselves. And there is a tremendous
amount of this sort of commentary in the drama of the period, not
only, by any means, in the plays of the novelists, but very noticeably in
theirs. It tends to be an explicit, unambiguous kind of dialogue.
Characters are always explaining themselves to each other, as Sydney
does in Maugham's *For Services Rendered* (1932): 'Oh, don't bother
about me, mother. I shall be all right. They say suffering ennobles. It
hasn't ennobled me. It's made me sly and cunning. Evie says I'm
selfish. I am.' Or Dr Kirby in Priestley's *Eden End*: 'You're rectifying
that mistake, my dear. And only you. Lilian's your mother over again.
As long as she's a house of her own – and a man in it – she'll be happy
in her own way. Wilfred's a good lad, but he's a bit weak and easy-
going. He'll never do much.'

Rather ironically, this taste of English writers for 'full' explanations
often coexisted with great admiration for Chekhov, master of incomplete, unclosed explanations. Priestley was one who felt that
Chekhov had influenced his own style: 'In such plays within the
tradition as *Eden End* and *The Linden Tree* I owe much to the influence
of Tchehov, notably in giving each act its own atmosphere (as if the
characters were fish swimming in different coloured bowls. . . .)'[1]
Arnold Bennett was another admirer: he was involved through his
connection with the Lyric Theatre, Hammersmith, with Fagan's
celebrated production of *The Cherry Orchard*[2] and was greatly impressed and also troubled by it. In one entry in his journals, he records
his pleasure on being told by a Russian that his *The Death of Simon
Fuge* was in Chekhov's style, going on in the next breath to agree with
the same friend's comment that he had never written the plays he
ought to and could have written.

It's easy to understand Chekhov's appeal for Bennett. *The Cherry
Orchard* is such a brilliant demonstration of how commonplace detail
can be used to bring out the complexity and pathos of ordinary lives,

---

[1] *Plays*, 1948, vol 1.
[2] He tells how after a poor initial reception, the play suddenly and mysteriously
attracted support: 'Tonight this most disconcerting and original play is going in a sort
of triumph to the West End, where no manager would have looked at it a month ago.'
Journals, 1933; entry for 22 June 1925.

the almost unbearable sadness of time's effects upon them. One of the most lyrical moments in *The Cherry Orchard*, when Mme Ranevsky looks out of the window at the moonlit orchard and sees her dead mother walking there, is the fullest expression of that time-haunted melancholy which Bennett communicated so touchingly in *The Old Wives' Tale* and other novels, but didn't manage, so he felt, to get into his plays. Priestley got it in less subtle form, and many other English playwrights of the period aimed at it. 'Chekhovian' became a stock epithet for plays which seemed to have this kind of pathos, like Ronald Mackenzie's *Musical Chairs* or Rodney Ackland's *After October*.[1]

Mackenzie and Ackland also tried to simulate the Chekhovian illusion of haphazardness, 'plotlessness' as it has misleadingly been called. They have a great deal of bustle on their stage, characters coming in and out, talking about breakfast or glasses of milk while other characters are trying to conduct a love affair or some business over an oil deal. Much of this reads tediously, and though it might possibly play better – little commonplace incidents usually need a stage to reveal their force – it's evident that it's a long way from the subtle counter-pointing of small things that makes up the rich Chekhovian texture. Yet the general fascination with Chekhov, the sense of affinity that so many playwrights feel with him, especially in his handling of pathos and nostalgia, is a striking and important phenomenon of the thirties. The Chekhovian form became, one might say, the ideal form of realism for the English theatre, strong in its power to attract, weak in its manifestations, as I began by suggesting was true generally of English dramatic realism in the period. What is almost totally missing from the English Chekhovian plays is, as one would expect, the subtext. Priestley, Ackland, Mackenzie share Chekhov's interest in the inner significance of little commonplace incidents but they can't leave them to speak for themselves: everything has to be fully talked out and made conscious: there hardly seems any awareness of the unconscious, certainly no technique for indicating its workings, no mesh of Freudian slips, idiosyncratic omissions or contradictions, above all, no deeply revealing silences. One might say that realism had to continue after the war if only because the Chekhovian ideal had been so incompletely realized in the prewar theatre, and an idea so potent couldn't die out until it had come to fuller expression.

---

[1] Both produced at the Arts Theatre, *Musical Chairs* 15 Nov 1931; *After October* 21 Feb 1936.

The odd fate of Joyce's *Exiles* certainly suggests that the process of assimilating ideas can't be hurried in the English theatre. This is really a more Chekhovian play than any of Mackenzie's or Ackland's, but it has been hard for people to see it in this way because it has taken so long for a Chekhovian mode of production and acting to establish itself in the English theatre – partly because there haven't been playwrights to encourage it. It's no accident that *Exiles* finally got the production it needed from Pinter. He is, it seems to me, the first English playwright to realize in bold, arresting forms those Chekhovian impulses which sounded so much more faintly in earlier drama, from Mackenzie to N. C. Hunter. This is an argument I shall develop at length in a discussion of *Exiles* and its affinities with Pinter's drama.

Now I want to consider other ways in which the realism of the interwar period looks either unfinished or obviously open to continuation and development, and to indicate where the lines of continuation run in the postwar period: it's along those lines that a good part of my discussion of present-day playwrights will go.

The most obvious line of continuance is through the simplest form, the 'slice of life' play, which relies fundamentally on its power to interest the audience in day-to-day processes of ordinary life, 'authentically' presented on the stage. The pure slice of life play doesn't try for – in a way can't do with – complexity of character or action. Chekhov wanted 'everything on the stage to be just as simple and at the same time just as complicated as in real life': this is the illusion he so marvellously sustains in *The Cherry Orchard*. The slice of life play normally wants only enough complication to make its simplicity convincing, not so much as to take the interest away from its centre, the social process itself. Slice of life realism is a form with infinite capacities for expansion; far from being finished by 1956, the year of the so-called 'revolution' in the English theatre, it had barely begun to stretch itself, and I should say that the present day is really its heyday.

For one thing, the illusion of 'life as it really is' is more convincing the more inclusive it is. Sides of life can be shown now which were barred in the interwar theatre not so much by the censor, though of course some topics, such as homosexuality, were taboo, as by prevailing notions of good taste and decorum. In his study of the English censorship, Richard Findlater singles out the period as one of exceptional complaisance: 'There was no single revolutionary influence comparable with Ibsen's in the earlier period and no one English dramatist was as dominant a rebel as Shaw had been. On the whole they played the game inside the censor's rules, without undue resentment.'[1]

Decorum isn't necessarily a disabling influence. A sense of obligation not to be decorous can be quite as disabling, as some present-day plays testify. But over-refinement in language and in treatment of delicate subjects certainly contributes to the muffled effect made by many plays of the twenties and thirties. Physical functions are gingerly handled. Illness tends to be clean, not messy; death occurs decorously for the most part. Maugham's drama has a good deal of illness and pain in it and he does sometimes get a really raw edge, a note of strong pain – in his handling of Sydney's blindness in *For Services Rendered* for instance, or in the nervous breakdown that ends the play. But more usually in the theatre of the time physical events like breakdowns and deaths are cast into less direct, harsh forms. The sting is to some extent taken out of them by their being turned into subjects for discussion. Of course there is a kind of pain in the conversations about pain, and the conversational method often seems the natural one. But there is often too a sense of shrinking from a more direct presentation of painful events or a tendency to sweeten and soften them, as Maugham does finally (after seeming to promise something rather different) in his handling of the father's death in *The Unknown* (1920), or in his presentation of Sheppey's death as a long, kindly conversation with a symbolic lady in black.

Sexual relationships get similar treatment: they too are pushed towards conversation rather than event. Lovers endlessly analyze their feelings, discuss the changes of partner they would like to make or feel guilty about making, give the impression sometimes (in Keith Winter's *The Shining Hour*, for instance) that they enjoy talking about sex rather more than practising it.

The bloodless quality of so much of the realism in the period comes partly from its impoverished language. Here the pressure of gentility is very strong and inhibiting. A scene in Edward Wooll's play, *Libel* (1934) rather neatly expresses it. A character giving evidence comes out with the line, 'Then the feathers began to fly, and I came out a God damned sight quicker than I went in', to be rebuked by the judge for his bad language: 'You must remember you're in an English Court, Captain Buckenham.'

The playwrights of the twenties and thirties seem to have no difficulty as a rule in remembering that they are in an English court.

---

[1] R. Findlater, *Banned!* 1967, p 127.

And they conform accordingly – or perhaps don't even have the sense of being called on to conform but work quite at their ease within the decorous convention. Realism had to get free of the limitations such attention to decorum imposed. It is just the process of getting free that has infused its simpler forms with so much new life during the last fifteen years.

A major limitation of realism in the period was its narrow range of subject and social interest. Subjects were almost always taken from middle class life and there is a marked shortage of 'work' plays, the kind that explore the interests and problems people encounter simply by having a certain kind of job. Again, as with so much else in the theatre of the period the possibilities in that type of realism are recognized and touched on without being taken far. Sometimes the will is there but no great power – Aimée and Philip Stuart's play about mannequins at work, *Nine till Six* (1930) might serve as an illustration – but more often the will seems to be lacking, or at any rate the life of work is not explored in any very serious way. It's rare to come across an extended working routine like this from Maugham's *Sheppey* (1933) which in its different style anticipates the kind of scenes Arnold Wesker specializes in, and David Storey. There's a pleasantly relaxed, natural feeling in the scene, with the manicurist chiding a regular for being 'unfaithful' to her – 'I shall have no end of a job getting your nails nice again' – and Sheppey demonstrating all his professional skills on stage, from lathering and shaving a customer to selling him a bottle of hair restorer.

BOLTON: You needn't mind telling me, you know. You'll never catch me if you try till doomsday. All these preparations of yours. A lot of damned nonsense. I wouldn't take one of them as a gift.

SHEPPEY: I know I couldn't sell you anything not in a hundred years. You 'ave to be a judge of character in my business and I know it would be just a waste of time to try.

BOLTON: Thank you for those kind words.

SHEPPEY: You see, we make our money out of the vanity of the 'uman race. And I don't mind telling you that men are every bit as vain as women.

MISS GRANGE: Vainer, if you ask me.

SHEPPEY: Now I don't think I'm wrong in stating that you 'aven't got a spark of vanity in your composition.

BOLTON: I daresay you're right.

SHEPPEY: I know I'm right. I mean, if you was vain you wouldn't want to look any older than you need, would you?

BOLTON: I'm only just over forty, you know.

SHEPPEY: Is that a fact, sir? Of course, being so grey over the temples makes you look more.

MISS GRANGE: Oh, I like the grey over the temples, Sheppey. I always think it makes a gentleman look so distingay.

SHEPPEY: I don't say it don't look distingay. I only say it adds a good five years to one's age. If Mr. Bolton 'adn't got that grey 'e wouldn't look a day over thirty-five.

MISS GRANGE: He wouldn't look that, Sheppey.

BOLTON: I'm not going to dye my hair to please you, Sheppey.

SHEPPEY: I don't blame you. I'd never recommend a gentleman to dye his hair. It seems unnatural somehow.

MISS GRANGE: I always think it makes a face look so hard.

SHEPPEY: What I mean to say is, I don't suppose you mind if you look thirty-five or forty-eight. Why should you?

BOLTON: I don't know that I want to look as though I had one foot in the grave, you know.

SHEPPEY: You know what I'm thinking of, Miss Grange?

MISS GRANGE: That German stuff.

SHEPPEY: Mind you, sir, I'm not trying to sell it to you.

The emphasis falls on the conversational aspects of the job when one reads the scene, but it's obvious that on stage the effect would be of a very complete slice of real working life.

The occupation that attracted most interest among playwrights of the period was predictably the middle class one of teaching. Boarding schools are favourite settings. But the professional area of the characters' lives is seldom examined very closely. Priestley attempts it in *The Linden Tree* (1948) where the whole action turns on Professor Linden's devotion to his work as a teacher in a provincial University and his wife's resistance to it. There's even a snatch of a seminar on stage, but it's so embarrassing for the credibility of the view the play invites us to take of the Professor's intellectual quality that on the whole one would rather it hadn't been there. Rattigan, perhaps wisely, confines his attempt to handle a teacher-pupil relationship in *The Browning Version* to a leave-taking in which the pupil's parting gift so affects the teacher that it gives him strength to turn on his nasty headmaster. Of course, although Rattigan may be more adroit in avoiding a real lesson on stage, his is a much slighter piece than Priestley's play, which does look seriously at the kind of problems an academic brought up in the humane tradition of the past might have in what seems to him the brash atmosphere of a new-style University.

Other playwrights like Van Druten and Keith Winter who dramatize school life are more interested in the characters' private lives. This is one reason why *Young Woodley* (1925) is such an anti-climax of a play: it avoids all the opportunities the situation offers to explore something real, the plight of a sensitive adolescent in the rigid grip of the English public school system, and chooses instead to be a trite piece about calf love. Similarly Keith Winter's *The Rats of Norway* (1933) although set in and around a staff room in a preparatory school and given touches of verisimilitude by ringing bells and grumbles about the timetable, succeeds in keeping the boys entirely off the stage and reducing the professional activities of the characters to a background of gossip: the real action consists in a couple of conventionally handled love affairs. The school environment provides local colour and, more important, a claustrophobic, protected situation in which the characters have plenty of time – despite the nagging bells – to concentrate uneasily on personalities.

This is one version of the typical situation of realism, a closed, tight situation, which in a way gives the characters very little freedom and in another way too much. They certainly feel oppressed by the chronic state of under-occupation most of them are in. The playwrights are deeply interested in that particular kind of boredom and malaise. Their biggest technical problem is to find means of communicating it without making it only too tediously real for the audience. Sadly, they often fail to get control over the tedious elements in their material: the language tends to be simply boring, over-saturated in platitude and cliché, and presented curiously straight so that we can't be sure whether it's meant to be taken satirically or seriously. They don't seem able to get at the right distance from their characters, whether because their techniques for framing and distancing the action are inadequate, or because they are too emotionally involved in it, isn't always clear.

Priestley usually seems deeply sympathetic to his characters, but with other playwrights it's not always easy to know when and where sympathy is being called for. Maugham, for instance, in *The Unknown*, seems at first to be very down on his conventional characters: their pious platitudes are questioned and attacked, most audaciously in the scene when a bereaved mother punctures the Vicar's pomposities – ' . . . who should know better than the Ministers of God that to err is human, to forgive, divine?' – with the bitter rejoinder 'And who is going to forgive God?' Yet for long stretches characters as platitudinous as the Vicar are seemingly approved of, or, rather, presented in such a neutral, cagey way that we can't tell whether they are or not. The result is that it's not very easy to approve of them as dramatic characters: they're too successfully boring; the need of a humorous or sharp perspective is too much felt.

This is strikingly true of Van Druten's *After All* (1929), a play I'd like to quote from because it is such an odd illustration of the tentative, uncommitted impression the realistic drama of the time so often makes. The ingredients for an interesting treatment are there, but the playwright's attitude seems to prevent him from making the most of them.

After All is the archetypal play of middle class family life. For scene after scene the trite conversations shuffle on at exactly the pace they would have in real life, as in this sequence between the mother of the family, Mrs Thomas, and Auntie Doe.

MRS THOMAS: More tea, Doe?

MRS. MELVILLE: I don't think Walter's looking at all well, Margaret.

MRS. THOMAS: I know. He isn't. It worries me. It's his blood pressure. It's all wrong.

MRS MELVILLE: Why doesn't he see a doctor?

MRS THOMAS: He has. Wilkinson. You know what he is. I've been trying to persuade him to see a specialist but he won't. Wilkinson's put him on a diet. No red meat – and he does get so tired of chicken. I rack my brains trying to think of new things. I wish somebody would invent a new food. No spirits. No wine. He misses it.

MRS MELVILLE: Is he any better for it?

MRS. THOMAS: Oh yes, I think so. A little. Wilkinson says he mustn't worry. As if one could avoid it!

MRS. MELVILLE: Is business bad?

MRS. THOMAS: No. No worse than usual, I suppose.

MRS. MELVILLE: Ralph must be a great help to him. Though I suppose he'll be giving it up for his drawing one of these fine days. It really does seem as if he had a turn for it. Do you see much of him now he's living away from home?

MRS. THOMAS: Not a great deal. He comes home to dinner once a week.

MRS. MELVILLE: And Phyl? I didn't think she was looking very well either. She seemed nervy to me. Gordon's not still worrying her, is he?

MRS. THOMAS: No. She doesn't see him.

MRS MELVILLE: Is she sorry, do you think, that she broke it off?

MRS. THOMAS: My dear, I don't know. She doesn't talk to us.

MRS. MELVILLE: Isn't that funny? But children are like that. They don't seem to realise that their parents are their best friends in the end. Doris is just the same. Not that I think she's got anything she wouldn't tell me.

This is banal enough to be almost disturbing. For a moment the shadow of Ionesco falls. One pictures him waiting in the wings to seize the dialogue as raw material for *The Bald Prima Donna.* Or N. F. Simpson looms up, out hunting fodder for the Groom kirbys. But does Van Druten intend any such 'absurd' effect? The question is made just feasible by the irony that does get into the play through the point of view of the young people. The son of the house is given to mildly mocking remarks like 'How time flies, as Auntie Doe would say'. By the end, though, this irony has quite gone and we're being invited to look back on the time that seemed so boring while it was happening with the same nostalgia that pervades Priestley's plays. It's not easy to do that: one wonders very much how easy it was for Van Druten and his audiences.

Certainly there was vast scope for the development of slice of life realism after the war. Like the neo-Chekhovian form, but for the different reasons which I've been trying to indicate, the slice of life form was in some ways a stunted growth. I shall go on to look at the way it burst into full flower after the war.

Another form of realism which has had an interesting post-war development is the type of comedy generally known as 'drawing-room' or 'cocktail' comedy: it needs a portmanteau title, really, for the two elements can't easily be distinguished, at any rate in the plays of Maugham and Noel Coward, chief exponents of the kind. 'Drawing room' places it socially – houses in Mayfair, butlers and personal maids, Anglo-Indian connections – and 'cocktail' sets the tone. It's never too early for one, as Florence Lancaster says in *The Vortex* (1924) when she offers drinks to guests in her drawing room at the time of afternoon tea.

Of course Coward has a foot in the musical theatre too, but I want to consider him now as a realist. His contemporaries had no difficulty in seeing him in this way. 'Drives at reality' was Ivor Brown's comment on *The Vortex* in 1924. Du Maurier agreed, though with dislike: 'The younger generation are knocking at the door of the dustbin'. He has many of the realists' characteristic preoccupations and sentiments, fascination with idleness and tedium, nostalgia for the past, divided feelings about the habits of the bourgeoisie. The split shows up in a more spectacular way in his plays than in theirs because he is so much the sharper stylist: at one extreme he produces a *Design for Living* (1933), at the other a *Cavalcade* (1931). But it's the same split. There's the same tendency, too, to over-saturate us in boring detail, banal conversations and tedious routines, though his are more often the cocktail party than the homely bourgeois kind.

But of course all this is redeemed in Coward's best work by the humour which brings out so gaily the absurdity of the routines and puts such a sharp perspective on the sentiment. Sharpness comes well before character consistency in the values of his comedy. In *The Vortex*, for instance, although Nicky Lancaster's is supposedly the sharp mind and his fiancée's the conventional one, it's she who rather disconcertingly is given some of the most cutting comments. 'I like you better clear cut, not blurred by sentiment' she says, after he's made a sentimental speech about his childish memories of his radiant mother kissing him goodnight. Her remark may not be quite in character, but certainly the cool perspective is what the scene needs. It's the lack of that perspective in the nostalgic scenes of the realistic drama generally that is so damaging to it.

Coward is much more ruthlessly selective than the other realists. The 'cocktail/drawing-room' form has a built-in selectiveness to start with – kitchens, bathrooms, back doors don't exist for it – and he makes the most of it. He brings out the ritualistic quality in the cocktail routine, making great play with pauses, sudden silences, snatches of fragmented half-heard dialogue and crossed conversational lines to suggest that the characters aren't even trying to talk meaningfully to each other but are involved in some esoteric ritual where each has his appointed role to fulfil.

One expression of their need for ritual is their passion for games: a great variety is played on his stage, from bridge and Mah Jong to the hilarious Alibis of *Hay Fever* (1925), and played with exactly the same kind of feeling that the players bring to their other relationships. The quarrel scene at the end of *Hay Fever* is an amusing instance. The Bliss family quarrelling are like initiates performing a rite to renew their psychic energy. They're so absorbed in it that they don't even notice their four unhappy guests sneaking across the stage to make their escape from the traumatic weekend. When the door slams and reality impinges, the quarrel is wiped away as if it hadn't been – which in a way it hasn't – and they settle down cosily to discuss their guests: 'People really do behave in the most extraordinary manner these days.'

These are lighthearted rites, but elsewhere the games are made to look rather more desperate, crudely in *The Vortex*, more deftly in later plays like *Design for Living*. The world of Gilda, Leo and Otto is a

thoroughly closed one. Apart from the necessary stooge, the bourgeois
Ernest who helps to define their style by contrasting so heavily with it,
no one else exists for them. They have no intimacies outside their
charmed threesome: the rest of the world is far away at the other end
of a telephone. This is Coward's stylized version of the classic, closed
situation of realism. The trio's dependence on each other is made
flippantly funny at first as Gilda switches from one lover to another and
back again, but towards the end its disturbing aspects begin to show:
the dread of loneliness, the insecure sense of personal identity. As
Coward puts it: 'These glib, over-articulate and amoral creatures
force their lives into fantastic shapes and problems because they cannot
help themselves . . . they are like moths in a pool of light, unable to
tolerate the lonely outer darkness, and equally unable to share the light
without colliding constantly and bruising one another's wings'.[1]

Style is immensely important to them: it's how they recognize
themselves, as their parting remarks to Ernest bring out:

> We're all of a piece, the three of us. . . . No one else's way is any good,
> we don't fit.
> Our lives are a different shape from yours.

When the curtain falls on a flood of abuse from him – 'You're shifty
and irresponsible and abominable' – there's a feeling of triumph about
their helpless laughter. They've forced him into self parody, an exaggerated style that makes it easier for them to recognize their own and
feel secure in it again.

Coward's characters are often supposed to be actors but even when
they're not, his 'initiated' ones are always aware of themselves acting
and amazed or amused that the uninitiated, the 'dull' ones don't
recognize that they're taking part in a performance.

'Fascinating to lift the roofs a fraction and look down into the houses',
Otto says at one point. 'Not when the people inside know you're
looking', Gilda corrects him, 'not when they're acting for you and
strutting about and showing off!' These are the bad actors, the ones
who strut. Gilda and her lovers are the accomplished ones. As for the
others, who don't know they're acting, they hardly exist at all.

In the way he uses these acting elements in his characterization and
in his handling of the ritualistic elements in social life, Coward anticipates an astonishing amount of present-day drama. There are striking

---

[1] Noel Coward, Introduction to *Play Parade*, 1934, vol 1.

connections with the drama of T. S. Eliot, Osborne and Pinter especially, and I shall have these in mind in my discussions of those playwrights.

I have been trying to indicate the special interest the realism of the interwar period has for students of the present-day English theatre, its inventiveness and also its strangely muffled, inhibited quality. Now I want to look at the development of some of the forms I have touched on, beginning with the simplest of them, the slice of life play.

1. *Texts*
   Maugham, W. S. *Collected Plays*, 1931–4
   Priestley, J. B.:
   Collected Plays, 1948–50
   Chekhov, 1970. International Writers series
   Rattigan, T. *Collected Plays*, 1953

2. *Anthologies*
   Contemporary British Dramatists, 1922–33
   Famous Plays of Today, 1929–39, 14 vols
   Great Modern British Plays (ed J. W. Marriott), 1932
   Plays of the Thirties, 1966–7

3. *Critical Writings*
   Ervine, St J. *How to Write a Play*, 1928
   Ervine, St J. *The Theatre in my Time*, 1933
   Marriott, J. W. *Modern Drama*, 1934
   Nicoll, A. *British Drama*, 1962 rev.
   Priestley, J. B. *The Art of the Dramatist*, 1957
   Sherriff, R. C. 'In Defence of Realism'. *Theatre Arts Monthly* 14, 1930
   Sutton, G. *Some Contemporary Dramatists*, 1924
   Trewin, J. C. *The Theatre since 1900*, 1951

II

Realism in new directions

Arnold Wesker, David Storey, David Mercer

Before 1956 N. C. Hunter's plays about sad gentility mouldering away in country houses or hotels were 'realism'. After the explosion of new talent triggered off by *Look Back in Anger*, realism was a play about working-class people in Salford or Liverpool; a new scene, a new style, but more often than not the same old form. The slice of life convention has held the stage for a surprisingly long time since – surprisingly, that is, if one thinks of all the pressure to change and open out into new forms there has been from plays like *Waiting for Godot*, from Brecht and Ionesco, from theatrical experiments like Joan Littlewood's at Stratford and Peter Brook's with Theatre of Cruelty.

From other points of view it isn't so surprising, of course. 'To put ourselves and our situations on the stage' is, as Raymond Williams puts it, a recurrent ambition of realism.[1] And there was all that leeway to make up from the more timid twenties and thirties, all those untapped or just touched-on subjects, all those interesting directions indicated but not really explored. There was a need for sequels and follow-ups in the fifties and authenticity was still a compelling concept. In some ways it's more compelling now than it ever was, to judge from the popular success David Storey has had recently with essays in total realism like *The Contractor* and *The Changing Room*. Arnold Wesker's drama is the most substantial, and to my mind the most moving, in this convention. He has made some brave experiments in the faithful recording of ordinary life which have given 'plain' realism, as one might call it, a great extension.

---

[1] R. Williams, *Drama from Ibsen to Brecht*, 1968, p 318.

But there have been changes too. Some of the new wine poured into the old, thin bottles has come near to exploding them. The forms of realism have begun to mix in a curious way with the forms of the alternative tradition, especially with farce. The threat of explosion, the urge to break out of the 'pretending it's not a play' framework is increasingly felt in the texture of the slice of life drama. David Mercer's plays provide some particularly curious illustrations of this compromise or transitional form.

The post-1956 slice of life plays were from the start more inclined to look out to the audience than the earlier realistic drama had been. Peter Cheeseman tells how affected he was during a production of Shelagh Delaney's *A Taste of Honey* (1958) when the actress playing Jo came downstage to the footlights and leaned against the proscenium to speak directly to the audience: 'The effect, visually and aurally, was quite electrifying for me.'[1] Perhaps what made it so electrifying was her coming out of the frame as an actor, not as a narrator/character, presenting the action in a more literary way, as, say, Peter Nichols' narrator does in *Forget-me-not Lane* (1971). The confrontation Peter Cheeseman describes was more anarchic than that; for a moment it must have threatened the whole real life illusion. It's toward that sort of tightrope balancing that we seem to be moving all the time in today's theatre.

Perhaps in the years just after *Look Back in Anger* it was easier to get a sense of openness and freedom without venturing far, if at all, outside the conventional realistic framework. It came in through the characters' own feelings of freedom. There is often a touching and exhilarating sense in the plays of that time of a whole people breaking out of their limiting frame. The 'dumb inarticulate classes', as Yeats called them, were finding a voice, as Beatie finds hers in *Roots*: 'D' you hear it? Did you listen to me? I'm talking. Jenny, Frankie, Mother – I'm not quoting no more.'

Nothing in Wesker's later drama has made quite the same impact as *Roots*. It was the play for the time and of the time. And yet it was also, of course, a play of the old time, in a tradition going back beyond Walter Greenwood's *Love on the Dole* (1934) to the Manchester School and D. H. Lawrence's plays of mining life. That *Roots* seemed so novel in 1959 was a sign of how much untapped vitality there still was in that tradition and in the whole convention of realism. New subjects were wanted but the old recipes hadn't lost their appeal.

---

[1] Peter Cheeseman writing about his work at the Victoria Theatre, Stoke on Trent. *Theatre Quarterly* 1, 1971.

The simple recipe used by N. C. Hunter and Priestley before him went on being useful to the realists of Wesker's generation. Take a group of people from some well marked social class, gather them together in a natural meeting place like a hotel lounge or family sitting room and leave them to reveal themselves – always within the limits of social probability – in response to small pressures from each other and from the environment. The meeting places got rather rougher and tougher after 1956 – the basement bedsitter set replaced the French window set – but the formula survived. It's above all a formula for conversation and discussion, for the sound of talk; and it was given an enormous boost by the new sounds that came into stage talk in the fifties from the regions outside London. Just to hear the Norfolk sound, the Liverpool sound, all those regional airs, seemed the experience the London theatre had been waiting for. The speed of Arnold Wesker's arrival in London was symptomatic. Two of the plays in his trilogy[1] were seen at the Royal Court within weeks of their opening at the new Belgrade Theatre, Coventry. Within a month *Roots* had moved to the West End and in the following year the trilogy was given in its entirety at the Royal Court.

> Waas matter wi' you then?
> I don' know gal. There's a pain in my guts and one a'tween my shoulder blades I can hardly stand up.
> Sit you down then an' I'll git your supper on the table.
> Blust gal! I can't eat yit.

Here was a full-blooded sound of a kind that had hardly been heard on the London stage since *Love on the Dole* and that was a swallow in the thirties summer. Wesker in his earnest way vouched for the authenticity of the dialect, providing a note on pronunciation to clinch it. Only the pedantic would have argued about it (some did, of course). The crucial thing for most people, to judge from recorded reactions, was the sense of authenticity that came through, a warm, lived in, believable quality which is a characteristic of Wesker's dialogue at its best. It was this quality in his play and in others like *A Taste of Honey* (the Salford sound) and Alun Owen's *Progress to the Park* (the Liverpool sound) that made them so attractive. The characters in *Progress to the*

---

[1] *Chicken Soup with Barley*. Belgrade Theatre, Coventry 7 July 1958; Royal Court 14 July 1958. *Roots*. Belgrade Theatre, Coventry 25 May 1959; Royal Court 30 June 1959; Duke of York's 30 July 1959. *I'm Talking about Jerusalem*. Belgrade Theatre, Coventry 28 March 1960. Complete Trilogy at the Royal Court summer 1960.

Park spend a fair amount of time talking about how they talk: they are as fascinated as critics and audiences proved to be by regional differences. This scene, where the young Liverpudlians discuss the provenance of their names is typical:

> HANNAH: I mean, if anybody's going to clout you, you can always tell them you're Manx.
> KELLY: Oh, I've found it very useful in the past.
> HANNAH: Yeah, I suppose so . . . but it's funny really, cos I always thought that Kelly was an Irish name.
> KELLY: What are you on about! Don't you know the song . . . (Singing rapidly) Has anybody here seen Kelly, Kelly from the Isle of Man!
> HANNAH (after a pause): Then it must be Manx.
> KELLY: It is.
> HANNAH: Well, you're all right then.
> KELLY: Aye . . . but how about you like?
> HANNAH: Oh, I'm all right! Y'know, you can spell my name backwards and it spells the same as frontwards. Hannah, H.A.N.N.A.H. . . . Either way it's the same.
> TEIFION: Scotch, isn't it?
> HANNAH: Dunno. The old fella came from Wigan.
> KELLY: But what about your mother?
> HANNAH: Her name wasn't Hannah until she got married.
> KELLY: Well, I know it wasn't, y'daft sodger! Was she Scotch?
> HANNAH: No. She came from Fazerckerley!
> TEIFION: Well, you're all right then.
> HANNAH: Oh aye, I'm all right.
> KELLY: And Teifion here, he's all right, he's Welsh.
> HANNAH: Well, that's what I always say, there's one good thing about being Liverpool Welsh, you don't have to join up with them lot.
> TEIFION: Well . . . as long as everybody knows about us . . . we're all right.

The leisurely pace of this scene was characteristic of the new regional realism. It was a reflection perhaps of the new sense of spaciousness that was spreading in the theatre. Everything was becoming more relaxed, freer. Subjects could be more freely chosen, areas of life formerly closed (if not by the censor, then by notions of decorum) could be newly explored. With all that went the urge to look out at the audience that struck Peter Cheeseman so forcibly in *A Taste of Honey*. Jo's mother, Helen, in that play, invites the audience to say what they would do in her situation; in Henry Livings' play, *Stop it, Whoever You Are*, a character introduces himself to the audience and comments on other characters in music hall style: 'Well I never.

Makes you think, doesn't it? She's nobbut fourteen, though you wouldn't think it. . . . '

There is a quite marked movement towards epic theatre and melo-drama in these plays. One can see why Shelagh Delaney's style would appeal to the creator of the epic documentary theatre at Stoke-on-Trent and why John Arden should single out Henry Livings when he was asked about contemporary playwrights who had influenced his work (less expectedly, perhaps, Christopher Fry was another).[1] Shelagh Delaney and Henry Livings were among the many play-wrights (Brendan Behan was one of the most interesting) who were encouraged to move in a musical/epic direction by Joan Littlewood at the Theatre Royal, Stratford East. O'Casey hovers (strangely unproduced) in the wings there. Henry Livings, for instance, acknow-ledges his genius. In a recent article[2] he quotes with approval his saying that theatre should contain all the arts, and certainly in his own plays he uses music with an O'Casey-like freedom: characters break into song as casually as speech.

And yet, interestingly, writers such as Livings have continued to feel the pull of realism: his plays often have a transitional look as if he wanted to get his audience into the conventional eavesdropping situa-tion as well as the more open one of epic. Much of the drama that has come out of Joan Littlewood's theatre has been gently persuasive rather than revolutionary: it has helped in the great opening-up process, helped to make a soil for plays like Peter Barnes' *The Ruling Class* to grow in without itself making the same violent break with the slice of life convention.

The convention retains its potency, there is still a fascination with the idea of accurate recording – getting the exact pace of ordinary social life on to the stage, the exact shape and sound of the kind of conversa-tions that might be overheard in ordinary homes or public places. The risk of reproducing its tedium too is as high as it was for the prewar realists. In a way it's become higher since the relaxation of official censorship set playwrights free to record more or less whatever they saw and heard in the social life about them; there are obviously hazards as well as advantages in that situation. For dramatic language, there is no doubt that the advantages have been overwhelmingly greater than the disadvantages. A living common speech has emerged, as full of

---

[1] John Arden, Interview in *Tulane Drama Review*, 11, 1966; rptd in *The Playwrights Speak*, ed W. Wager, 1969.
[2] Henry Livings, 'Let's Make a Theatre for Real People', *Theatre Quarterly* 2, 1972.

rhythm and flavour in its own astringent urban style as the nuts and
apples speech of the Irish peasants which Synge thought the last expression of natural poetry that English-speaking Europe could expect to
hear. From the hopelessly impoverished speech of the proletariat (as it
seemed to him) has emerged the most truly poetic English drama of
our time, prose plays that haunt the imagination with the force of
poetry – *Waiting for Godot*, *The Caretaker*, *The Entertainer*, Bond's *Lear*.

But when the flame burns less fiercely, freedom to let characters
talk as they would in 'real, real life' can be rather disastrous. Keith
Waterhouse and Willis Hall say about a character in one of their plays,
Billy Liar (1960) – 'he uses the adjective "bloody", so frequently that it
becomes completely meaningless.' True indeed, and dramatic force is
regularly sacrificed by the realists in this way. Some kinds of language
have begun to lose their power: the four letter words, for instance,
whose open usage nowadays is lamented by Pinter; what was, in his
phrase, the 'dark, secret language of the underworld' withers away
when it's overexposed in the common light of day.

Pinter's is a romantic's attitude, of course. Today's realists tend more
often to be unromantic or anti-romantic materialists who don't care
for mystery: they like everything out in the open. They have certainly
opened up the house of realism in a way that would have startled the
thirties. More rooms have come into view: the house has acquired a
bathroom and lavatory (strange how long it managed to do without
them) and total frankness in representing all sides of life is rapidly
becoming an acceptable goal. There may have been some coarsening of
dramatic fibre in the process, but the realists' achievement in the last
fifteen years has been impressive: they have tried to give us the whole
life of social man, including his ordinary bodily functions – boring
perhaps, but needing notice – and his working life, which, as I suggested
earlier, hardly existed in any very solid way for the prewar playwrights.

That underworked area, work, has become the great stamping-
ground of present-day realists. All kinds of working routines have been
explored for dramatic interest – the day-to-day tasks in a hotel kitchen,
an architect's office, a factory lavatory, on a building site. Sometimes it
seems that the drama is being required to function not so much as a
mirror to nature but as a species of social history. This is the impression
given in the introduction to one of the Penguin anthologies of new
playwrights when the editor praises a play about a comprehensive
school for its documentary interest and suggests that more plays of

this type are needed – 'There are still many large gaps in the portrayal of the social scene by contemporary British dramatists.'[1] Certainly he liked Barry Reckord's play, *Skyvers* (1966), at least partly because it gave him 'a clearer insight into the attitudes of the early school leaver than most educational articles do'.

Clearer insights into unfamiliar or puzzling social behaviour are what audiences today seek with rather touching eagerness. It's an eagerness that has given a new lease of life to old-fashioned forms of realism, even when their language isn't especially vigorous or interesting. A play like Charles Dyer's *Staircase* (1965), for instance, doesn't command attention by the quality of its language or its incidents – both are rather flat – but by the odd and awkward social situation of the two characters, the pathos of their attempt to make a homosexual marriage and somehow to fit it into the pattern of their working lives. So far as form goes, there's a distinct lack of excitement. The play is one long drawn-out conversation between the two men; as it ambles along, one begins to wonder if it's not too quiet and jogtrot a piece for the theatre, whether television wouldn't be its more natural medium.

That is a question that often comes up nowadays. Television, with its insatiable appetite for near-documentary drama and its love of discussion – people endlessly interviewing each other – has given a great fillip to old style realism. In one way, of course, the medium has encouraged a new style, helped in the great loosening-up process, with its preference for loosely constructed plays, quick cutting from scene to scene, visual movement rather than plot. But it can work the other way too and push the action into a frame of its own, the frame of the conventional 'talking it over' pattern: from box set to little box can involve some narrowing down and thinning. It has obviously been very helpful to new playwrights to have this other stage, and television has been a good patron, but plays written out of television rather than theatre experience can look rather small and faint in the theatre proper. This was the case with a recent play, *Siege* (1972) by a promising young playwright, David Ambrose. It was the epitome of quiet realism, a long conversation between two old men, an ex-Prime Minister and the current one in a London club, and it badly needed a camera, one felt, to give those glimpses of the happenings outside the sheltered room – buses without numbers, naked young revolutionaries – which as it was only got into the action in the most shadowy form,

---

[1] M. Billington, Introduction to *New English Dramatists* 9 (Penguin Plays series) 1966.

filtered through the polite, mannered conversation. The shadowiness was appropriate in a way, since the whole action was a dream, but it was tantalizing rather than the satisfying kind it might well have been if more sense of stage had got into it.

It is interesting to find the stage still welcoming gentle conversational forms of realism such as this. Today's is no longer the domain of the novelist as it was in the thirties: quiet narrative no longer has the same pull. Most of our leading playwrights have been actors or workers of some kind in the theatre and write almost exclusively for the stage (sometimes also the screen). Peter Brook makes the point very firmly in his discussion of the new theatre he sees emerging[1]: ' . . . the relationship between the man who sits at home working it all out on paper and the world of actors and stages is getting more and more tenuous, more and more unsatisfactory. The best English writing is coming out of the theatre itself: Wesker, Osborne, Arden, Pinter, to take obvious examples, are all directors and actors as well as authors – and at times they have even been involved as impresarios.' And yet – partly through the influence exerted by television – the theatre door is still very much open to novelists and writers with a novelistic background. David Storey, outstandingly among today's writers, moves between novel and drama with a Maugham-like ease. 'Storey, Novelist or Playwright?' is the sort of title that critics find appropriate in discussing his work[2]: significantly, one of his plays, *Home*, transferred with great ease to the television screen. In fact, in watching the filmed version[3] of the original production without having seen it on the stage, it was hard to envisage what the play would gain from stage presentation.

Storey has provided some interesting information on the genesis of *Home*: 'You remember the white table at the end of *The Contractor*? Well, this play starts from there, from the image of that white table'.[4] It's no surprise to learn this. In the television production the white table established itself immediately as a tremendously important place, the focal point for a series of meetings between the two gentlemanly old men and the two elderly ladies from a poorer, rougher social class who chat the day away in the grounds of their 'home'. Everything happens at the table and as the happenings are all conversations,

---

[1] P. Brook, *The Empty Space*, 1968, p 34.

[2] M. Bygrave, 'David Storey: Novelist or Playwright?' *Theatre Quarterly* 1, 1971.

[3] The film made by National Education Television USA was broadcast by the BBC in 1972.   [4] Quoted by J. R. Taylor in his *The Second Wave*, 1971, p 144.

the television screen seemed exactly the right size for the requirements of the action. In the opening sequence, the festive-looking white table set elegantly on a spacious terrace created a fleeting illusion of normal well-being; the melancholy strain in the tangential fragmented conversation of the two old men might have been no more than the ordinary melancholy of the N. C. Hunter/Priestley mode. It was only gradually that one realized how seriously and sombrely the disconnectedness had to be taken, that the lofty, courtly old men and the edgy, lost-looking women who joined them were all equally patients in a home of quite another sort, with no kind of cosiness about it. The moments of revelation, the 'big' moments of the play, were all physically tiny ones – the expression on one old man's face when he sees there is no chair for him (a gentle, subnormal young giant takes them away at intervals to practise weight lifting); the changes of tone and look when they settle at the table – in pairs or all four together – and try with immense difficulty to make contact with each other. Expressions of remoteness or of suspicion and hostility (in the women for the men, especially) give way to expressions of sympathy and understanding: communion builds up, holds for a few poignant moments, then is broken by some uncontrolled movement of the face or tongue.

The camera's sharp focus on the subtle changes of facial expression brought a kind of emotional coherence into the incoherent, desultory dialogue which expressed their pathetically fractured personalities. It was hard, as I said, to envisage what the play might have gained from having a stage, easy to see what it might have lost. But with another play of Storey's, *The Contractor*, the opposite is true. Physical movements are still immensely important here, but they are very large ones, so large that the small screen could hardly accommodate them and still get the total view – panorama *and* close up – which was the great feature of the stage performance.

The focal point in *The Contractor* is the lifesize marquee which the contractor's men put up from scratch on the stage – or rather, in the grounds of the contractor's home where his daughter's wedding reception is to be held (the mode is so lifelike that the word 'stage' comes to seem incongruous). The wedding party happens between acts, so that we move straight from the scene of the marquee's triumphant completion to the scene where it is being grumpily taken down, a wry arrangement which seems to be the play's deepest meaning. Not the wedding but the putting up of the marquee was the central event, and a spellbinding event it was. Audiences were fascinated by the sheer process of construction, as Storey's minutely detailed stage directions suggest that he was himself:

> They've begun to attach the rings, fastened to the necks of the canvas, round the poles. They're secured with a bolt, like a collar. The collar itself is then shackled to the pulley rope above and the ridge pole underneath. The guys they fasten off to the "pegs" in the wings.

These are directions for a spectacular transformation act which is also – though it may not be easy to feel it in the text – a poignant emotional experience, even a poetic one. Out of the rough old jumble of the stage scene – the noisy, confused effect of men at work, the fights, the swearing, the broad jokes, the simple animal behaviour (Ewbank, the contractor, has to warn the foreman against letting the men relieve themselves on the lawn in full view of the house in their usual, uninhibited way) – out of all this comes the lovely, delicate thing, the marquee, with its white ironwork tables, its pots of flowers, its air of elegance and festivity. Like the white table in *Home* it's a place where moments of tranquillity and communion are achieved by people who find such moments hard to come by. There are two high points of this kind: before the wedding, when the family come to inspect the finished marquee and are prompted by the spirit of the scene to uncharacteristic, impromptu dances among themselves (son with mother, husband with wife), and after the wedding when Ewbank serves the men with champagne and wedding cake before they leave for their next job.

In both scenes the tensions that have been building up ease; in the last a character who has been out of things, the much-teased 'half wit' is brought by the men into the centre and made much of: 'He's a damn fine lad. He is, he is. You're right.' These are moments of warmth and tenderness but we feel most sharply, perhaps, their fleetingness, that sadness which the men themselves had groped to express earlier on:

> FITZPATRICK: I remember the first day I came here, now, to work. At the beginning of the summer.
> MARSHALL (looking at the sky): It's damn near the end of it now.
> FITZPATRICK: Except in the army. I'd never seen a tent before.
> BENNETT: Aye!
> FITZPATRICK: We were driven out of the town, on one of the trucks ... Up the valley, past a lot of trees and hills. And suddenly ... looking down ... this field. Full of tents. White canvas, everywhere you looked.
> MARSHALL: Big as a balloon.
> FITZPATRICK: Big as an elephant ... Aye.

(They work for a moment in silence. Then:) When we got down here, and we got out of the cab . . .
MARSHALL: One of the favourites . . . Not riding on the back.
FITZPATRICK: I stood there, looking up at them and thinking, 'It's a damn great pity it is, to take them down at all.'
MARSHALL: I remember that day very well. Almost four hours before he did a stroke of work himself.

The last comment characteristically punctures the sentiment, keeps it in perspective, allows us to go on taking the action as lifelike (though sometimes only just, for there is a decided note of strain in the dialogue). The ending is touching in a human way as well as, clearly, ripe for allegorical interpretation. Ewbank and his wife, left alone after the men have gone, convey with moving simplicity the sense of anticlimax, the sadness of a phase of life ending:

MRS. EWBANK: . . . . . . They had a drink, then.
EWBANK: Aye. Wet the baby's head . . . (looks up at her expression) Well, I don't know, do I? These days . . . one damn thing . . . (Pause. Then:) Set an example there'll be no stopping. They'll be wanting a sup on every job from now on . . . I don't know. (Looks down at the view, standing beside her.) You'd think you'd have something to show for it, wouldn't you. After all this time.
MRS EWBANK: Well, now . . . (Abstracted)
EWBANK: I don't know . . . (Looks round. Then down at the lawn.) Made a few marks in that.
MRS. EWBANK: One or two . . .
EWBANK (Shivers. Looks up): Autumn . . .
MRS. EWBANK (Abstracted): Still . . . It's been a good summer.
EWBANK: Aye, Comes and goes.

The spare, hesitant words, the visual impact of the empty stage and bare poles where the marquee once stood make up an elegy, an elegy for the men who put up the tent, perhaps, or for the coming on of old age, or the transience of things. Storey himself recognizes all these and other possibilities: 'I see it more and more as being about – or somehow related to – the decline and fading-away of a capitalist society. Or I have seen it as a metaphor for artistic creation: all the labour of putting up this tent, and when it's there, what good is it?' There is, as J. R. Taylor comments, a 'teasing and elusive feeling' that a great range of interpretations is open.[1] And yet the words are so slight and often so

---

[1] Storey quoted by J. R. Taylor in his *The Second Wave*, p 145. His comment on the play is on the same page.

clumsy, on the whole so true to the clumsy, disoriented personalities they express. It's from the spaces around the words and their relation to the poetically expressive visual effects that the play draws its potency. Interestingly in a novelist/playwright, there is a strong pull towards silence and the mute language of the body: Storey is closer to Joyce (as playwright) here than to the majority of novelist/playwrights who write in the realistic mode.

The same pull towards the physical is felt very strongly in the drama of Arnold Wesker. Curiously, Wesker hasn't attracted much in the way of extended critical study yet, although (or perhaps because?) he invites it by his willingness to enter into critical controversy (as in his recent analysis of the critics' analysis of *The Friends*[1]) and by the remarkable openness and candour of his comments on his own creative processes.

Wesker is, up to a point, a thoroughgoing thirties style of realist. His characters are immensely voluble: they everlastingly analyze themselves, seem to imagine, as Ronnie Kahn says of himself, that they can solve things by talking about them. He specializes in that favourite type of thirties realism, the family play, handling the subject with an affection and respect[2] that is rather unusual in today's theatre where parodic treatments like Giles Cooper's *Happy Family* (1966) are rather more the rule. The key figure of the prewar family drama, the fiercely possessive mother, has an especially sympathetic role on his stage. Sarah Kahn, for instance, may be laughed at and sometimes resented by her family for her excessive preoccupation with their physical well-being – 'Food and sleep and you can see no reason why a person should be unhappy' – but the action makes a hero of her: she is continually drawing life out of the grip of illness and time's corrosions.

But of course there are striking differences too between his interests and methods and those of his predecessors. One major difference is the much greater awareness his characters have of political and social issues. His families are still intensely family-centred but they live in a political dimension too, very actively in *Chicken Soup with Barley*, in this scene, for instance, where the Kahns in their East End basement flat prepare for clashes with Mosley's Fascists, who are expected in the streets just outside their home:

DAVE: Comrades! You want to know what the plans are or you don't

---

[1] Arnold Wesker, 'The Critic in the Theatre', *Theatre Quarterly* 1, 1971.
[2] He writes interestingly on the value of the family in a recent article, 'From a Writer's Notebook', *Theatre Quarterly* 2, 1972.

want to know? Again. As we don't know what's going to happen we've done this: some of the workers are rallying at Royal Mint Street – so if the Fascists want to go through the Highway they'll have to fight for it. But we guess they'll want to stick to the main route so as not to lose face – you follow? We've therefore called the main rally at Gardiner's Corner. If on the other hand, they do attempt to pass up Cable Street –

SARAH: Everything happens in Cable Street.

HARRY: What else happened in Cable Street?

SARAH: Peter the Painter had a fight with Churchill there, didn't he?

MONTY: You're thinking of Sidney Street, sweetheart.

HARRY: You know, she gets everything mixed up.

SARAH: You're very wonderful I suppose, yes? You're the clever one.

HARRY: I don't get my facts mixed up, anyway.

SARAH: Per, per, per, per, per! Listen to him! My politician!

MONTY: Sarah, do me a favour, leave the fists till later.

DAVE: If, on the other hand, they do try to come up Cable Street then they'll meet some dockers and more barricades. And if any get through that lot then they still can't hold their meetings either in Salmon Lane or Victoria Park Square.

SARAH: Why not?

PRINCE: Because since seven this morning there's been some of our comrades standing there with our platforms.

MONTY: Bloody wonderful, isn't it? Makes you feel proud, eh Sarah? Every section of this working-class area that we've approached has responded. The dockers at Limehouse have come out to the man. The lot!

PRINCE: The unions, the Co-ops, Labour Party members and the Jewish People's Council——

SARAH: The Board of Deputies?

HARRY: There she goes again. Not the Jewish Board of Deputies – *they* asked the Jewish population to keep away. No, the Jewish People's Council – the one that organized that mass demo against Hitler some years back.

This family view of horrific political events is just the view that was missing from the thirties stage: it was left to Wesker twenty years after to express 1936 as no one then had been able or wanted to do. The eye-witness feeling he manages to get into the play is one of its most impressive effects.

It might seem to be undermined in the scene I have quoted by the amount of teaching and informing that goes on in it, rather beyond what is natural, one might think. In a way it *is* natural, though, or so we realize as the play goes along and it becomes clear that it is the nature of Wesker's characters to give and seek information: this is one of their great central drives. The effect can be irritating, even like a parody of the discussion mode – that wearisome analysis of marital troubles in *The Four Seasons*, the oppressive reiteration of principles in *Their Very Own and Golden City*. But the craving for knowledge is a source of poignancy too, especially when the viewpoint is the learner's, rather than the teacher's; when Beatie discovers her voice, for instance, or when Sarah Kahn wistfully contemplates the power of education: 'If I were young, oh, what wouldn't I study! All the world I would study. How properly to talk and to write and to make sentences. . . . '

Poignancy of this kind is a characteristic note, perhaps *the* characteristic note of Wesker's drama, stronger in the end than the other strain of Utopian confidence and optimism that also runs through it (his Shavian strain, one might say). The pattern of feeling in *The Four Seasons* is from this point of view characteristic: the emotional movement, corresponding with the cycle of Nature, is from winter – through a brief outbreak of passionate, summery feeling – to a sad autumnal end. Even the buoyant *Roots* has inertia and decay in it – 'whatever she will do they will continue to live as before' is Wesker's final dry comment on Beatie and her family – and it is flanked by two plays heavy with a sense of mortality and disappointed hopes. We don't know whether Ronnie will be able to respond to Sarah's exhortations at the close of *Chicken Soup with Barley*: – 'You'll die, you'll die – if you don't care you'll die. . . . Ronnie, if you don't care you'll die.' And *I'm Talking about Jerusalem* ends with the failure of an attempt to lead the good life in the humane tradition of William Morris: the strains of Beethoven's Ninth symphony heard at the beginning of the piece give way at the close to the sound of crying:

> RONNIE: Well Sarah – your children are coming home now.
> SARAH: You finished crying, you fool you?
> RONNIE: Cry? We must be bloody mad to cry, Mother. (*Sarah goes leaving Ronnie to linger and glance once more around. Suddenly his eye catches a stone, which he picks up and throws high into the air. He watches, and waits till it falls. Then he cups his hands to his mouth and yells to the sky with bitterness and some venom –*)
> RONNIE: We – must – be – bloody – mad – to cry!
> (*The stage is empty.*
> Soon we hear the sound of the lorry revving up and moving off.
> A last silence.
> Then –*)
>
> A LAST SLOW CURTAIN

In its leaning to melancholy and nostalgia Wesker's drama has a deep affinity with those plays of the twenties and thirties that sought to express the sadness of time's ordinary pressure on ordinary lives. Like Priestley, Wesker uses some elaborate time schemes to bring out this sadness, especially in *Their Very Own and Golden City*, where the echoes of Priestley are remarkably strong. The title recalls *They Came to A City* (1944) that other play about building the new Jerusalem, and the time structure recalls the structure of *Time and the Conways*, which is also, incidentally, haunted by the concept of a Utopian city: one thinks of Kay Conway in the far future scene replying to her sister's malicious question about the book she has never written with a sad question of her own, 'What about you, Madge? Are you building Jerusalem – in England's green and pleasant land?' The bitter contrast between youthful dreams and adult achievement that Priestley got by sandwiching an act set in the future between two in the present, Wesker gets by taking a series of running jumps into the future. The characters' youthful time is a kind of continuing present: we leave them there in Durham Cathedral dreaming of the splendid cities they will build, and go into their future in what Wesker calls flash-forwards (as opposed to flash-backs), always returning to find them still dreaming, and planning, untouched by knowledge of the disillusionments in store. There is achievement too – they do build cities – but the sharpest impression made by the time scheme is one of irony and melancholy.

A very similar effect is got by the arrangement of the plays in the trilogy, an exultant, optimistic middle action coming out of and leading into disillusionment. In *Chicken Soup and Barley*, the chronology is straightforward but the same kind of sadness builds up: enough years are covered – 1936 to 1956 – for an emphatic downward curve to show, with the exuberant militancy of the opening scene and the bustle of family life in it giving way to the deep melancholy of the end when all the young people, except Ronnie, have left the scene, the father is destroyed by strokes, and Sarah, though still fighting, is drained and exhausted. 'It's all broken up, then', says one of their old friends, who calls on them at this stage; mournfully he says to his wife, 'I wish you'd have known us in the old days; Harry there used to have a lovely tenor voice. All the songs we sang together, and the strikes and the rallies. I used to carry Ronnie shoulder high to the May Day demonstrations. Everyone in the East End was going somewhere. It was a slum, there was misery, but we were going somewhere. The East End was a big mother.'

Echoes from the past ring loudly here. The voices of Priestley's Conways drift into the mind's ear, asking each other where all the good times have gone, raging against what Time has done to them:

> KAY: . . . You see, Alan, I've not only been here to-night, I've been here remembering other nights, long ago, when we weren't like this. . . .
>
> ALAN: Yes, I know. Those old Christmasses . . . birthday parties . . .
>
> KAY: Yes, I remembered. I saw all of us then. Myself too. Oh, silly girl of nineteen-nineteen! Oh, lucky girl!
>
> ALAN: You mustn't mind too much. It's all right, y'know. Like being forty?
>
> KAY: Oh no, Alan, it's hideous and unbearable. Remember what we once were and what we thought we'd be. And now this. And it's all we have, Alan, it's *us*. Every step we've taken – every tick of the clock – making everything worse. If this is all life is, what's the use? Better to die, like Carol, before you find it out, before Time gets to work on you. I've felt it before, Alan, but never as I've done to-night. There's a great devil in the universe, and we call it Time.

'What's happened to us? Were we cheated or did we cheat ourselves?' The question is put by Ronnie but it could have been asked by almost any character in the melancholy, time-haunted drama of the English realists. Wesker's people are in a way more hopelessly trapped than Priestley's. They aren't allowed the consolation Alan offers Kay in *Time and the Conways*, when he tells her that time is an illusion; it 'merely moves us on – in this life – from one peephole to the next'; the 'real' person is immortal, has soul as well as body. For Wesker's characters 'soul' has no meaning except as a function of body. They are deeply serious materialists whose struggle to be idealists is constantly being defeated by the great, sad weight of matter.

This earthy feeling makes for melancholy but paradoxically for vigour too, and for a salty kind of humour that is much needed to counteract the earnestness and abstractness that can hang rather heavy on Wesker's drama. It needs a character like Sarah Kahn in it to bring the broody theorists down to earth. 'My thoughts keep going pop, like bubbles. That's my life now – you know? – a lot of little bubbles going pop' says Ronnie. And she deflates him with her, 'Pop! pop! pop! pop! pop! – schmop!' What a relief to be able to laugh at him for a moment, and how one longs for someone to do the same service for the two intensely earnest, self-analyzing characters who have the whole play to themselves in *The Four Seasons*.

Humour is one aspect of Wesker's earthiness; another is his candour and bravery in showing ordinary bodily life and functions on the stage. It's a candour that goes far beyond anything earlier English realists had attempted: probably it is something entirely new in the history of English theatre. From this point of view Wesker has been one of the most influential of our postwar playwrights. The importance of food and drink in his drama is one expression of his intense feeling for the life of the body. Meals are great, warm events on his stage; the preparation for them a ritual, sometimes a nerve-racking one, as in *The Kitchen*, but more often joyful in the vein of the apple strudel sequence in *The Four Seasons*. The making of the apple strudel is a bravura physical performance. 'Actors learn to fence', says Wesker, 'why not to cook?' He calls for beautiful movements in the manipulation of the pastry – the cook moves round and round the table, not too quickly – drawing comparisons with other masters of bodily skills, the doctor with his scalpel, the ballet dancer, the clown; the best chefs clown while they do it, we are told. It's hard to estimate the dramatic effect of this strange performance without having seen it done, but it seems quite likely that it would work as Wesker intended, like yeast in dough, quickening the whole action and providing needed relief from the long verbal strain of the analysis Adam and Beatrice so grimly practise on each other.

In Wesker as in playwrights like Mercer who have followed him, volubility coexists with a strong drive to silence, to dumb, physical forms of expression. His dumb scenes are usually contained in realistic limits: the long silences in *The Friends*, for instance, are there, so he says, because rehearsal experience showed them to be natural and inevitable in the situation of the play (which is a true-to-life situation). There is *some* pressure from his strong physicality to turn his drama expressionistic, as *Chips with Everything* shows. This piece plays far better than it reads, partly at least because so many of its climactic moments are expressed non-verbally, in boldly theatrical, physical terms. The young recruits' virtuoso raid on the R.A.F. coke store, for instance, came over in the theatre as Wesker said it should; it was, 'silent, precise, breathtaking, and finally very funny'; it convinced one far more effectively than their dialogue did that they were the intelligent, lively beings Wesker thinks them – and that their officers refuse to admit they might be. Other 'breathtaking' episodes of this kind were the scene of the upper class recruit's sickeningly sudden reversion to type – demonstrated by his whipping out an officer's jacket and putting it on in the middle of a sentence, his whole manner changing to match – and the brilliant final episode of the passing-out parade. In this scene the men stood rigidly to attention while the national flag was slowly hauled to the top of a very tall pole ('very tall' was Wesker's instruction) and *God Save The Queen* was played. For audiences in 1962, still accustomed to stand to attention themselves for the playing of *The Queen* at the end of theatre performances, this was an uneasy moment: people could be seen struggling to their feet and then embarrassedly sitting down again. Wesker had wickedly forced them into a subversive, non-standing position, forced home his suggestion that not standing was the appropriate position – in the deepest sense – in relation to the brutal events depicted in the R.A.F. training unit, which clearly represented the hierarchical class structure of English society as Wesker saw it.

It seemed with *Chips with Everything* that Wesker might be striking off in a new direction, towards out-and-out expressionism. But that didn't happen: in the best of his later plays, dumb, physical effects were again (and more characteristically) turned towards faithful realism. And 'faithful' seems the right word for what Wesker tries to do. He is faithful to the harsh facts of physical life as well as the joyful ones. What earlier realists like Maugham had interestingly indicated but kept muted or out of view, Wesker is prepared to place centrally on his stage: such things as illness and death are not softened nor hushed up but allowed to show their cruel edges as they would in life. Harry's first stroke in *Chicken Soup with Barley* doesn't occur off stage, as it could easily have done: there, in full view of the audience, he begins to choke and lose control, reverting to the language of his childhood and calling out distressingly for his mother. In the last act, when further strokes have brought on premature senility, he has an attack of incontinence on stage and has to be helped out, almost dragged, by Sarah. It is all there as it might be in life: the sense of squalor and resentment, the embarrassment – 'In front of Monty and Bessie. I'm so ashamed' – and the wretchedness. And under it all the touching sense of human caring – Sarah giving her last drop of energy to keeping Harry going in whatever decency is possible, the friends shocked and sad. It is a bleak and tender recording of the ordinary pains of life.

The most difficult thing of this kind Wesker has yet attempted is the representation on stage of a death from cancer in *The Friends*. Esther is slowly dying of leukemia throughout the play. Her bed is a focal point, the place where her friends (including her brother and her lover) gather to hold their long conversations and practise activities like

Yoga exercises, playing the guitar, sewing on buttons. On the occasions when Esther compels attention by speaking or (tense moments these) getting out of bed, she is an interesting character whom we want to know about; but for most of the time she is such a static, silent or sleeping figure that the interest tends to move away from her and settle where there is more happening, on Roland and Crispin, on Simone massaging Tessa's feet, on Manfred's perorations. It's easy for the audience to forget, as her friends do, what she is suffering physically; even her lover, Roland, tells himself that she feels no pain, is simply tiring and wasting away. But he is forced to know – and so are we – when she wakes from her doze in an irritable state (an extremely life-like moment), her self discipline temporarily broken, and reveals the state she is in: 'Look, Macey, bruises. My body, full of bruises, look at me, my arms, my legs, full of pain. I'm racked with pain and you all stand around.' Roland responds by rushing out to inflict pain on himself; he comes back with blood seeping through his shirt, having cut himself with a razor and rubbed salt into the cuts. A fool's act, as Manfred says, or a clown's, sad in the ludicrous way that a clown's lonely antics in a great circus ring are sad.

'Clown' is one of Wesker's favourite words. He uses it about apple-strudel making and he uses it in *The Friends* about Manfred's enormous speech, his précis of the revolutions in scientific thought which are changing man's concept of the universe although most individual men, such as the friends, have probably never heard of them. Wesker directs the actor playing Manfred to make as much sense of the précis as possible 'while at the same time clowning the story'. It's this willingness to clown, to let themselves be seen as clumsy and totally exposed and inadequate as well as masterfully fluent that forces respect for Wesker's characters, it seems to me (as well as for Wesker himself). *The Friends* ends with an extraordinary scene in this semi-ludicrous vein. To the refrain, 'She wanted to live', repeated on different notes and finally shouted exultantly, the friends break through their inhibitions about death; they lift up the dead body, embrace it, seat it in 'Esther's chair' at the centre of the stage, and raise the dead hand in a salute to the facing portrait of Lenin. Then they go about the small ordinary tasks of clearing up, folding away blankets and so on, with the dead girl sitting bolt upright among them. Like Roland's self-wounding, it is a ludicrous and rather terrible gesture. He *would* feel her physical pain (something we can't do for each other); they *will* keep the loved body alive. Esther herself was trying to keep the dead alive in a different way:

early in the play she was seen at work cutting out old sepia photographs to add to the family mosaic she has made on an old screen. This screen, Wesker says, is an 'area of the set rich in brown, black and white tones and nostalgia'. Nostalgia; that key word of English realism. But here the soft nostalgic mood mixes with a new raw physicality out of which comes the painfully grotesque ending – a desperate materialistic resurrection.

Wesker's curious mixture of clowning and pain, of wordiness and physicality, has set the pattern for much of today's realistic drama. In David Pinner's *Dickon* (1966), for instance, a man dies on stage of lung cancer while a voluble analysis flows around him; he taking his own part in it, charting his own symptoms[1] and so on (on an increasingly feverish, delirious note) until the bitter end. In David Storey's early play, *The Restoration of Arnold Middleton*, the characters turn events into analysis so smoothly that the central episode, the neurotic hero's apparent seduction of his mother-in-law comes through in a rather unsatisfactorily blurred way, but even here the action moves to a sharp physical climax when Arnold's recovery of sanity is represented as a 'happening', in the direct way that Harry's stroke is represented in *Chicken Soup with Barley*. He suddenly starts to shout:

> ARNIE: Oh! (Cries out.)
> JOAN: Arnie.
> ARNIE: Oh! There's something coming out!
> JOAN: Arnie . . .
> ARNIE: Oh, dear, Joan.
> JOAN: Arnie . . . It's all right.
> ARNIE: Oh, dear, Joan. There's something here . . . that's very hard . . . Merciless.
> JOAN: Arnie . . . It's all right.
> ARNIE: Oh, dear, oh!
> (He covers up his head.)
> JOAN: Arnie.
> ARNIE: Oh, dear. Oh, dear. There's something. What? Oh, dear. There's something coming out.
> JOAN: Arnie.
> (He looks up, still holding his head.)
> Come on, now.
> ARNIE: Oh. Oh.

---

[1] There is a Gothic note of comic horror in some of this; for instance, his account of the loss of feeling in his feet: 'They're not there! Don't tell lies! They've cut them off – like pig's trotters – pink pig's trotters – someone's eaten them – gobble – gobble. . . .'

(His hands are clasped to the top of his head.)
What am I to do?
JOAN: Here.
(She holds out her hand.)
ARNIE: Oh. *Now*. (Screams, hugely. Then:)
JOAN: It's all over.

It sometimes looks as though these realists are deliberately setting out to prove Freud wrong in his assertion that physical – as distinct from psychic – illness – was not a suitable subject for dramatic treatment. Like Wesker, they feel the need to clown in handling their painful material: indeed they need it more: no one else, I think, has taken quite the straight, head-on approach that he does to events like Harry's strokes or the death of Esther. Generally, the pressure from this kind of material has pushed the forms of realism nearer to farce. The 'heartless' techniques of that form have proved immensely valuable for controlling and distancing experiences that press too heavily on the heart to make dramatic pleasure easily possible (pleasure must always be an element in the theatrical experience, after all). One can't tell whether Peter Nichols would have been able to handle his harrowing subject – the pain of having a spastic child – in *A Day in the Death of Joe Egg* (1967) without the help of the comic patter the child's father is given to put him at some distance from the pain. But without the lift this comedy gives, it would certainly have been harder for us to respond as Nichols wants us to respond to the sight of the afflicted child, not with the kind of pity that is also a shrinking but with the fuller sympathy that might come out of a whole evening willingly spent in contemplating the distressing subject. Nichols has made other interesting explorations in this area of painful farce, notably in *The National Health* (1970) where pantomime techniques come into play at the most serious moments, at the kidney operation, for instance, when the surgeon rises up on a stage trap, spotlit like a prima donna taking the centre of the stage for the big aria; a disturbingly absurd effect.

It's not only for handling harsh physical material though, that farce is proving so attractive to present-day realists. It offers, too, release from the pressure to analyze and formulate in the over-explicit way that has for so long been the bogie of realism. It isn't easy to shake off the habit, of course. Pedagogic situations and characters stay top favourites with today's realists: clergymen, schoolmasters, psychiatrists abound, analyzing themselves, battling with their schizophrenia, fulminating against the tyranny of reason and ordered language but very much slaves of reason; able to break out usually only by breaking down. Farce is often used as a way of showing breakdown – and also in a more lighthearted way as an expression of the normal, intuitive, anarchical self, still alive there under the weight of all those words. We get a significant number of plays showing us high jinks in the academic world: from the student's viewpoint in David Halliwell's *Little Malcolm and his Struggle against the Eunuchs* (1965), from the school teacher's in *The Restoration of Arnold Middleton* (where a suit of armour grotesquely figures), from the University teacher's in Simon Gray's *Butley* (1970).

These are rather desperate though often very funny exercises. The excessively analytical hero can't stop himself analyzing and in a way doesn't want to. He's not a true farce hero, who can let himself be carried along by the irresistible flow of events, in the way of, say, Orton's opportunistic Dr Prentice in *What the Butler Saw*. The pedagogues of the realistic drama can't give up being pedagogues; they always have to be creating the situations, controlling the dialogue. There is some nice fun and free-seeming improvisation in plays like *Little Malcolm and his Struggle against the Eunuchs* and *Butley* but the tight, controlled, analytical situation of realism stands firm, even against the waves flung at it from the anarchical sea of farce.

David Mercer's is some of the oddest in this odd mixed mode. He is a very prolific writer for both television and stage, and interesting from several different points of view; in his handling of politics, for instance, or as an adaptor of television techniques for the stage. But what I am concerned with is the curious way he uses farce, both as a means of expressing inner fantasies and as a way of containing them within an ordered, reasoning structure.

Mercer is an analytical realist to the core, although violent physical actions occur on his stage and strange fantasies (often to do with animals and their uninhibited life) are acted out there. His farcical technique functions as a defuser, taking the heat out of the wild events, allowing us to contemplate them coolly and rationally: paradoxically, farce in his drama isn't a turning away from motive and the analysis of motive but a way of leading back into it.

The scene of Esme's murder in *Flint* is typical. Victoria comes on in this scene pushing her sister-in-law in her wheelchair in her accustomed style and stands talking to her, hands on her shoulders: 'I had such a lovely dream last night, Esme. Though it was upsetting at first. (Pause.) It all took place in Dieppe and it was about the second coming.

(Pause.) I've never been to Dieppe. But it makes me think of ships, and cranes, and those green French trains waiting for all the travellers from England.' Dieppe is the triggering-off word for the stream of consciousness that follows. Dieppe stands for Esme's catastrophic honeymoon with Flint, her discovery of her frigidity (expressed in the hysterical paralysis that has kept her in a wheelchair during her married life) and Flint's reaction to this, his liaison with Victoria, which is now a thing of the past to him though not to her.

> VICTORIA: You could walk *before* the church burnt down. (Pause.) Couldn't you, Esme? (Pause.) You've always had periods of – what do the doctors call it? – spontaneous remission. (Pause.) Whenever he took a new woman. (Pause.) The painter Sickert painted some lovely pictures in Dieppe. And that was where Jesus came again, in my dream. (Pause.) I was in a shabby little hotel. I was waking up. I'd set my alarm to ring exactly at dawn. (Pause.) But the sun didn't rise, Esme. (Pause.) There was no light of any kind. (Pause.) Then it happened. (Pause.) Down from the sky. (Pause.) A thousand feet tall. A thousand feet at least. (Pause.) Jesus descended. (Pause.) There was a brilliant aura round him. (Pause.) Owing to his enormous size, one could easily perceive each detail. (Pause.) He wore a blue velvet cap with a little brim, Esme. And a white cricket shirt. And white cricket trousers. . . . I looked at the heavenly cricketer floating gently from the black sky, and I cried with love and gratitude. But. D'you know, Esme. As those monumental blancoed shoes of His touched the ground – he disappeared in a great flash of light and smoke. (Pause.) Like the demon king at the pantomimes only, of course, not the same at all, being Jesus. (Pause.) And the sun was in the sky. And I suddenly knew that we were all immortal now. But immortal on this earth. (Pause.) Now I know it was only a dream. But it leaves me with the feeling that Dieppe must be an extraordinary place.

There's a touch too much elaboration and contrivance in this to make it quite convincing in either realistic or farcical terms. But then we move into a passage of farce which does make a real impression of a mind wildly out of control:

> FLINT: Victoria – Esme doesn't look at all well.
> VICTORIA: She *isn't* well, Ossian.
> FLINT: Hadn't we better phone Patrick Colley?
> VICTORIA: That won't be at all necessary. I was telling Esme all about my dream last night.
> DIXIE: We were wondering where you were.
> FLINT: goes towards *Esme*, reaching his hand out.
> VICTORIA: Don't touch her!

FLINT (stops): I want to know what's wrong with her.

VICTORIA: I expect my silly old maunderings sent her to sleep. We've been out in the sunshine, you know. And the air's rather fresh. (Pause.) She didn't like that policeman who came to see you. (Pause.) I bought her an icecream in Kensington Gardens. Then I brought her home and kept her in the kitchen. Didn't you look in the kitchen.

DIXIE: I did.

VICTORIA (smiling): We were in the pantry.

FLINT: Why don't you make us some tea, Victoria?

VICTORIA: Sly one! You're only trying to get rid of me. (Pause.) But my sister needs me.

FLINT: Dixie will look after her, whilst you make the tea.

VICTORIA: Esme and I have had a beautiful relationship for many years. Don't think you know everything, Ossian! (Pause.) She loathes you.

FLINT: Well. I do know that.

VICTORIA: She hoped you'd be sent to prison.

Dixie steps forward close to Victoria.

DIXIE: Will you bloody well wake her up?

Victoria looks from Flint to Dixie, smiling. Then, almost coyly, she gives Esme a push from behind. Esme slumps forward across her own knees: there is a knife in her back.

The characteristic movement of the play is the movement we get here between explanations – with a fair amount of dotting i's and crossing t's – and freewheeling revelations. Flint has a gift for creating anarchical situations as when he and Dixie are almost caught making love in their underwear in the church vestry, he having forgotten that it's the night for choir practice: in the confusion that follows when the church is set on fire by his pipe, he and Dixie clad in cassocks make their escape through smoke past the incredulous choir – And who was *them*? Ghosts? – and the scene ends in a great pandemonium, with firemen rushing through the vestry, setting up ladders and unreeling hoses, while the choirmaster dementedly tries to save his harmonium and the stuffy curate announces: 'Well, since the fire brigade's here, you might as well get on with your fatuous priorities. *I* intend to save the Parish register.' As the Bishop comments, Flint is rapidly turning a dying institution into chronic farce.

But still, he's not a clergyman for nothing: he can sermonize with the best of them. Oddly, he moves out of farcical scenes like the vestry affair into long, moralizing speeches which are not set up for mockery, as when he reflects on the difficulty of faith: 'Injustice, poverty, exploitation . . . well, they've led more than one scrupulous and compassionate cleric from the Sermon on the Mount to the works of Vladimir Ilyich Lenin.'

In other plays, the pull to explanation and exhortation is stronger still. Mercer's characters are always looking for somebody to sell their self analysis to: the hero of *Ride a Cock Horse*, for instance, goes from wife to mistress to whore, endlessly comparing his responses and examining his motives, as when he says to his wife about his mistress: 'I think it's very odd. Very interesting. That I should go for somebody who's past having children. A mother figure's one thing. A sterile mother figure's gruesome.' They seem hardly capable at all of unselfconscious actions. Even the seventeen-year-old Claire in *After Haggerty* has to examine her emotional state (though humorously) in the very act of eloping – 'I mix my vernaculars because I am an adolescent in a condition of revolt.' The fearful volubility of Mercer's characters is often convincing as a symptom of the mental disturbance so many of them suffer from, but it can become very unpersuasive dramatically. It's a relief when the closed, analytical situation opens up and we get something freer, either by way of cinematic swoops and leaps (such as those out of Bernard's room to public platforms in Moscow and Havana in *After Haggerty*) or through farce.

This freewheeling strain has got stronger in Mercer's drama: some of his recent work has taken on a decided look of Joe Orton; *Flint* especially has much in common with *Funeral Games*,[1] including a manic clergyman (Orton has two) at the centre of the action and the use of a clipped, comically deadpan style for some peculiar discussions of peculiar events. Here is Flint talking to his curate, Swash:

FLINT: Do you find God fun, Eric?
SWASH: Oh stop it!
FLINT: I've been agnostic for over forty years. Ever since I was ordained. I doubt if I could have survived without a complete lack of faith.
SWASH: I hear they're going to cut your electricity off next. (Smugly) *And* the water.
FLINT: I shouldn't think God finds *you* much fun, eh?

And this is one of Orton's clergymen, Pringle, receiving a visitor:

CAULFIELD: My name is Caulfield. We spoke over the telephone.
PRINGLE: I remember you distinctly. Do come in.
Caulfield closes the door.

---

[1] *Flint* was first produced on 5 May 1970 (at the Criterion Theatre). *Funeral Games* was produced by Yorkshire Television 25 Aug 1968, though not published till 1970.

PRINGLE: Sit down. Or kneel if you'd prefer. I want you to behave naturally.
(Pause.)
Shall I ring for a hassock?
CAULFIELD: These chairs look comfortable.
He sits.
PRINGLE: They're unsuitable for trances. Are you a praying man?
CAULFIELD: I'm lost in thought occasionally.
PRINGLE: We've a house of contemplation, in the Arcade. Pay us a visit. (Pause.) Have you heard of my group? The Brotherhood. We hang about on street corners.
CAULFIELD: I've read of your activities in the Press. Weren't you had up for causing an affray?
PRINGLE: We were waylaid after conducting a 'God and You' meeting. Several of our members were arrested due to Jesuit intrigue. (He takes a cigarette box from the desk.) Have a herbal?
CAULFIELD: I'd rather smoke my own.
He takes a packet of cigarettes from his pocket.
PRINGLE: Would you like to chew a bit of root I dug up in the garden of Gethsemane?
CAULFIELD: No. If it's all the same to you. (He lights a cigarette.)
PRINGLE: I never have to worry about dental decay since my Holy Land trip.

Mercer doesn't ever get right out into this free, zany dimension that Orton can sustain throughout the full length of a play. His farce has to keep explaining itself. After the murder of Esme, Victoria says to Flint, 'There *is* a thick mist in my head sometimes, but you roll it away, Ossian.' We often go with his characters inside that mist and experience in a very direct way the disappearance of reason's landmarks, but we always emerge to the sound of the analyst's voice pointing out directions for us.

In attempting as they increasingly do, bizarre, mixed forms of this kind, the English realists are responding, it seems, to the Dionysian spirit that is invading the present-day theatre. Whether the forms of realism will break down in the process or assimilate and survive is a question for the future. But whatever the answers may be, the achievement of the last fifteen years has its own value: it has been a time of great opening up which has produced both interesting new growths and some good fruit with a new full-bodied flavour in the old mode of faithful realism.

1. *Texts*
    Mercer, D.:
    The Generations: Where the Difference Begins; A Climate of Fear; The Birth of a Private Man, 1964
    Ride a Cock Horse, 1966
    Three Television Comedies, 1966
    Belcher's Luck, 1967
    The Parachute, 1967. Also *Let's Murder Vivaldi; In Two Minds*. Television plays.
    The Governor's Lady, 1968
    After Haggerty, 1970
    Flint, 1970
    On the Eve of Publication and other plays, 1970

    Storey, D.:
    The Restoration of Arnold Middleton, 1967
    In Celebration, 1969
    The Contractor, 1970
    Home, 1970
    The Changing Room, 1971

    Wesker, A.:
    The Wesker Trilogy, 1960
    The Kitchen. First version in *New English Dramatists* 2 1960, rev; published separately by Cape 1961
    Chips with Everything, 1962
    The Four Seasons, 1966. (In *New English Dramatists* 9)
    Their Very Own and Golden City, 1966
    The Friends, 1970
    Fears of Fragmentation. 1970, Essays
    Six Sundays in January, 1971. Stories etc, and the television play, *Menace*

2. *Critical Writings*
    Armstrong, W. A. (ed) *Experimental Drama*, 1963
    Brown, J. R. and B. Harris (eds) *Contemporary Theatre*, 1962
    Hayman, R. *Arnold Wesker*, 1970. Contemporary Playwright's series.

    Kitchin, L.:
    Mid-Century Drama, 1960
    Drama in the Sixties, 1966
    Leeming, G. and S. Trussler. *The Plays of Arnold Wesker*, 1971
    Taylor, J. R.:
    Anger and After, 1969 rev.
    The Second Wave, 1971

III

Joyce via Pinter

The continuity of English realism was interestingly illustrated when Pinter's production of Joyce's *Exiles* was given at the Aldwych by the Royal Shakespeare Company in 1971.[1] Here was a play of the twenties – its first London production was in 1926[2] – that seemed completely at home in the world of Pinter. It was well in his world: he had directed it and his own new play, *Old Times*, was in repertory with it.

Exiles took so easily to Pinter's direction that as the reviewers were quick to point out, it might almost have been written by him. It was common to hear people wondering whether Pinter really *had* written it, in the sense, they would explain, of cutting or rearranging or, above all, of introducing un-Joycean silences so as to manoeuvre it into a more Pinteresque position.

If one did have any doubts of this kind, a very quick re-reading of the text would be enough to dispel them and show that Pinter had followed his directions with exactly the same kind of scrupulous accuracy that Joyce put into devising them. To read the play with the production fresh in mind is to get an uncanny sense of two minds functioning as one; Pinter, one feels, must have loved the meticulousness of Joyce's stage directions, enjoyed making the scene look exactly as it is said to look, open window on left, framed crayon drawing of young man on the wall above the sideboard, faded plush upholstery. Was this upholstery green, as Joyce says, and did Bertha make her first entrance in a lavender dress with cream gloves knotted round the handle of her sunshade?

---

[1] First produced at the Mermaid 12 Nov 1970; at the Aldwych 7 Oct 1971.

[2] It was written in 1915 and first produced abroad: the first London production was by the Stage Society 14 Feb 1926.

These would be rather absurd questions to ask as a rule, but Pinter's production made them seem natural. It is clear from the text, though, that the play badly needs a stage to bring its tiny detail alive, to get us interested and involved in it in something like the way the characters themselves are. On the page the meticulous stage directions are dull reading. There is no attempt to liven them up for the reader in Shavian style or to treat them in a novelistic way as so many of the stage realists do. The tone is cool, expressionless, as of one recording what is happening on some actual stage in front of him: 'BRIGID goes out on the left. BERTHA goes towards the double doors and fingers the curtains nervously, as if settling them. The hall door is heard to open.' And so on.

One notices the importance of pauses and silences in the text after having seen the production, but it would be easy to overlook them without that help. Joyce doesn't draw attention to them by the typographical layout as Pinter does: he sets it all flatly down, dialogue, pauses, directions for every tiny move, and leaves the reader to do his own production. Even one of the best readers he ever had, Ezra Pound, found it hard to see the action in his mind. 'It takes about all the brains I've got to take in (the) thing, *reading*,' he wrote to Joyce in 1915, and 'even read it takes very close concentration'. As his phrasing implies, it was hard for Pound to imagine that it might be less rather than more difficult to follow on the stage. He hadn't much sympathy with the theatre – 'a gross, coarse form of art' – and assumed that the average audience would be quite incapable of concentrating as he had needed to do. Still, with his good instinct for possibilities, he admitted that he might be wrong about this and that 'the actual people moving on a stage might underline and emphasize . . . . the changes of mood.'[1] He would surely have thought, if he had been able to see it, that this was exactly what happened in Pinter's production; it might even have converted him to a radically different view of the play as a piece essentially theatrical and needing to be seen rather than essentially literary and needing to be read.

This at any rate is how it seems to me. The play on the page is misleading in all sorts of ways: its humour doesn't show much, the interest of some of the smaller details, especially around the character of Beatrice, isn't clear, the poignancy of the silent moments, particularly Bertha's long-held silence at the end of the 'seduction' scene, is almost missed.

---

[1] This and the other comments are from Pound's letter to Joyce of 6 Sept 1951; rptd in *Pound/Joyce*, ed E. Read, 1968.

On stage it was a different matter. The silences became subtly and movingly expressive in a way that Joyce had prepared for but couldn't in the nature of things realize in print. He brings down the curtain in the second act, for instance, on Robert begging Bertha to stay with him: 'Do not go, Bertha! There is time still. Do you love me too? I have waited a long time. Do you love us both – him and also me? Do you, Bertha? The truth! Tell me. Tell me with your eyes. Or speak!' Then follows the stage direction: 'She does not answer. In the silence the rain is heard falling'.

The words are banal but on stage the situation wasn't. After two acts of tightly held tension and probing, with every action being turned into food for analysis, this non-verbal moment came as an exquisite relief, almost in itself the consummation that Bertha and Robert were looking for. The direction 'In the silence the rain is heard falling' suggests that Joyce was aiming at just that impression of lyrical sadness that Pinter brought out so delicately.

And yet it was also a moment of deep frustration. 'She does not answer'. In this simple sentence, which needs a stage to realize its force, Joyce seems to be anticipating almost the whole of Pinter. A drama of silence and 'not knowing' is contained in *Exiles*, though it's enclosed in the framework of a wordier and more knowing kind of realism.

To see *Old Times* just after Joyce's play was a curious, almost ghostly experience. There again was the silent woman, the probing husband, the jealousy of the past and the nostalgia for it. The play opened with an inquisition: Deeley forcing his wife back into her memories, pressing her to recall details about the friend of her youth:

> KATE (Reflectively): Dark.
> Pause
> DEELEY: Fat or thin?
> KATE: Fuller than me, I think.
> Pause
> DEELEY: She was then?
> KATE: I think so.
> DEELEY: She may not be now.
> Pause. Was she your best friend?
> KATE: Oh, what does that mean?
> DEELEY: What?
> KATE: The word friend ... when you look back ... all that time.
> DEELEY: Can't you remember what you felt?

In the process of this investigation – the friend makes a mysteriously sudden appearance to take her part in it – the memories of all three tangle and merge in such a way that it becomes difficult for us, as for her husband, to separate what is said about one woman from what is said about the other. At times the wife, Kate, seems to fade out. At other times it's the husband who appears not to exist: the women's memories take them into an intimacy so deep that it is hardly possible to see them any more as separate beings; they complement each other, seeming to make up a whole, perhaps the woman the husband thinks or wants to think he has married.

A good deal of this looks as though it could have come out of hints in *Exiles* though Pinter's style is so distinctive and bold that it seems rather more natural to think of Joyce's play as Pinteresque than Pinter's as Joycean.

One of these 'Pinteresque' moments is the bizarre dialogue between Richard and Beatrice when he takes her point by point through Robert's supposedly secret lovemaking. It has a strong resemblance to the opening of *Old Times*:

BERTHA: He was very nervous. You saw that?
RICHARD: Yes. I saw it. What else went on?
BERTHA: He asked me to give him my hand.
RICHARD (Smiling): In marriage?
BERTHA (Smiling): No, only to hold.
RICHARD: Did you?
BERTHA: Yes (Tearing off a few petals.) Then he caressed my hand and asked would I let him kiss it. I let him.
RICHARD: Well?
BERTHA: Then he asked could he embrace me – even once? . . . And then...
RICHARD: And then?
BERTHA: He put his arm round me. . . .
RICHARD (As before): . . . And then?
BERTHA: He asked for a kiss. I said: 'Take it.'
RICHARD: And then?
BERTHA (Crumpling a handful of petals): He kissed me.
RICHARD: Your mouth?
BERTHA: Once or twice.
RICHARD: Long kisses?
BERTHA: Fairly long. (Reflects.) Yes, the last time.

The comical and the troubling were subtly blended in this strange dialogue. Bertha's accurate replies – those 'fairly long' kisses – were very funny: the laughter they started up put an ironical focus on Richard's obsessional questioning. But the scene was disturbing too, suggesting a tormented voyeurism in Richard and a complicity in Bertha, which could seem perverted too or could be put down to her simplicity, the 'virginity of her soul' as Richard calls it.

Perhaps it was rather difficult to take the 'simple' interpretation from Vivien Merchant's playing, which was in her most finished Pinter style, suggesting a less artless character. But Bertha is something of a riddle too. She has hidden depths, as the strange scene with Beatrice shows, when first she harasses her and then woos her. This came to life on the stage as it hardly does on the page: it was one of the episodes that most needed to be seen. Beatrice became a much more rounded and interesting character – her nervous hesitations, pauses, retreats into silence helped to define her – and the relationship between the two women came over not as the peculiar, strained affair it can seem in reading but as a deeply feminine encounter of half-expressed feelings, delicate nuances. There was a pathetic note about it, too: Bertha's lapse into girlishness gave a sense of her relief at the momentary freedom from masculine pressure; both these women, one remembered, were in a way victims of the same man.

The Bertha/Beatrice relationship brings us again into the sphere of *Old Times*. Joyce's saying about Bertha – 'A faint glimmer of lesbianism irradiates this mind' – seems just the right delicate wording for the impression the Kate/Anna situation makes. And the doubts that come up in *Old Times* about whether the two women really do have a separate existence come up in *Exiles* too about Richard and Robert, in a more muted form.

They were very much *there* in Pinter's production as independent characters. That was what made the confessional scene between them so touching. There was a sense of real human contact between two people who found real contact difficult, the introvert who tended to analyze feeling away and the extrovert actor, never sure whether his feeling was quite real. At this point *Exiles* opened up into a tenderer, warmer kind of realism; a Chekhovian note sounded.

Yet there was a faint suggestion too of something more like Beckett than Chekhov, just a hint that these two opposites were the elements of one divided being, a Richard/Robert, comparable to the Kate/Anna who seems to be continually dissolving and reforming in *Old Times*. This was one of the moments when Joyce began to look a rather important progenitor, despite the obvious weaknesses of *Exiles* as a self-

Vivien Merchant as Bertha and John Wood as Richard in the Royal Shakespeare Company's production of James Joyce's Exiles, *directed by Harold Pinter, at the Aldwych Theatre.*

Photograph: John Haynes

PLATE 1

Colin Blakely as Deeley and Dorothy Tutin as Kate in Peter Hall's production of Old Times *by Harold Pinter, at the Aldwych Theatre.*

Photograph: Dominic

PLATE 2

Fay Compton as Ruth, Kay Hammond as Elvira, and Margaret Rutherford as Madame Arcati in Noel Coward's Blithe Spirit *at the Piccadilly Theatre.*

PLATE 3

Dorothy Tutin as Kate, Colin Blakely as Deeley, and Vivien Merchant as Anna in Peter Hall's Royal Shakespeare Company production of Harold Pinter's Old Times *at the Aldwych Theatre.*
Photograph: Dominic

PLATE 4

contained work, its anti-climactic last act, its occasional descents into total banality.

There are certainly a remarkable number of lines out from it to Pinter's plays. The motive of wanting to 'know' is central in a similar way. Joyce almost seems to have invented Pinter's technique for expressing it, a more sadistic version of Ibsen's inquisitory method. His own phrase for *Exiles*, 'three cat and mouse acts' has an obvious appropriateness to Pinter, and there are some interesting similarities of detail in the way the technique is applied. The scene in *The Homecoming*, when Lenny cruelly plies Teddy with pseudo-philosophical questions, or in *The Collection* when James and Bill fence over the 'seduction' of Stella – this last particularly – are startlingly like the first dialogue between Richard and Robert, when Robert 'plays' with Richard, taking him to be in the dark, and Richard all the time is playing with him, watching and setting traps.

Knowing and wanting to know lead into 'not knowing' in *Exiles*, as in all Pinter's plays, though here Joyce's method separates and starts to look more like the expository method of the realism of his time. This is true at any rate of the third act. If the play had ended where in some ways one rather wishes it had, on the fine close of Act 2, it would have made an impact much more in Pinter's style. It's a fruitful state of doubt we're left in there: all the revelations, all the nuances of the preceding scene are drawn into it. We have the material to interpret Bertha's silence for ourselves, to see why it could mean response, why in a way it *should* mean that, and why it could and probably does mean refusal.

Of course Joyce could have made dramatic capital out of the non-event as Pinter does out of our not knowing whether there is or is not an act of adultery in *The Collection*. But he doesn't do this. The third act is a rather painful anti-climax, it almost looks like a concession to contemporary standards of respectability; no one need feel too uncomfortable about the possibility of Bertha having committed adultery: there's too much laborious evidence to show how little time there was for it to leave the question a very open one.

The characters turn very didactic too, once the burning issue is no longer ablaze. It's true that from the start they had more knowledge of themselves and were allowed to expound it more openly than Pinter would ever let his characters do. Here Joyce was writing very much in the manner of the standard Ibsenite realism of his day. But in the earlier scenes this method worked. The confessions Richard and Robert make to each other came out naturally, stimulated by the bizarre situation, husband and would-be lover waiting for their victim. She *is* their victim. What they confess to is a greater interest in each other than in her. Richard enjoyed thinking of her being seduced by his friend: 'in the very core of my ignoble heart I longed to be betrayed by you and by her – in the dark, in the night – secretly, meanly, craftily.' Similarly Robert wants her because she is Richard's creation: 'You are so strong that you attract me even through her.' At least this was how it started: when he makes love to her later it begins to seem a more straight-forward desire, less insulting to her.

All this is absorbing in a live dramatic way. But when the tension goes out of the situation in the last act the tendency of the characters to explain themselves rather drags down the dramatic vitality. It also raises doubts about their credibility in a way one isn't quite sure Joyce intends. There's a stagey note in Richard's summing up of the situation that leaves one uneasy: 'I have wounded my soul for you – a deep wound of doubt which can never be healed. I can never know, never in this world. I do not wish to know or to believe. I do not care. It is not in the darkness of belief that I desire you. But in restless living wounding doubt. To hold you by no bonds, even of love, to be united with you in body and soul in utter nakedness – for this I longed. And now I am tired for a while, Bertha. My wound tires me.'

Bertha's rhetoric is stagier still, but at this late point in the play we have to accept it, as we have to take Richard's: this is the 'truth'. 'Forget me, Dick', she says, 'Forget me and love me again as you did the first time. I want my lover. To meet him, to go to him, to give myself to him. You, Dick. O, my strange wild lover, come back to me again!'

This was sadly banal after the subtle and poignant climax of the previous act. Yet the situation was still full of interest and again it pointed in directions that Pinter has explored. *The Lover* and *Landscape* seem almost like projections from her speech. In both plays her dream of a lover/husband is acted out, in *The Lover* threateningly, in *Landscape* more gently and lyrically. There's even a faint visual echo of *Exiles* in the scene of *Landscape*, a woman sitting, withdrawn, lost in reverie while a man desperately tries to get a response from her.

Bertha and Beth are both pathetic figures, driven into this melancholy fixation on the past, it seems, by some deep failure in their marital life (the cruelty of both Richard and Duff is obviously an element in it). Nostalgia, as it's expressed through these characters, seems the mood of a deprived, even crippled condition.

But the feeling of nostalgia in both plays goes much beyond this. We seem to be invited not just to pity but to sympathize and even identify with it. This is rather what the elaborate lyricism of Beth's language suggests, and the way it's protected from irony by the monologue structure. While in *Exiles* there is strong reinforcement for Bertha's romanticism from the rest of the play. Richard and Robert are equally preoccupied with the past, saddened by the falling away they see in themselves from their youthful ideals. 'Yes, it is the language of my youth', Richard says when Robert quotes his own words to him in support of his right to love Bertha freely. The line comes over with a wistfulness which is very much the prevailing mood of the play. They are all exiles from the golden age of their youth.

So are Pinter's characters in *Old Times*, the play which brings out his affinity with Joyce perhaps more strikingly than any other. The note is sounded by Anna, when she reconstructs *their* golden age of the thirties: 'We sat hardly breathing with our coffee, heads bent, so as not to be seen, so as not to disturb, so as not to distract, and listened and listened to all those words, all those cafés and all those people, creative undoubtedly, and does it still exist I wonder? do you know? can you tell me?'

In this mood – which has become very strong in the last few plays – Pinter joins Joyce in the centre of the English realist tradition. Their fascination with the small detail of domestic life is another link with each other and with the playwrights of the interwar period, and it's in this area that *Exiles* seems – in its low key, tentative way – something of an innovatory piece. It offers a technique which no one had used in quite that way before in the English theatre for keeping the banal material taut and turning it towards a searching reading of character; a version of Ibsen's 'investigation' technique with silence, pauses, visual movement used in something more like the Chekhovian way.

That Joyce had hit on a method of real value for extending the limits of realism is shown by the way Pinter has been able to make use of techniques that are often so strikingly similar. Some of the innovations in *Exiles* anticipate *The Family Reunion* too, and that in its turn anticipates a great deal of Pinter. Here is a strong line of continuity, in fact, from Joyce to Pinter; from *Exiles* through *The Family Reunion* to *Old Times* and *The Homecoming*. Oddly, the titles of their plays are often interchangeable, a fact that seems of some significance.

Although a weak play in some ways, *Exiles* has a more important place in the tradition than has commonly been agreed. It can't be seen since Pinter's production as a dead end, a flat exercise in an outworn form of realism. It remains difficult to read, and perhaps over-dependent on production, but in a theatre tuned to Pinter's style it should have better prospects of getting produced and given the chance to show its peculiar kind of delicate interest.

1. *Texts*
   Exiles, 1918, 1952 (with Joyce's notes and introduction by Padraic Colum)

2. *Critical Writings*
   Read, F. (ed) *Pound/Joyce*, 1968
   Mason, E. and R. Ellmann (eds) *The Critical Writings of James Joyce*, 1959
   Cunningham, F. R. *Joyce's Exiles: a problem of dramatic stasis, Modern Drama,*
   Feb 1970

IV

T. S. Eliot

At first glance Eliot's progress as a playwright seems to be a movement away from experiment. His most modern-looking piece, a jazz melodrama, was published in 1926; his last play, produced in 1958, looks more like a piece of staid neo-Ibsenism. Many of his critics saw the postwar plays as a regression: even Martin Browne, who produced them all and was deeply in sympathy with his playwright, was inclined to take that view. He thought them an unconscious reversion to the style of theatre Eliot had known as a young man. Eliot did jokingly say himself about some improvement suggested for *The Cocktail Party* that every step seemed to take him nearer to Lonsdale.

But experiment of some kind is going on all the time in Eliot's drama. He had an extraordinarily keen sense of new theatrical possibilities. *Sweeney Agonistes*, his most radical experiment (of the plays not written for religious occasions) was so far ahead of orthodox theatre practice that for years it was thought of as a poem rather than as what it now clearly looks to be, an exciting (if unfinished) piece of theatre. *The Cocktail Party* has a claim to be considered the first black comedy in the postwar English theatre and *The Confidential Clerk* indicated some interesting new directions for farce. Both these plays, and in its own way *The Elder Statesman*, explore subjects that fascinate the modern theatre – role playing, the search for identity – with techniques that foreshadow those of Albee and Pinter.

Eliot's central characters suffer from a troubling sense of division between their real and their acted selves. 'Real' self is a concept that still has force in his drama – here he separates from successors like Pinter – but the performing self is very much in the foreground,

uneasily conscious of its liability to be taken over by the 'speechless self', the mute, tough one.

Eliot finds some interesting answers to the problem of how to represent these selves, with their different voices. To a great extent, of course, he relies on the traditional means of verse drama, imagery. There is a tremendous amount of acting imagery in the plays, a fact that Martin Browne draws attention to in his absorbing account of his collaboration with Eliot; an indispensable book, this, for anyone concerned with the drama of the period as well as with Eliot's work.[1] Through all the plays runs a chain of nightmarish images to do with losing one's part, being in the wrong play, having a sense of existing only in a part.

The Chorus in *The Family Reunion* resent being summoned to 'play an unreal part in some monstrous farce, ridiculous in some nightmare pantomime'. Harry comes home prepared for one part and finds 'another one made ready – The book laid out, lines underscored, and the costume / Ready to be put on', and Lord Claverton, who describes himself as a broken-down actor, dreads the moment when he will have to walk off the stage 'without his costume and makeup. / And without his stage words.'

Other more direct methods are tried out too. In one interesting sequence from an early draft of *The Cocktail Party*, much cut down in the final version, Peter Quilpe is invited by the other characters to imagine roles for them in the film he is supposed to be making about a country house murder. 'Very few people can act the thing they are', he says, and goes on to cast accordingly. Edward can't be a lawyer in the film, though he is in the play, because he doesn't look secretive; neither does Alex, so he can be the Secret Service character; as for Reilly and Julia, they can't be in it at all: nothing about them is ordinary enough for what an 'ordinary' murder film requires. The effect of this – trying to imagine characters as characters – is unsettling. Even in the unsatisfactorily verbose form it has in the draft, the scene takes us to the edge of that phantasmagoric region where Edward exists, not sure whether he is really there, except in his role as husband to Lavinia: 'Without her, it was vacancy. / When I thought she had left me, I began to dissolve, / To cease to exist.'

The feeling of being an actor is closely related to the feeling of being spied on which Eliot's characters suffer from. Roles, false names and

---

[1] E. M. Browne, *The Making of T. S. Eliot's Plays*, 1969.

identities are protection against being known. The characters are terribly repressed and inhibited by the polite society they live in: the point is made in that way in *The Family Reunion*. They have to be shocked into opening up and revealing themselves. A violence comes in here which takes Eliot's drama very close to Pinter's. Characters are subjected to painful, mysterious inquisitions, the Furies appear at a window, bringing their victim near to total nervous collapse; an un-invited guest arrives at a cocktail party; with the aid of two spies he manoeuvres three of the characters to a consulting room for 'treat-ment'[1] which ends in the violent death of one of them; two unwanted visitors descend on an elderly man taking a 'rest cure'[2] and badger him into confessing past faults; he collapses and dies.

Of course these summaries are misleading, omitting as they do the 'bright angel' aspect of the inquisitors and the emphasis Eliot puts on conversion and reconciliation. But perhaps all the same they hint at a truth about the plays, that their greatest theatrical vitality is just in those dark and icy areas where they draw so near to Pinter's drama. *The Birthday Party* seems to take over where they leave off: it's a very live connection.

Eliot is certainly good at suggesting suppressed violence. He manages at times to look like a forerunner of the theatre of cruelty without ever allowing an act of physical violence to erupt on his stage. He can manoeuvre the audience into a worrying sense of complicity with sadism, for instance with the jokes in *The Cocktail Party* about Christians eating monkeys and pagans eating Christians. They are nasty jokes but the audience usually laughs at them, to their embarrass-ment when they learn that Celia was one of the victims. Martin Browne was relieved when Eliot agreed to cut out some of the horrific detail[3] that outraged the first audiences in Edinburgh. He was surely right in thinking that the emphasis on physical horror would distract attention from Celia as a person. I'm not so sure, though, that Eliot did think of Celia as a person in quite the way Browne himself did: it was he who had advised Eliot to build up sympathy for her: 'She is the character whom above all we want to love – the heroine, the play's necessary focus of sympathy.'[4] But that last scene was first written as an epilogue:

---

[1] M. C. Bradbrook draws attention to this anticipation of Monty's in *The Birthday Party* in her *English Dramatic Form*, 1963.
[2] *The Rest Cure* was Eliot's original title for *The Elder Statesman*.
[3] References to Celia's body being smeared with a 'juice attractive to ants' and to its decomposition.   [4] Browne, op cit, p 176.

the germ of the play was the marriage of Edward and Lavinia and, to my mind, it's in that Strindbergian dance of death relationship that the strongest dramatic interest lies. The prevailing mood is grotesque; masked actors in a cruel harlequinade, decidedly in tune with the modern spirit which encourages the rewriting of *The Dance of Death* in the near-farcical terms of Dürrenmatt's *Play Strindberg*.

I began by referring to the extremely modern look of Eliot's first dramatic piece, the unfinished *Sweeney Agonistes*. If he had continued to write in that vein he would have been in the front ranks of the anti-realists and I would probably have been discussing him now along with O'Casey and Arden and other makers of the alternative tradition rather than in relation to Pinter and Priestley.

Even as it is, *Sweeney Agonistes* has had some influence on the play-wrights who have made the sharpest break with realism, on Auden and Isherwood, and on John Arden, who tells us that his first schoolboy attempt at dramatic writing was a play inspired by the death of Hitler written in the style of *Sweeney Agonistes*.

It's odd that this seminal piece should still be included among the poems in the collected edition of 1969, especially as it has had a number of interesting productions. In Peter Wood's 1965 production[1] – with Cleo Laine as Dusty and jazz by Dankworth – it came over as an exhilaratingly open piece of theatre, with its evocative changes of rhythm, its easy, swinging movements out of dialogue into soft shoe turns and musical comedy numbers like 'My little island girl.' Osborne seems to be recalling this in *Look Back in Anger* when he has Jimmy and Cliff go into one of their turns as T. S. Eliot and Pam, 'Bringing quips and strips to you'. There's the same feeling here that knockabout is a blessed means of breaking out from an oppressive atmosphere of sexual tension – what Pinter's characters, for instance, can't ever do – nor Eliot's own in later plays.

Sweeney is very much a play of breaking out and acting out rather than talking out. There's a feeling that anything could happen: it's in key for an old gentleman looking like Father Christmas to turn up, as he did in Peter Wood's production, with an alarm clock in one hand and a champagne bottle in the other, to close down the proceedings.[2] Violence is *in* the action, not just something heard about. Sweeney's tale of his friend who did a girl in and pickled the body in a bath of

---

[1] Globe Theatre 13 June 1965. In a memorial programme, 'Homage to T. S. Eliot'.
[2] A transcript of this scene (discarded from an early draft) was included in the programme to the 1965 production.

Lysol comes over as a kind of sleep-walking preliminary to the real thing, the murder of a woman such as Dusty by a man driven by a mysterious loathing of women: 'Any man has to, needs to, wants to, / Once in a lifetime, do a girl in'. It's the world of Jack the Ripper, or of the Grand Guignol theatre – which was active in London in the twenties[1] – illuminated by the understanding of a poet who is deeply involved in Sweeney's complex feelings about women and violence.

Whether because the method of *Sweeney* was too direct and physical for the subject he wanted to handle or because he saw no hope of getting the right production for this style of play in the theatre of the time – these are questions to which there are as yet no answers. Certainly there wasn't a regular theatre company in London in 1926 (the year *Sweeney* was published) geared to the style of production the play needed. Eliot knew this well: it was in these years that he was enthusing in the pages of *The Criterion* about the superior training in bodily discipline and expressiveness that ballet dancers had; the ballet was the great potential source of the truly modern drama of the future, (a remark which seems to point straight to Beckett's mimes and the ritualistic movements of *Endgame* and *Krapp's Last Tape*). The other acting qualities he admired – and aimed to bring into *Sweeney* – came from another kind of non-realist theatre, the music hall. Eliot was fascinated by the directness of entertainers like Marie Lloyd, their openness to their audience, their capacity for improvisation. His account of her 'searching in her handbag' turn[2] shows a feeling for the music hall art that makes one understand why a writer like John Arden should have been so drawn to *Sweeney*: something of that feeling got into the play.

It seems rather sad that Eliot couldn't find an outlet for these sympathies in the theatre of the twenties and that *Sweeney* had to remain for so long a fragment on a page. When he did see it performed by the Group Theatre[3] in 1935 he apparently wasn't very enthusiastic: one can't tell whether it was because the production was poor or because his interest in the method had waned.

Perhaps the closed form of the fourth wall play better expressed

---

[1] See G. Sutton's 'The Shocking business in the Adelphi' in his *Some Contemporary Dramatists*, 1924, for an account of these Grand Guignol seasons.

[2] 'Marie Lloyd', *Dial* 73, 1922; rptd (rev) in *Criterion*, 1923 and in his *Selected Essays*, 1932.

[3] See J. Isaacs' account in his *An Assessment of Twentieth Century Literature*, 1951, pp 135–6.

his state of mind at that time. Certainly one feels that the special force of *The Family Reunion* comes from the sense of the lid being held on so tight: the moments when the repressed feelings trickle through in delicate verbal music are poignant just because the context is so stiff and anti-musical.

Eliot has, I think, a stronger interest in the 'ordinary' part of his material, the non-mystical part, than he's usually credited with. There are striking resemblances of detail between his play and the typical family plays and detective plays of the thirties, and some interesting indications that he was aware of experiments being made with the material by contemporaries such as Priestley.

The first audiences of *The Family Reunion* had an opportunity of seeing the standard family play and Eliot's adaptation of it playing almost side by side. Dodie Smith's *Dear Octopus*, the epitome of the popular family drama, opened at the Queen's Theatre on 14 Sept 1938, while Eliot was finishing his play. For a time there was even the entertaining possibility that Gielgud who was playing Nicholas Randolph in *Dear Octopus* might take on Harry as well in matinée performances of *The Family Reunion*. Harry in the afternoon, Nicholas at night – a mind-boggling prospect, as the advertisements for *The Mousetrap* have it! Gielgud was looking forward to bringing out the contrasting treatments of 'the same characteristics, the family theme, the return of the prodigal, etc. . . . '[1] He would have had plenty to work on.

In each play, as he indicates, a prodigal returns home for a family anniversary: in *Dear Octopus* it's a daughter who, like Harry, has been kept abroad for years by an unhappy sexual relationship. Both have to come to terms with fiercely possessive mothers and with families obsessively taken up with their own past. About here the resemblances end and the obviously much more important differences begin. One wonders how Gielgud's performance as Nicholas would have survived the cold light thrown on that cosy family from the other one. Just occasionally the irony might have gone the other way, perhaps: one of Dodie Smith's child characters has a line nicely pointing out to *The Family Reunion*: 'I wish we didn't have any dead people in the family. It sort of spoils the party.' But it seems safe to assume that *Dear Octopus* would have been the play to shrivel under the comparison!

The uncanny thing about it – viewed alongside *The Family Reunion* – is its deep unselfconsciousness. The characters manage to evade real

[1] See his letter to Martin Browne in E. M. Browne, op cit, pp 145–6.

scrutiny, as they do in most of the family plays of the time, even those, like Van Druten's *After All*, which ask to be taken rather more seriously than *Dear Octopus*. Eliot seems to provide the critical focus for the whole genre, to give it full selfconsciousness for the first time.

His way of forcing his characters to examine themselves is to put them in the framework of an amateur detective play, borrowing from another popular type of thirties drama, which was represented in the London theatre at the time he was writing by Anthony Armstrong's *Mile-Away Murder*.[1] He sets the play up as a probe into the causes of Harry's breakdown; witnesses come forward in turn – Agatha, Mary, the family doctor, the chauffeur – even the stolid country policeman is brought into the scene, and we hear of the off-stage brother getting into trouble with the police. Some of the conventional elements – the bucolic sergeant, for instance – make an uneasy fit, but they function usefully as a means of keeping some sort of connection with the outside world – clearly important for Eliot – and of emphasizing the family's dread of publicity, the strength of their will to keep everything closed and hushed. One after another of the witnesses brings out this governing principle:

WARBURTON
Harry, there's no good probing for misery.
There was enough once: but what festered
Then, has only left a cautery.
Leave it alone.

CHORUS
Why should we stand here like guilty conspirators, waiting for some revelation
When the hidden shall be exposed, and the newsboy shall shout in the street?
When the private shall be made public, the common photographer
Flashlight for the picture papers: why do we huddle together
In a horrid amity of misfortune? why should we be implicated, brought in and brought together?

In applying pressure from the detective play to the 'matter' of the family drama Eliot had hit on a technique with rich possibilities. He was taking up where Joyce left off in *Exiles* but going much beyond him into the area where feelings are nameless, the sense of guilt obscure and undefined.

---

[1] Duchess Theatre 2 April 1937.

His true heir in this sphere is Pinter. Contemporaries seem to have picked up hints too, though: Priestley in *An Inspector Calls* (1947) uses the detective technique in a similar way. And Eliot in turn picks up from Priestley, to judge from the striking similarities between *The Family Reunion* and *I Have Been Here Before*.[1]

This particular comparison brings out interestingly, I think, how Eliot tried to move away from the analytical, narrative methods of the thirties novelist/playwrights into a more direct and physical kind of drama. Priestley's play is about a moment of fatal choice on the Yorkshire moors. An unhappily married couple, a young schoolmaster and a German doctor meet at a country inn. A love affair develops between the wife and the schoolmaster; the husband reacts violently, threatens to wreck his rival's career: his own suicide seems inevitable. The German doctor intervenes: he has come to this obscure inn simply to avert the tragic outcome which – so he claims – he has witnessed in another dimension of time.[2] Watching now, he says, is 'like watching the performance of a play that one has first read carefully'. The other characters are sceptical, then resentful. Are they just marionnettes, the wife asks, with no minds and wills of their own? No, says the doctor, now they have knowledge from the 'past', they have freedom too: this is the 'great moment' of choice: 'In the end the whole universe must respond to every real effort we make. We each live a fairy tale created by ourselves.'

There are some rather remarkable anticipations already here of Eliot's themes and situations, even his way of putting things. And when Dr Görtler speaks of 'what seems to happen continually just outside the edge of our attention', we are getting very close to Harry's account of the Eumenides as something sensed, 'Here and here and here – wherever I am not looking, / Always flickering at the corner of my eye, / Almost whispering just out of earshot.' Priestley's Ormund too is a haunted man: the knowledge he doesn't know he has casts its shadow:

> All my life I've had a haunted sort of feeling . . . as if, just round the corner, there'd be a sudden blotting out of everything.

Dr Görtler is his mentor, as Agatha is Harry's: he offers a way out from under the 'spell':

---

[1] Royalty Theatre 22 Sept 1937.
[2] The idea came from Ouspensky's *New Model of the Universe* which Priestley describes as 'an idea of modified recurrence'.

You can return to the old dark circle of existence, dying endless deaths,
or you can break the spell and swing out into new life.

It's at this point of greatest closeness that one is reminded how much
more direct and physical the 'haunting' is in *The Family Reunion*.
Whether the Eumenides are given some tangible shape or indicated by
changes of light – Eliot's final preference – they are a real presence in
the play, something that enters the action and freezes it in a moment of
terror: 'Come out! Where are you? Let me see you, / Since I know
you are there, I know you are spying on me.' It is confrontation, not
narrative. But yet they are not there: Mary, for instance, doesn't see
them. So the audience is involved directly in the experience of being
haunted without having to lose belief in the solid, ghost-free world.

These are the places where Eliot now looks so modern. It's just those
experiments that seemed to cut him off from the mainstream in the
thirties theatre that bring him back into it in the theatre of the seventies.
His method of indicating 'unvoiced' thought, for instance, by changing
from one rhythm and verbal style to another has been followed up by
writers as diverse as Pinter and Charles Wood, Pinter keeping to prose,
Wood often using a strange patterned colloquial speech which is as
poetically free from normal restraints in its own way as Eliot's 'duets'
and 'arias'.

In the postwar plays Eliot took over forms from the other main area
of the tradition, smart drawing-room comedy. Again he darkened the
material, put it into ironical focus and drew out forcefully implications
that the early master, Coward, had just touched on. The rituals of the
cocktail party world are given a push in a sinister direction. Reilly
sipping gin and water is a Coward character poised for a leap into a
Pinter scene. No wonder Eliot was appalled when he once dropped in
on a performance of *The Cocktail Party* to find Rex Harrison getting an
illicit laugh by sneaking an extra gin and water when he was alone on
the stage; how easy to wreck the effect of machine-like inevitability in
the sequence of invitation, response and refusal that makes up the gin
and water ritual.

This sense of an unstoppable machine at work seems to me the
strongest single impression made by the play. Behind every small move
in the social game there's the shadow of a dark manoeuvre in the sub-
conscious: every word is being registered and scrutinized by someone or
something: an 'obstinate, unconscious sub-human strength' – Edward's
phrase for Lavinia – is felt to be taking over the action. Of course
Eliot intended his guardians to be seen as benevolent figures and the

detailed working out of Celia's conversion – the nursing order, the missionary work, the crucifixion – push a Christian interpretation forward. But there's so much to undermine it; the black magic element in the consulting room ritual – the moon is invoked, Celia is to be 'fetched' at full moon and so on – and the overbearing ways of the guardian-intruders. Martin Browne speaks of the difficulty of knowing how far nosiness like Julia's could be taken without ceasing to seem comic and benevolent: for some people, he recognized, it had passed that point. That is certainly how it seems to me: what we get from Julia, I should say (and from Reilly and Alex rather less forcefully), is a perfectly chilling demonstration of what happens when the genie is loosed from the bottle, to prise and probe – like Ibsen's Rat Wife again – into the dark corners the characters want to keep hidden. Julia has some very undermining habits, including the Pinterish one of unsaying what she has just said, as when she makes a joke about Lady Klootz (opens the play with it, in fact) and a little later professes never to have heard the name: 'Who is Lady Klootz?' Her whimsies have a nightmarish tinge – that vision of the missing Lavinia being all the time in the pantry 'listening to all we say'. 'I don't want to probe', she says, and gets a laugh, almost the kind a harmless Coward gossip might get, but well on the way to being the uneasy laughter drawn out by a Mick or a Lenny.

The Coward convention is immensely useful to Eliot in his attempt to strike a balance between outer and inner reality. It's such a highly selective arrangement of material from ordinary life, instantly re-cognizable as 'real' and yet, as a context for living, worryingly incomplete and unreal. What sort of beings can exist only in a cocktail party context, as the guardians seem to do? When they move on to the Gunnings (poor Gunnings!) at the end of the play, it's a neat, Coward-ish joke ending and at the same time a powerful reinforcement for the subterranean impression of the guardians as genie who only exist in one dimension – perhaps really inside rather than outside the self. Given the bias of the convention towards caricature and silhouette, it's remarkable that Eliot gets as much solid human interest into the play as he does: it's an indication of how committed he is to the drama of character and motive. One may not be so sure about Celia; she seems something of a dream. But Lavinia and Edward sitting side by side having their 'nervous breakdowns' diagnosed – this ludicrous and sad scene remains in one's mind as a compelling human episode, perhaps even the reason for the whole play.

The innovatory force that makes *The Cocktail Party*, like *The Family Reunion*, such a seminal play, can still be felt, though more faintly and intermittently, in Eliot's last two plays. He was still seeing possibilities in the old forms for new types of drama. In *The Confidential Clerk* he rediscovered farce – one remembers Maugham deploring its disappearance from the theatre of his time – and gave it a new, Pirandellian look that propelled it well into the future. Joe Orton is one of his (unlikely) successors in this sphere: he follows up audaciously and grotesquely in directions gently indicated by Eliot. And the trend is strongly carried forward by plays like David Mercer's *Flint*.

No doubt the idea is better than its working out in *The Confidential Clerk*, but still there are moments when the comic losing and finding of parents leads into genuinely disorientating effects and the precariousness of identity becomes an experience rather than a theme. The farcical structure sets the characters free to express their sense of being 'characters' in a spontaneous, direct way. B. Kaghan can come on saying 'Enter B. Kaghan'. Colby can be given a choice of identities: a selection from a number of possible parents and the roles that would be their legacy. He is rather a good farce hero, with a touch of the cool opportunism the type requires; 'a certain deliberate ambivalence' was Eliot's phrase for him. When he does choose from Mrs Guzzard's alternatives a 'dead obscure man' for his father, the absurd takes on a sombre, troubling quality, the kind of effect modern audiences have come to recognize and respond to; farce in a new dimension, to borrow N. F. Simpson's phrase for his own play, *One Way Pendulum*.

Even in *The Elder Statesman* which comes closest of Eliot's plays to being a piece of flat, conversational realism in thirties style, there are interesting shadowings of new techniques for a new type of realism. Touches of farcical exaggeration in the characters of Gomez and Mrs Cargill reinforce the impression made by their name changing that they are masks or ghosts rather than solid beings. The flamboyant new identities they have acquired don't ring true, but what else are they? They bring home with chilling persistence how close Lord Claverton's situation is to theirs. He has had three sets of names and identities, is almost as disconnected as they are. Names always have magic force for Eliot's characters. The way they are used in *The Elder Statesman* – as something to hide behind and to attack with – points, as so much of Eliot does, to Pinter and the swoops in and out of different names that his characters practise so alarmingly.

Although Eliot doesn't carry through his ideas with the sustained force of successors like Pinter and Orton, he seems to me an important precursor and model maker. His innovating instinct was so strong that it almost took him right out of the realist tradition with *Sweeney Agonistes*. Chiefly, though, it has operated within the tradition, extending and enriching it to the benefit of present-day playwrights. Apart from its intrinsic value – and *The Family Reunion* seems to me one of the truly haunting plays of our time – his drama must surely always have interest as the melting pot where the old forms were recast and made new.

1. *Texts*
   The Complete Poems and Plays of T. S. Eliot, 1969

2. *Critical Writings*
   Browne, E. M. *The Making of T. S. Eliot's Plays,* 1969
   Jones, D. E. *The Plays of T. S. Eliot,* 1960
   Martin, G. (ed) *Eliot in Perspective,* 1970

Background: Maggie Smith, Robert Stephens, Lynn Redgrave and Robert Lang; foreground: Anthony Nicholls, Celia Johnson, Derek Jacobi and Louise Purnell in the National Theatre production of Noel Coward's Hay Fever *at the Old Vic.*

Photograph: Angus McBean

PLATE 5

Nicol Williamson as Bill Maitland and Cyril Raymond as Hudson in John Osborne's Inadmissible Evidence *at Wyndham's Theatre.*

Photograph: Dominic

PLATE 6

John Kane (1st *Soldier*), *Bruce Myers* (*Barney Bagnal*), *Ben Kingsley* (*The Croucher*), *Patrick Stewart* (*Teddy Foran* = 4th *Soldier*), *Robert Oates* (3rd *Soldier*) *and Phillip Manikum* (*The Corporal*) *in Act 2 of the Royal Shakespeare Company's production of Sean O'Casey's* The Silver Tassie *at the Aldwych Theatre.*

Photograph: Reg Wilson

PLATE 7

*Students in George Hall's Central School of Speech and Drama
production of* Maria Marten *at the Embassy Theatre.*

PLATE 8

V

John Osborne

'Revolutionary' was a word much used about Osborne in the days of
Look Back in Anger and one can still see why, even though in form that
was anything but a revolutionary play. 'Old fashioned', Osborne's
own term for it, was nearer the mark. Both adjectives were needed –
and still seem needed – to describe the strangely mixed impression his
drama makes: the sense of the past and the spirit of change tend to be
equally strong in it.

In his recent drama the balance has shifted a little and the weight
come down rather more heavily on the traditional elements. So it was
in *West of Suez*: it looked much closer to Shaw's play, *Geneva*, which
was revived at the Mermaid in the autumn of 1971 while Osborne's
play was still running than to the new plays by interesting contemporaries – Bond's *Lear* and Heathcote Williams' *AC/DC* – that opened
at the same time.

Of course it was no surprise to recognize Shavian echoes in Osborne's
drama: they have been sounding there from the start along with others
from Coward and that whole comic mode. It was rather surprising,
however, to find him using such a very static version of the Shavian
conversational form, picking up from discursive, 'quiet talk' plays
like *Geneva* rather than more dynamic pieces like *Heartbreak House*
which stand in the background of his earlier work.

Osborne seems to enjoy occasioning this sort of surprise. Un-
popular forms have a great attraction for him. Often his characters are
nostalgic for old theatrical styles, and although he sometimes makes it
easy for us to share their feelings – who wouldn't sympathize with old
Billie Rice reminiscing about the golden age of music hall? – there are
other times when he seems almost to refuse us the chance. Pamela in

Time Present is made a rather remote figure for most people, one would guess, by her very special addiction to plays with Ouida-ish titles like *The Call of Duty*, *The Undecided Adventuress*, *The Real Thing*. It's hard to envisage the splendour of her father's acting style – the style she thinks of as 'the real thing' – in these plays or to enter sympathetically into her nostalgia for it. She finds one character in the play to do this (it is almost his only function) and together they look through old playbills, quote bits of dialogue, dwell with pleasure on details like the old world settings of *The Call of Duty*: Nutley Towers; The Conservatory, Nutley; the Marksby Drawing Room, Fitzroy Square. One begins to wonder if Osborne is deliberately flinging back in the critics' faces the compliments they paid him in the *Look Back in Anger* era, when Tynan, for instance, hailed him as the hero who had freed the English stage from 'those fabled dododramas that begin with a telephone ringing in the library of Colonel Bulstrode's country house in Lower Nattering, Bucks.'

There's a kind of aggressiveness in the presentation of Pamela, a flaunting of her off-key nostalgia that is very characteristic, the expression of a fiercely individualistic and romantic temperament. Perhaps 'revolutionary' goes on seeming an appropriate word for Osborne even in the phase of *West of Suez* and *The Hotel in Amsterdam* because the feel of this temperament is never quite lost from his plays. He loves what is fixed and past – his characters are haunted by the concept of the past as a Golden Age – but he loves change too, to judge from the way the forms of his drama are constantly changing – from the claustrophobic interior of *Inadmissible Evidence* to the sweeping historical sequences of *A Patriot for Me*, from the epic austerity of *Luther* to the jokey fantasies of *Under Plain Cover*.

For some of his critics, this versatility is suspect, a sign that he has no style of his own – has made none his own but the tirade, as one recent critic puts it.[1] It's true, of course, that it's a difficult style to pin down; it's not instantly recognizable from a line or two of dialogue as Pinter's is. Osborne's is at the other extreme from that chiselled, meticulously edited style. It has a rough, impulsive, unpredictable quality, gives the impression of being totally unedited. A remark of Edward's in *West of Suez* describes the effect rather well. When Frederica complains that she hasn't understood his train of thought, he says, – 'Nor me. But there was some bacteria jumping about in there if you can be bothered

---

[1] G. Gersh, 'The Theatre of John Osborne', *Modern Drama* 10, 1967.

and neither of us can.' The bacteria do jump about in a lively way in Osborne's dialogue, but we have to stay on the alert to catch them and there are some awkward patches to get through: the style works cumulatively in torrents rather than drop by drop. Like O'Neill and Tennessee Williams – he has much in common with both – Osborne has to be judged by the impression his plays make as wholes: they have something of that ungainly power that in a play like *Long Day's Journey into Night* forces one to recognize how delicate the movements of feeling are behind the often clumsy and sentimental language.

Almost any play of Pinter's picked at random could represent him well to someone coming newly to his work. But what would one choose to represent Osborne? *Look Back in Anger, Luther, Under Plain Cover, A Patriot for Me*? It wouldn't be easy to choose, and it's not always easy, either, to define the style within particular plays. Take for instance the little television play, *The Right Prospectus*. It starts off looking like a mildly satirical piece of social observation, the line of country that was thought to be Osborne's own in his early days. A young to middle-aged couple are choosing a boarding school, for their son, we presume. They study form from prospectuses, have interviews with Headmasters: there are jokes about Harrow – 'full of pushy spivs' – and progressive schools – 'those scruffy boy and girl places, where they all smoke and have affairs and call the teachers Alf and Mary'. They settle for a boys' public school – 'Victorian, post-Arnold but humane, open atmosphere' – and then proceed to enrol, not the imagined son, but themselves; it's all done in a supremely matter-of-fact style, no one at any point seeming to notice anything unusual. The pair are assigned to different houses; she – slightly pregnant by now – to the crack house, where she turns out a regular chum and a star at everything, he to a second-rate house where he's a dismal failure. In the delicate production BBC Television gave it, the little piece came over as comical and yet faintly disturbing too. Everything was so tremendously solid and jovial, so much *there*, and yet so unreal. We went with Newbold into a traumatic experience, watching his wife flashing jauntily by, surrounded by the school élite, while he floundered from one trouble to another. He seemed trapped in something more permanent than a dream. By the time they drove off together at the end of the term (or day?) in a mysterious quiet, she radiant as ever, he thoroughly demoralized, his one friend vanished, no one to wave goodbye – a ghostly melancholy had filtered into the absurd action: it had become strangely touching.

Osborne out of character? It might seem so to anyone coming to
The Right Prospectus straight from the previous Coward-like plays,
Time Present and *The Hotel in Amsterdam*. But then one would have to
remember that haunting play, *Inadmissible Evidence*, which opens with
the stage direction: 'The location where a dream takes place. A site of
helplessness, oppression and polemic. The structure of this particular
dream is the bones and dead objects of a Solicitor's office.' And think
too of the nightmare cone in *Luther* 'like the inside of a vast barrel,
surrounded by darkness', where Luther releases his innermost fear:
'I'm afraid of the darkness, and the hole in it; and I see it sometime of
every day!' A dream location is very much Osborne's territory, in
fact. It's the area where he comes close to Pinter, but his dream land-
scapes are entirely distinctive. They have more 'world' in them, more
topical allusion, a stronger sense of history. And yet they can exude
solitariness, seem cut-off places, the 'intense interior' envisaged in
Luther. This is certainly true of *Inadmissible Evidence*: its strange
double vision effect is one of Osborne's most impressive achievements.

Osborne's chameleon quality doesn't at all mean, to my mind, that
he lacks style. On the contrary, I think, whatever he touches is invested
with his strong – and puzzling – personality. One of the striking
features of this personality as it comes through in the plays is its exceptional openness. It's a kind of unwilling, tortured openness. Words
like 'raw' and 'rude' that were used about *Look Back in Anger* go on
seeming appropriate to the middle-aged characters in later plays.
They keep their raw responses, can't close their minds to painful
impressions or keep them on the surface, as the journalists they so
detest do. In a way they *are* journalists without the journalist's power of
detachment. Wyatt in *West of Suez* says fretfully at one point to the
rest of the group, 'I wish I noticed things like you all do'. To which the
answer is – 'I think you do, really, Daddy. You don't miss the tricks.'
True enough. He doesn't miss the tricks nor do any of Osborne's central
characters. They're fascinated by social change, however disagreeable;
they seem compelled to take it into their consciousness and try to grasp
it. A tremendous amount of recording goes on in *West of Suez*, as in
this scene where the Wyatts try to 'fix' their recollections of India:

> EVANGIE: A timetable of the South India Railway, the oars of Jesus College;
> *In China with the British* – two vols. 'Setting sail aboard the Rawalpindi.'
> WYATT: Old *Pindi* – torpedoed first month of the war.
> EVANGIE: Taking arsenic instead of baking powder. Talk in the mess.
> The club.

FREDERICA: In the club. Mummy four times. Lizards on the ceiling above the mosquito net, sweat, the mail. Knick-knacks. Junk and boa constrictors . . .

Wyatt's comment, 'I'm surprised you remember so much. *I* don't. You were all such *children*.' draws attention to the oddness of this very characteristic sequence. It's characteristic too that time past should be registered in such an affectionate tone of voice. Time present prompts a more hostile kind of recording, like the diatribe against modern youth Bill Maitland flings at his silent daughter:

> Oh, I read about you, I see you in the streets. I hear what you say, the sounds you make, the few jokes you make, the wounds you inflict without even longing to hurt, there is no lather or fear in you, all cool, dreamy, young, cool and not a proper blemish, forthright, unimpressed, contemptuous of ambition but good and pushy all the same.'

This is social history registered on the raw, tender spots of the mind. It's because they give this impression so strongly that Bill's immensely long monologues – mostly spoken into the telephone – are dramatically forceful. We're kept wondering about the nature of his relationships with the unheard speakers at the other end of his line, what went wrong, what are the connections between those painful emotional experiences and his way of observing and thinking about life in general. We can't separate his feelings from his thoughts any more than he can. It seems to him, though, and it's an element in his suffering, that other people do succeed in making that kind of separation. He lives at the fiery emotional centre of his life all the time and half envies, half despises those who are able to rest on the cool periphery of theirs.

Whether they really do or only seem to is one of the unresolved questions that tantalize him and us. His nightmarish day at the office is a series of humiliations and rejections: the typists he's had casual affairs with, the colleagues who are beginning to look elsewhere for safer employment, his unseen wife, his mistress, his daughter, all appear to him to be turning colder and harder as he gets more hopelessly entangled in feeling. Some of the coolness comes over as real – there's plenty of reason for it – some may be an illusion, a projection of his despair, or perhaps just a deep difference of style. His daughter, for instance, is described in the stage directions as 'cool' but also as 'distressed and scared'. As she is given no lines at all to speak, it's the coolness, the lack of response that registers, but the exaggeration of the technique – the unreal effect of her total silence – carefully suggests that the coolness may be all in the mind of the beholder. There's a similar ambiguity in the representation of his mistress. Her patience with Bill – which finally gives way in the scene – has been admirable, we may think; yet it's related to something less attractive, a kind of cool disdain that comes out in her attitude to his terrible sense of guilt. She despises it – a 'real peasant's pleasure' – congratulates herself on being free of such feelings, won't attempt an act of imaginative sympathy.

It's this kind of cool self-containment that Osborne's heroes are constantly scenting out in people and fighting against, as Archie Rice humorously fights the indifference of his music hall audience: 'Blimey, that went better first house. I've taken my glasses off. I don't want to see you suffering.' Archie is another great noticer. When he goes into his performance, the audience have no hope of hanging on to the traditional eavesdropping role of the audience in the realistic theatre. An uneasy feeling develops that he might suddenly pick on us individually, 'fix' us in the way of music hall comedians, bring us into his patter along with the leader of the band – 'the only boy soprano in the Musicians' Union' – and his wife – 'She may look sweet, but she's a very cold woman, my wife'. We mightn't fancy our chances if he carried out the offer he makes at the end of the play: 'Let me know where you're working tomorrow night – and I'll come and see YOU.'

Like Bill Maitland and the rest, Archie has one eye turned sharply outward and the other deeply inward. All these characters seem in a way thoroughly in touch with the world: they certainly bring what Shaw called 'the bustle and crepitation of life' on to the stage. Osborne is inventive in devising situations that give their rhetorical powers full range; they interpret and present society to us, give us lessons in history. And yet at the same time they're strangely cut off from the world, separated by the intensity of their imaginative responses. Disconcertingly – for us and for them – they take headers into obscurer waters, below the reach of reason and argument. In the middle of a sharp exchange of social observations, they're liable to come out with remarks such as Edward makes in *West of Suez*:

> Sometimes I don't feel I can understand a word of anything anyone says to me. As if they were as unclear as I am.

The lessons in history are always subordinate, in fact, to the lessons in feeling – that territory Osborne staked out as especially his at the very start of his career:

I want to make people feel, to give them lessons in feeling. They can think afterward. In some countries this could be a dangerous approach, but there seems little danger of people feeling too much – at least not in England as I am writing.[1]

In putting this sort of emphasis on suffering and the dark 'unclear' elements of consciousness, Osborne moves a long way from the masters of his comic tradition. Not, of course, that the drama of Shaw or Coward or Maugham is without strong feeling or dark elements. One thinks of Shotover lamenting the waste of his creative intelligence or the hysterical, feverish strain in plays like *The Vortex*. But on their stage the comic mask is held more firmly in place. Osborne's is constantly slipping to show the naked, suffering features beneath. At the moments when it seems most settled in a Shavian or Coward-like mode, his drama is liable to break out into direct and violent confrontations of a kind that are alien to the mode.

His attitude to the staging of his plays reflects these polarities. He has said that he is happy for the most part working inside the proscenium. But at one time he hankered after its exact opposite, imagined himself writing 'something for a circus, something enormous and immense, so that you might get a really big enlargement of life and people'.[2] The ideal theatre, he went on, would be one that combined 'the intimacy of the Court with the grandeur of a circus'.

Intimacy and grandeur; the proscenium frame enclosing the little room and the open area where actors and audience confront one another directly. Impossible to marry these opposites, one might say. And yet this is what happened in *The Entertainer*. It was that movement between the two stages – the cramped private one where sad events like the son's death occurred and the glaring, public one where they were translated into 'performance' – that made the play such an exhilarating as well as moving experience. Osborne hasn't moved as far out of the fourth wall since, though there's just a hint in the ritualistic style of *A Bond Honoured* that he might have wished to. As Martin Banham suggests, the style 'might have been more fully realized on an open stage than was possible on the rather awkward stage of the National Theatre at the Old Vic.'[3] His normal method is to work for size and openness within the limiting frame – through language (as he suggests

---

[1] John Osborne, 'They Call it Cricket', *Declaration*, ed T. Maschler, 1958. Rptd in *Playwrights on Playwriting*, ed T. Cole, 1960, p 141.

[2] John Osborne, 'That Awful Museum', *Twentieth Century*, Feb 1961.

[3] M. Banham, *Osborne*, 1969 (Writers and Critics series).

himself); through moments of music and spectacle and 'turns'; through
abstract settings like the cartoon backcloth in *Luther*; through violently
unexpected physical movements.

Similarly, he opens out the comic styles he inherits from Shaw and
Coward and Maugham, turns them to expression of passionate feeling.
The mix is seen at its oddest in *A Bond Honoured*. Osborne says about it:

> The acting style is hard to discover or describe, I will just say: it must
> be extremely violent, pent-up, toppling on and over the edge of animal
> howlings and primitive rage. At the same time it should have an easy,
> modern naturalness, even in the most extravagant or absurd moments.
> It requires actors like athletes who behave like conversationalists.[1]

'Actors like athletes who behave like conversationalists.' This reads
like a grotesque parody of the classical Shavian mixture of physical and
mental acrobatics. Osborne has an immense amount in common with
Shaw – his socialist sympathies, his fondness for England and im-
patience with her, his urge to educate his audiences (*Plays Unpleasant*
and *Plays for England* could be interchangeable titles). He always wants
his conversationalists to hold the floor, but at the same time, he wants
to move away from Shaw to more violent and also more oblique and
poetic, means of expression. His celebrated letter to *Tribune*, 'Damn
you, England', was inspired he tells us by a pacifist appeal from Bertrand
Russell in *The New Statesman*. It moved him that an old man could be 'so
concerned with the survival of everybody else' but he felt sceptical about
the chance of sane, logical arguments like those making anything happen. Something more violent was needed – a metaphor – 'something
the English people would respond to, because I think English people
are violent, and I think they respond to this kind of poetic content'.[2]

These comments are very illuminating: they bring out both
Osborne's responsiveness to the 'reasonable' tradition and his need to
push it towards more directly emotional forms. When he doesn't
push it far enough the Shavian conversational model is a rather bad one
for him. *West of Suez*, for instance, looks like an attempt at 'cool'
Shaw and it is certainly far from being Osborne at his best. Shavian
echoes are very strong. There is the general conversational set up –
talking people strung out across the stage in the emotionally disconnected way of, say, the restaurant scene in *Geneva*. And there are more

---

[1] Stage direction in *A Bond Honoured*, 1966.
[2] John Osborne, Interview with John Freeman, BBC Television 21 Jan 1962; rptd in
Wager, 1969, pp 84-5.

specific likenesses too, especially to the situation and characters of *Heartbreak House*. In Shaw's play an ageing inventor is cooped up with his siren daughters and their spouses and friends for a conversational weekend in a symbolic house; it represents England and also, as Shaw said, 'cultured, leisured Europe before the war'. In *West of Suez* another type of inventor, a writer (also ageing) is frivolling away his time with *his* daughters, their spouses and visitors on a sub-tropical island, once a British colony, now independent and tolerating grudgingly as tourists the people who formerly ruled there. Wyatt Gillmann and his family, like Shotover and his, are drifting: the sense of lost function, directionless movement is the most striking thing the two plays have in common. There is a Brigadier who has nothing to do but entertain and cook, a writer who wastes his time on interviews and literary quiz games: an awful inertia prevails. Everything is felt to be representative: it is the situation of *Heartbreak House* updated: England – and perhaps too 'cultured, leisured Europe' – still further at sea, drifting to the rocks without a skipper's hand at the helm or a voice to exhort, 'Learn navigation or be damned'.

As in *Heartbreak House*, the characters' lengthy and leisured analysis of their situation is brought to a violent conclusion. In Shaw's play bombs drop from a Zeppelin and two characters are killed. In Osborne's a hysterical and obscene verbal attack by a foul-mouthed hippy student is followed by a physical attack, when Wyatt is killed by native guerillas, for no reason whatever that one can see. The freakish un-expectedness of the violence, the bizarre contrast it makes with the 'cultured leisured' mood of the scenes before is another striking similarity between the two plays. In this instance Shaw's violence is more compelling. Osborne's hippy student is disturbing in a dis-jointed sort of way but the shooting of Wyatt came over as a blurred, confused event, an accident seemingly without significance. One would guess that this was at least partly because the emotional temperature throughout the play had been too low for Osborne's style to start working properly. He needs a thicker air: Shaw's lucid ether isn't really his climate.

Far more characteristic is the emotional texture of *The Entertainer*, another play that has strong affinities with *Heartbreak House*. The ship-like look of Shotover's house was a visual metaphor for England, the ship of state, the ship we are all in, as Hector says to the others, the 'soul's prison we call England'. Archie Rice's music hall theatre stands for England too; a run-down version of the glorious halls of the past, a place where we can't be too energetic – clap too hard – because it's such an old building. 'Yes, very old. Old.' Osborne's will to establish a circus type of relationship with his audience comes out in his very different handling of this similar metaphor. Shaw's characters shut away behind the proscenium, are in the drifting ship on their own: the audience may choose to identify with them but they don't absolutely have to. Osborne gets his audience into the same position as the actors: we become actors in the sense that we can't help but act out the metaphor. There we are in the Royal Court – or better still for the analogy an old theatre like the Theatre Royal, Newcastle, where the play has been given – and suddenly it has turned into that other theatre, we are Archie's audience now, reacting with him to the larger-than-life nudes and the inscription 'Rock'n Roll Newd Look' plastered across the front cloth and to the nude Britannia with the bulldog and trident. We can choose to laugh or not to laugh at her and at Archie's jokes in the vein of 'Madam with the helmet on is sagging a bit'. But either way our response is prepared for and taken into the play. The feeling of being *really* in it together is uncomfortably communicated.

Shaw's audiences are never brought into such directly uncomfortable situations as this. There is rather more reliance on their willingness to respond to reason. Saint Joan, for instance, draws us, by her 'divine commonsense', whereas Osborne's equivalent character, Luther, batters us disagreeably with his inflamed Protestant conscience. Saint Joan wins easily on sympathy. But as Shaw himself points out in the Epilogue she's also easy to canonize away into a romantic legend, a feat that would be difficult indeed with rude, constipated, unstable Luther. He makes his impact partly by confronting the audience so directly, haranguing them from his stage pulpit:

> I need no more than my sweet redeemer and mediator, Jesus Christ, and I shall praise Him as long as I have voice to sing; and if anyone doesn't care to sing with me, then he can howl on his own. If we are going to be deserted, let's follow the deserted Christ.

The aggressive tone is decidedly liable to irritate: if it does, then that is the kind of active response that Osborne is working for. Plays unpleasant for a new age.

Osborne often seems to be supplying the missing notes in the Shavian debate, the elements that don't respond to reasonableness. He doesn't altogether part company from Shaw, though, when he explores into areas of unreason and obscure psychic disturbance. Rather curiously they share an interest in certain kinds of sexual hysteria and ambivalence. In *Mrs Warren's Profession*, for instance, Shaw sketches an odd situation which faintly foreshadows the still odder one in *Under Plain Cover*. Vivie Warren and her young man, Frank, are represented as being so thoroughly at home with each other that the distinction between family feeling and sexual feeling seems to have become shadowy to them. At any rate, it's a curiously undefined feeling that comes through the scene where they play at babes in the wood shortly before they learn that they may in fact be brother and sister. He nestles against her 'like a weary child':

> FRANK: Let's go and get covered up with leaves.
> VIVIE (rhythmically, rocking him like a nurse): Fast asleep, hand in hand, under the trees.
> FRANK: The wise little girl with her silly little boy.
> VIVIE: The dear little boy with his dowdy little girl.

The nursery rhyme flavour of this nicely expresses the Peter Pan mix-up of feelings (strange how long a shadow Peter Pan throws over the modern English stage).

A very similar note is struck in the erotic games of *Under Plain Cover*. When the postman calls or one of their off-stage babies is heard crying, Jenny and Tim behave like adults, camouflaging their fantastic get-up, picking up their responsibilities. Then they rush back to the nursery to get on with the serious business of playing. They go into masquerade to get more fun out of the sexual game; he becomes an upper class employer, 'silky, menacing, authoritative', she a palpitating housemaid, he a patient under her orders as a stern hospital nurse, and so on. They have fun mimicking the censorious grown-ups (parodying the BBC critics) and in swapping items in their collections – knicker advertisements instead of stamps or marbles. The tone is friendly, jolly. 'Oh is this the nineteen thirties?' she asks, when he starts to bully her in her housemaid role, threatening her with dismissal and unemployment, 'When did you think of that? . . . Oh, what a good idea.'

The brother and sister note in their relationship is well established, in fact, before the news that they really *are* brother and sister is broken to them by Stanley the reporter. By that time it's become hard for us to see it as he does, as a piece of sensational headline news, calling for labels like 'incest'. Probably we feel, as Osborne evidently means us to, that it shouldn't really matter to us if it doesn't to them. As Frank says to Vivie in Shaw's play, after they've learnt what might be the truth about her parentage, if it is true, it only makes them babes in the wood in earnest. Pathetic seems, finally, the word for what happens in *Under Plain Cover*. Although it's not a well-constructed play—there is a sequence of rather uncoordinated scenes when Jenny and Tim are separated and she is pushed towards a 'normal' marriage – it ends strongly with them back together but living behind locked doors to escape the intrusiveness of people like Stanley. He is seen hammering on their door, trying vainly to get a response from them. They have been prisoners for nine years and he too is a prisoner, hopelessly trapped in his public relations response to life: in one breath he speaks personally, a friend asking for help, in the next he is talking out to the media: 'The world is still interested in *them*, and, yes, wants to help.' In the lightweight terms of the play, this is a rather worrying end; it's a little sad and disturbing to think of the jokey pair who were so conscious of their luck in having all those wavelengths open to each other being shut away and narrowed down, forced to live behind locks.

Plays that mix jokes and sadness have become the mode in the modern English theatre, but Osborne's mix is very much his own. The well-used term 'black comedy' doesn't really apply. Much of the time his jokes are real buoyant ones; they may have an edge to them but not a consistently dark tone: they give the impression of being in for the fun of it, and because it's the sort of language that comes naturally to his ebullient, talkative actor-characters.

It's here that the likenesses to Coward begin to thrust themselves on one's attention. There are several lines of connection to him as to Shaw – feeling for England again, fascination with her Imperial history and some nostalgia for it, interest in the different styles of different social classes – but I suppose the most striking is the similarity of their wit, above all its intense theatricality.

> He's probably the only man living whose unconscious desires are entirely impersonal.
> He's very keen on a lot of American plays, sort of about leaving nude girls in plastic bags at railway stations.

So far as tone goes, jokes like this would be well at home in *Hay Fever*. They are actors' jokes and Osborne's characters *are* actors, in a solid, real professional way more often than not, rather than in the unnervingly unreal way of Pinter or Eliot. They tend to think of themselves and others professionally, in terms of parts and styles; they divide themselves into groups of 'in' and 'out' people along the line of style, very much as Coward's characters do. 'Scornful' is a key word. George Dillon sees himself as a player of scornful parts and Constance in *Time Present* thinks of Pamela in that way:

CONSTANCE: Why are you so scornful to me?
PAMELA: I'm not.
CONSTANCE: It's as if you hate what I do, what I am, everything about me. I know a lot of it seems funny and wasted effort but a lot of effort *is* funny and wasted.
PAMELA: I don't mind effort. I'm not so keen on strain.
CONSTANCE: You make me feel very shabby and inept and all thumbs sometimes.

The 'all thumbs' people, the characters of limited imagination and coarser sensibility are set in sharp contrast with their opposites, the perceptive, witty ones whose minds and feelings, as George Dillon puts it, 'are all finger tips'. The Coward note is very strong here. One thinks of Gilda and company roaring with laughter at poor pompous Ernest, and Gilda telling him, 'Our lives are a different shape from yours' – and of the patterns of separation (dull/witty, earnest/subtle) that run through his comedy.

Osborne's 'finger tip' characters have a shape and a language of their own too. They can communicate obliquely through jokes and nuances of idiom: they 'understand the content of tone of voice'. Earnest Constance doesn't understand anything but what is said, so Pamela tells her (scornful *was* the right word). She belongs in the large category – all Americans are in it, ipso facto – of the non-elect, characters who strain hard to find meaning they will never get because they haven't the ear. They can't enter into the esoteric pleasures – or pains – of the others' world, which depend so much on a highly developed sense of style. The finger tip characters are often gourmets of style; they taste it, Jenny and Tim, for instance, sampling knicker advertisements, deploring the sad falling off from 'cami knickers' to 'bikini briefs' or Frederica and company conjuring up the elegant style of Anglo-India: 'Yes I can see all that. Can't you? The lady in waiting; the umbrellas; the marquee?'

Their exclusiveness is often cruel. 'All thumbs' characters are brought in to serve as foils and mocked as clumsy Gillian is mocked in *The Hotel in Amsterdam*. She is in a direct line from clumsy Jacky who was annihilated by the witty actors of *Hay Fever*. This same cool, mocking

Coward-like tone shows too in the handling of sexual relationships. *Look Back in Anger* looks back not so angrily to *Design for Living* with its musical chairs changes of sexual partner from Alison to Helena and back to Alison, pointed by a real Coward joke, the changeover of girls at the ironing board, a moment of visual comedy that always gets a laugh in the theatre.

And yet, characteristically, out of all this flippancy and theatrical sharpness, the idiom he is so at ease in, Osborne draws a drama of passionate feeling. The jokes keep leading into emotional shocks, as when Jimmy breaks out into his Strindbergian screams against Alison and women in general – 'I want to stand up in your tears, and splash about in them, and sing' – or on a lower level of feeling, when we learn in *Time Present* that Pamela's apparently limitless candour co-exists with the ability to deceive her friend: Constance's lover, subject of so many friendly jokes between the two women, has been Pamela's lover too, has given her the child she is making preparations to get rid of at the end of the play.

It seems typical that a child has to be destroyed in this way. Osborne's characters aren't sublimely free of ordinary hazards and obligations as Coward's are: they don't really live in that conventionally childless, family-free world. They have to suffer consequences like common 'all thumbs' mortals. Osborne's point, indeed, is that they suffer more in every way. Pamela suffers in her imagination with her father who is dying in a hospital room while she fights her rearguard action on behalf of his style: the suicide of the film tycoon casts a long shadow over the frivolities of *The Hotel in Amsterdam*.

Osborne's aristocrats pay a high price in nervous strain for the 'privilege' of their exclusiveness. It's this sense of what they have to pay that strikes a note of seriousness in *The Hotel in Amsterdam* which is otherwise the most light and effervescent of all Osborne's comedies in the Coward mode. It has a characteristically exclusive situation: a group of film artists stealing a weekend in Amsterdam to relax in each other's congenial company out of reach of the non-artist, the 'dinosaurus' tycoon who milks their talents and reduces them to exhaustion. They can't quite shake him off, though: the strain of trying and not succeeding is very much in the play, as well as the rather touching sense of ease and warmth which – in the first London production, with Paul Schofield as Laurie – spread across the stage as the weekend took its course. Laurie, the writer/entertainer at the centre of the play, is the magician who works the charm: from time to time he lifts himself and his stage audience out of the dinosaur's sphere into a new, free dimension – by his jokes, his actor's patter, his elaborate anecdotes, the forms of expression his creative insight takes. As Pamela says of herself, he has a superficial manner sometimes for saying serious things; but he is more fortunate than she is: he has listeners who understand the content of tone of voice. They know the kind of struggles that lie behind his jokey presentation of himself as a conjuror:

> What I do, I get out of the air. Even if it's not so hot always, I put my little hand out there in that void there, empty air. Look at it. It's like being a bleeding conjuror with no white tie and tails.

And presumably they understand and are in sympathy with the romantic feeling that lies behind a passage like this:

> Those endless clouded days by the pool even when it's blazing sun. . . . The deadly chink of ice in steaming glasses all day. Luxury, spoiled people. Lounging together, basting themselves with comfort, staring into pools. A swimming pool is a terrible thing to look into on a holiday. It's no past and no future. You can stare into a stream or a river or a ditch. Who wouldn't rather die in a ditch than in a pool?

The atmosphere of brittle smartness gives way in such moments to something softer and more complex. A tentative spiritual communion seems to be forming.

This is a rare experience in Osborne's world, 'bloody unnatural' as Laurie ironically says. More often his characters are shown trying for it and failing: the failure is Osborne's great subject. Perhaps its bleakest expression is in *A Patriot for Me*, a play not 'about' homosexuality as it was sometimes taken to be (the Lord Chamberlain's refusal of a licence for public playing encouraged the view) but rather, one would say, about a man who can't find a congenial style to live in. Redl doesn't know where he is at home, all his impulses are at war. He has a full share of 'finger tip' exclusiveness, a point made in an early scene with the Countess:

> REDL: I don't agree that all men are brothers, like Colonel Mohl. We are clearly not. Nor should be, or ever want to be.
> COUNTESS: Spoken like a true aristocrat.
> REDL: Which, as you must know, I am not.

He means by this that he comes from a lower social class but it's true in a deeper sense: he is an unorthodox rebel in his soul. It seems at one point that he may find a way out of his terrible sense of isolation by recognizing his homosexual impulses for what they are. There is a great sense of release and relief in the movement from the style of the Establishment ball – stiff, military, formal – to the louche, whimsical, musically light and charming style of the drag ball.

But the drag style is as alien to Redl as the other one, a point made with a fine theatrical flourish at the close of the ball scene, when he is so irritated by the affectations of one flirtatious young man that he strikes him violently, then takes leave of his hosts with a military click of his heels in his best Establishment manner. When he is blackmailed into turning spy, the word 'traitor' seems to have no application to his case. He is a man without a country to be true to. 'You want my style', he says to the young soldier, Victor, in the last of his love episodes. 'Want' seems to be used in a double sense. Victor, it suggests, both desires and lacks what Redl has. It's the lack, the poverty of response in him as in his other lovers that drives Redl into the state of reckless despair that ends in his suicide. He is another, like Laurie, who has to put his hand out into the air 'that void, there, empty air', and try to draw something out. But for him nothing comes.

A capacity for despair has always been a hallmark of quality in Osborne's characters, from Jimmy Porter telling how he learnt despair as a boy at his dying father's bedside to Wyatt Gillman saying to his interviewer that for him 'real sin' is 'an incapacity for proper despair'. But the despair isn't usually so total as in *A Patriot for Me*. More commonly, Osborne's heroes keep their power to laugh as well as to suffer; Bill Maitland, for instance, joking into the telephone even when there is no answering voice and a terrible abyss of loneliness is opening up under him. Most clearly of all in this play, the jokes are a lifeline, bridges thrown out across the abyss: 'Some jokes are addressed to himself, some bravado is deflated to himself, some is dialogue between real people.'

A very delicate balance is held in *Inadmissible Evidence*, a balance characteristic of Osborne's drama, between inner anguish and solid, variegated outer reality; between despair and jokes; between old style and new style. The distinctiveness of the blend comes through, I think, in this scene towards the end of the play. Bill is taking one of his women clients through a mechanical rehearsal of her statement. He is very far gone in nervous collapse by this stage: her case merges in his mind with the other divorce cases he is handling (the point is stressed by having the same actress play all three clients) and with his own marital troubles:

MRS. A: Our marriage seemed normal for a time and reasonably happy. There were difficulties owing to the fact that we were living at my mother's house, 148 Chadacre Road, for two years.

(BILL makes a massive effort to assemble the facts in his mind. It is very difficult.)

BILL: Two years. You know, you mustn't expect people to behave well towards you, Audrey. You mustn't. I know you have and I know you will.

MRS. ANDERSON: There was discord when I was pregnant with the little boy Patrick John.

BILL: Patrick John.

MRS. A: My parents persuaded me to return to him.

BILL: You must always ask yourself. Is it dangerous or is it safe? And then make your choice. If you can, if you can.

MRS. A: Things became increasingly unhappy and difficult when my husband gave up his job and became a traveller for a firm in electrical fittings. He was able to be at home most of the time, but when he was away, never more than for the odd day or two, he would accuse me of going out with men.

BILL: Well. She thinks I've got mistresses all over London. They both do. And it's not even true. Worse luck. No, thank God.

MRS. A: He said I ought to go on the streets.

BILL: You might have met me then. You might have been worse off.

MRS. A: I have never been with anyone apart from my husband.

BILL: That's what's wrong with all of you, you dim deluded little loving things. You listen to promiscuous lady journalists and bishops and your mother. And hang on to it.

MRS. A: But he's always saying these things.

BILL: He listens.

MRS. A: It's as if he can't help it. When he wanted to, he would have intercourse two or three times a day. He would, he would go as far as he could but that was all. But it's not only that, it's not even that. If it were only that I could put up with all kinds of things. Because I know he is a good man, really, and a kind man. He can be, and he has been kind to me.

BILL: I love you. He never said, he hardly ever said, he stopped saying, he found it difficult to say I love you. It has to be heaved and dropped into the pool after you, a great rock of I love you, and then you have to duck down below the surface and bring it up, like some grasping, grateful, stupid dog.

MRS. A: He loves the children, and is always making a fuss of them, and giving them things. My sister used to come in to watch T.V., but I hardly ever went out while she was there. We went to the doctor and he made me go to Weymouth for two weeks for a complete rest.

BILL: I often think of my dying. And her, I mean. Of her being a widow.

7

As opposed to a wife. A blackened wife. Of the kind of suit she would wear and wear and where she would get it from. She hasn't got a useful black suit. Liz has, but I don't think she'd get there. Which worries me. Because the idea of her not being there is disturbing. I've asked her to be there, and she's promised me, which is damned silly and a lot to ask, especially if you think of her having to face Anna in her black suit. I wonder if they'd notice what the other was wearing. In the crematorium with all that G-Plan light oak and electrical department brass fittings and spanking new magenta hassocks. And the pink curate sending me off at thirty bob a head as I go rattling on little rails behind him and disappear like a truck on the ghost train at Dreamland, in the Amusement Park, behind the black curtains, and all the noise.

Much of what gets through to him here from the client is deflated to himself, in Osborne's phrase, but not all. The line to the outer world still holds, though the dream state the play opened with, the 'prison of embryonic helplessness', is gradually closing in. Yet the clients remain real people to him, and in a way more real because he has sunk so deep into his own suffering: it's this that allows him to enter into theirs. His sympathy – practical as well as moral – goes beyond what anyone else in the play is capable of giving. He keeps their cases in mind still when he's involved with his own troubled affairs, shows concern for their distress, has fellow feeling even for the boy, Benet (in Wormwood Scrubs on a charge of indecent assault) whom no one else has time for. The temperament that cuts him off from other people and shuts him in on himself is the same temperament that keeps him open in imaginative feeling.

These moments of rough communion at the bottom of despair – Phoebe's arrival with Archie's hat and stick at the close of *The Entertainer* is another – are the deeply touching moments of Osborne's drama. Remarkably, he gets to them by way of the comic mode: it's his ability to do that, to push the comedy of masks towards the naked drama of feeling without losing comic ebullience that gives his style its distinctiveness. It's also, I think, a reason for his being seen as a revolutionary force in the English theatre. But if that is debatable, there can hardly be doubt about his power to draw out feeling in his audiences – on one level perhaps only by irritating, making them feel the joke is an uncomfortable one, but in plays like *The Entertainer* and *Inadmissible Evidence* on a level of feeling that makes a comparison with Bond seem as natural as the ones I have been drawing with Shaw and Coward. That to my mind, is a measure of Osborne's power, certainly of his exceptional range. What sort of play his next will be is always a peculiarly open question, as open as in its massive, quirky way his drama continues to be.

1. *Texts*

    Look Back in Anger, 1957
    The Entertainer, 1957
    Epitaph for George Dillon, 1958
    The World of Paul Slickey, 1959
    A Subject of Scandal and Concern, 1961
    Luther, 1961
    Plays for England, 1963. *The Blood of the Bambergs. Under Plain Cover*
    Tom Jones: a Screenplay, 1964
    Inadmissible Evidence, 1965
    A Patriot for Me, 1966
    A Bond Honoured, 1966
    Time Present and *The Hotel in Amsterdam,* 1968
    The Right Prospectus: a play for television, 1970
    Very like a Whale, 1971
    West of Suez, 1971
    Hedda Gabler, 1972. Adaptation of Ibsen's play

2. *Critical Writings*

    Banham, M. *Osborne,* 1969. Writers and Critics series
    Carter, A. V. *John Osborne,* Edinburgh 1969
    Hayman, R. *John Osborne,* 1968. Contemporary Playwrights series
    J. R. Taylor (ed). *Look Back in Anger: A Selection of Critical Essays,* 1968
    Trussler, S. *The Plays of John Osborne,* 1969

VI

Harold Pinter

Pinter is the conjuror who comes into the realist tradition, takes over the well-worn material of the family play, the detective play and the cocktail comedy and works a dazzling transformation act with it. Of course to the reviewers who were bewildered by *The Birthday Party* when it was first shown in London in 1958 – 'What all this means only Mr Pinter knows'[1] – the term 'realist' would have seemed a ludicrous one to use about him. It still would, if it were applied in a simple, unqualified way as it might reasonably be to playwrights like Alun Owen or Willis Hall. Pinter's brilliantly oblique and haunting drama is so unlike theirs that it might well seem to belong in a totally different mode.

There has been a critical tendency in the past to assume that it does, and to discuss him in terms of the absurdist, anti-realist drama: Martin Esslin's essay of 1963, 'Godot and his children: the theatre of Beckett and Pinter'[2] was followed by many in the same line. 'Isolated elements in his plays are intensely realistic,' says one critic, 'the combination of elements is utterly absurd.'[3]

Certainly Pinter has always made plain his enormous admiration for Beckett. It may be that he was aiming at Beckettian effects in early plays like *The Room* and *The Dumb Waiter* – the symbolism does seem derivative – and there are still unmistakable echoes in recent plays. *Silence*, for instance, with its three characters in their separate 'areas' telling over their past, points pretty clearly to the three sad heads-in-urns of *Play* and to the pattern of movement among the three seated women in *Come and Go*; they break up into twos for intimate con-

---

[1] *Manchester Guardian Review*, 20 May 1958.
[2] M. Esslin, in *Experimental Drama*, ed W. A. Armstrong, 1963.
[3] V. E. Amend, 'Pinter – some credits and debits', *Modern Drama* 10, 1967.

versation rather as Bates and Ellen move out of their own areas, Bates to Ellen's, Ellen to Rumsey's, in Pinter's play.

But if the method – and the sad, backward-looking mood – is sometimes similar, the kind of interest Pinter raises is very different. His interest gathers round the revelation of character: he focuses attention on the subtext, the Freudian slips, compulsive repetitions and so on that give the characters away: we are drawn into 'reading' them and this usually involves looking back into their past as well as guessing about their future with the kind of curiosity that would be wildly inappropriate to Estragon or Clov or Winnie. Even *Silence* with its lyric-like structure and diaphanous texture offers solid character interest. A familiar real world can be sensed behind the shadowy recollections: one wants to piece the fragments together and reconstruct it: there's a feeling that it might turn out to be something like the Edwardian world of an L. P. Hartley novel with nice social distinctions (Bates lower class than Rumsey, Ellen somewhere in between) and wistful personal relationships. It was no surprise after *Silence*, at any rate, to learn that Pinter was actually working on the screen play of Hartley's *The Go-Between*.

This side of Pinter has begun to attract more attention lately. In his recent full-length study of the plays, Martin Esslin stresses their Chekhovian aspects, referring to Chekhov, indeed, as Pinter's master.[1] It is a comparison Pinter would not be likely to quarrel with, to judge from the way he commonly speaks of his own work. 'I regard myself as an old-fashioned writer,' he said in an interview in 1967,[2] 'I like to create character and follow a situation to its end. I write visually – I can say that. I watch the invisible faces quite closely. The characters take on a physical shape. I watch the faces as closely as I can'.

With remarks like this he places himself pretty firmly in the nineteenth century Ibsen/Chekhov[3] tradition. One thinks of Ibsen's acute visual sense of his characters, the way he gropes after better knowledge of them in a detective-like manner (fascinatingly recorded in the various drafts of his plays) and then turns the groping into dramatic process. It's this analytical 'investigation' form that Pinter has inherited via Joyce and Eliot, as I suggested in speaking of them. He brings it right into our

---

[1] M. Esslin, *The Peopled Wound*, 1970. A richly informative account of Pinter's career: records interviews and dealings with BBC as well as productions, etc.

[2] 'Talk of the Town', *New Yorker*, 25 Feb 1967.

[3] Hugh Nelson points out that structurally Pinter's drama is closer to the well-made Ibsenite play than is generally realized in his essay, 'The Homecoming': 'Kith and Kin' (in *Modern British Dramatists*, ed J. R. Brown, 1968).

time, ruthlessly speeds it up and strips it down. When it emerges as the
intense staccato form of *The Birthday Party* it's not surprising that its
ancestry should go unrecognized. It is a long way from the stately in-
vestigations of *Rosmersholm* to this knockabout third degree sequence:

> GOLDBERG: Webber, you're a fake. . . . When did you last wash up a cup?
> STANLEY: The Christmas before last.
> GOLDBERG: Where?
> STANLEY: Lyons Corner House.
> GOLDBERG: Which one?
> STANLEY: Marble Arch.
> GOLDBERG: Where was your wife?
> STANLEY: In ——
> GOLDBERG: Answer.
> STANLEY (turning, crouched): What wife?
> GOLDBERG: What have you done with your wife?
> MCCANN: He's killed his wife.
> GOLDBERG: Why did you kill your wife?
> STANLEY (sitting, his back to the audience): What wife?

And yet there is a recognizable clear line running back from Pinter
through Eliot to Joyce and the Ibsenian drama: the figure of the Rat
Wife probing Rita's wish to be rid of the 'little gnawing things' in her
house is a shadow in the background of Eliot's Reilly and Pinter's
Goldberg and McCann. Other elements come in to make up Pinter's
full inheritance, of course, from Chekhov and – very important, it
seems to me – from Noel Coward. Pinter's most audacious strokes,
those that make him look so dazzlingly new, are often developments
from Coward or solutions to problems that Eliot wrestled with,
solutions that allow him to remain inside the forms of realism.

His will to do this is most obviously demonstrated in his commitment to the proscenium stage. He told L. M. Bensky once: 'I *am* a very
traditional playwright – for instance I insist on having a curtain in all
my plays. I write curtain lines for that reason!'[1] When Bensky asked if
he'd ever thought of trying freer techniques like those in the Weiss
Marat/Sade, as a means of stimulating himself to write, he said cate-
gorically that he hadn't. Exceptionally, almost uniquely among the
playwrights of the new wave, he seems to feel no pull towards an open
stage, mixed forms, improvization. All that 'jamboree', he says, is so
noisy; what he likes is quietness.

---

[1] Interview with L. M. Bensky, *Paris Review* 39, 1966; rptd in *Writers at Work*, New
York 1967.

'Quietness' is a key word for Pinter. His most characteristic effect is one of violence exploding with alarming unexpectedness into an almost equally alarming quietness. The entry of Ruth and Teddy in *The Homecoming* is quiet in this troubling way: they come into a sleeping house and stand there, making no move to disturb the silence. When Ruth suggests a normal action: 'Shouldn't you wake someone up? Tell them you're here?' Teddy refuses; instead he goes up the stairs 'stealthily' to look at the state of his room, coming back to tell her triumphantly: 'It's still there. My room. Empty. The bed's there.'

The weird touch of Peter Pan in this is a subtle preparation for the bizarre events that follow, when Teddy stands by, watching his wife taken over by his brothers and father, assimilated into the home as a kind of sensual Wendy-goddess. There's a very deep connection between the uncanny quietness of that first scene and the shock of the revelation – 'Old Lenny's got a tart in here!' Something repressed and unadmitted comes out in a form which is odd and perverse somehow because of the stillness that went before: the dam bursts and the waters flood out anarchically.

The scenes that tend to stay in one's mind from Pinter's drama, it seems to me, are those where the relation of quietness to violence is particularly sharp and meaningful. I think of Mick hurling the buddha to the ground in *The Caretaker*, a traumatic event in a play of such deep and melancholy quietness, or in a quite different, more feverish mood, the irruption of terrifying party games into the cosy, dull routines of *The Birthday Party*. Or in a more recent play, *Landscape*, Duff's desperate chat flowing under pressure from Beth's silence towards an outburst which is felt to be as much a relief as an attack:

> You stood in the hall and banged the gong.
> Pause.
> What the bloody hell are you doing banging that bloody gong?
> Pause.
> It's bullshit. Standing in an empty hall banging a bloody gong. There's no one to listen. No one'll hear. There's not a soul in the house. Except me.

The force of this partly depends on the obscenity having the right effect. Pinter has made an interesting comment on this point. He objects to what he calls literal-minded persons' attempts to 'open up obscene language to general comment'. It should be, he says 'the dark secret language of the underworld'.[1]

---

[1] Interview with Bensky, op cit.

This is very revealing. Secrecy is Pinter's great subject, his most compelling reason for always using the proscenium, the closed, framed stage where the characters can be shut up and spied on. It's the only way of getting at the sort of beings he is interested in, tightly closed characters who turn most of their energy to keeping themselves hidden from view, protecting the 'dark secret language' of their underworld. An open stage would be as wrong for them as it would for the characters in *Ghosts* or *Exiles* or *The Family Reunion*. The whole 'closed' situation has to be there, the frame the characters can't break out of, the eavesdropping audience. Pinter sometimes takes up the eavesdropping position himself in talking about his characters. Again like Ibsen, he tends to speak of them as though they are real people, having a life stretching before and after the action of the play: he professes to make guesses about what really happened to them. About *Landscape*, for instance, he says in a tentative, open-to-correction tone of voice that he 'believes' the man Beth is dreaming of is her husband: ' . . . the man on the beach is Duff. I think there are memories of Mr Sykes in her memory of this Duff which she might be attributing to Duff, but the man remains Duff. I think that Duff detests and is jealous of Mr Sykes, although I do not believe that Mr Sykes and Beth were ever lovers.'[1]

If this happens to be one's own view, as it was mine, it's tempting to take Pinter's as the last word. He always does his best to prevent this kind of fixing, though, seldom being as explicit as this, and when he is, being careful to use words like 'believe' and 'think'. He hesitates nowadays to direct his own plays, he tells us, because he might be in danger of conveying to the actors – 'This is what's meant'. His great point is, after all, that motives can never be fully known. As he rather pedantically informed one of his first audiences: 'The desire for verification is understandable but cannot always be satisfied.'

It especially can't be satisfied in the area of strongest feeling. 'The more intense the feeling, the less articulate its expression.'[2] Pinter takes his exploration of this area as far as he can without undermining too drastically the sense of solid social reality: he almost always seems to want that in. It's in his techniques for getting both – the inner and the outer reality – that he often comes remarkably close to Eliot, as I suggested earlier. They meet in the middle of the terrain from opposite

---

[1] Letter to German director of *Landscape* (performed Hamburg 10 Jan 1970). Quoted in Esslin, p 192.

[2] Pinter's note in programme for *The Room* and *The Dumb Waiter* production at Court Theatre 8 March 1960.

ends, Eliot arguing that intense feelings tend to express themselves in
verse and using a near-prose verse as a ground to take flight from;
Pinter starting with the idea that intense feeling makes for incoherence
and using a sharply stylized prose as his means of suggesting it. Pinter
is often described as a poet: he has published verse, but he doesn't let
his characters use it; the nearest they approach it is in the prose poem
effects of a play like *Silence* or in imagery such as Ruth uses in *The
Homecoming* to express her frustration. She is supposedly speaking of
America:

> It's all rock. And sand. It stretches . . . so far . . . everywhere you look.
> And there's lots of insects there. Pause. And there's lots of insects there.

This is moving quite a way towards 'open' verse: it even sets up a
faint verbal echo from *The Cocktail Party* – Celia telling Edward that
his voice seems like an insect's:

> Dry, endless, meaningless, inhuman—
> You might have made it by scraping your legs together.

It's in a Chekhovian type of subtext, though, that Pinter finds his
real equivalent for Eliot's verse medium. I said in speaking of the thirties
playwrights that they sometimes seemed to be aiming at Chekhov
without the subtext. Pinter's drama might be called all subtext: I
suppose this is really what makes it so un-Chekhovian in mood and
feeling despite the similarity of the technique. There's no sense of throw
away, no casualness. Everything is pointed; even the humour, which is
certainly relaxing in a way, as all good humour is, has its sharp edge
uppermost pretty well all the time. The quarrel between Lenny and
Ruth over the glass of water in *The Homecoming* is characteristic:

> LENNY: And now perhaps I'll relieve you of your glass.
> RUTH: I haven't quite finished.
> LENNY: You've consumed quite enough, in my opinion.
> RUTH: No, I haven't.
> LENNY: Quite sufficient, in my own opinion.
> RUTH: Not in mine, Leonard.
>> Pause
> LENNY: Don't call me that, please.
> RUTH: Why not?
> LENNY: That's the name my mother gave me.
>> Pause
> Just give me the glass.
> RUTH: No.

Pause

LENNY: I'll take it, then.

RUTH: If you take the glass . . . I'll take you.

Pause

LENNY: How about me taking the glass without you taking me?

RUTH: Why don't I just take you?

The kind of social manoeuvring that is going on here is familiar enough. To go outside the theatre for a moment, one thinks of Trollope explaining why Mrs Proudie makes Mrs Quiverful sit down while she herself stands and how Mrs Quiverful responds to the manoeuvre without being able quite to 'translate' it.

The realism of the similar behaviour in Pinter's scene isn't destroyed, I think, though it's certainly affected by the heavy stressing he gives it. This and the many scenes like it in his drama usually seem poised on the edge of realism: we can recognize what is going on from our ordinary social experience – we all spend a good deal of time reading subtext after all – but we're made to feel uneasy and dubious by the bizarre, theatrical element in the style. The careful pauses have something to do with this. Pinter himself worries about these not seeming natural: he has found actors trying to time them like musical notes, as if they were 'formal conventions or stresses'. But this is not how they are intended. 'The pause is a pause,' he says, 'because of what has just happened in the minds and guts of the characters. They spring out of the text.' If the character is being properly played the actor should find the marked pause natural and inevitable: a silence should simply mean that 'something has happened to create the impossibility of anyone speaking for a certain amount of time – until they can recover from whatever happened before the silence'.[1]

The stylization, then, is a means of reading character. There are many different degrees of it. Like Eliot, Pinter shades off from the credible and the 'voiced' to the fantastic and 'unvoiced' but his transitions are smoother: one of his greatest skills is his ability to keep us doubtful about when we have moved from one plane to another. His first level, corresponding to Eliot's verse dialogue, is 'straight' subtext in the Chekhovian mode: tangential conversation, revealing pauses and so on, all heightened and pointed to take on the faintly unreal quality of the scene between Ruth and Lenny over the glass of water, but still credible in ordinary social terms.

---

[1] Interview with Mel Gussow, *New York Times Mag*, Dec 1971.

Then comes the level of sharper stylization where distortion from the characters' inner life creeps in – and yet still there is a way open to taking the action as in some way actually happening in the outer world. In this area one becomes very aware of Pinter's highly developed filmic sense. Techniques adapted from film are important in creating his peculiar illusion of things being real and yet not real, happening in an observable way and happening only at a deep level of the mind.

The spectacularly sudden appearance of Anna in *Old Times* has this filmic quality. She walks from the unlit area at the back of the stage into the middle of the conversation between Kate and Deeley, talking as though she has been with them all the time. Is she only there in the sense that Pirandello's Signora Pace in *Six Characters in Search of an Author* is there, summoned up by other people's memories of her? Or is she there in the flesh, and is the startling leap into her opening lines to be taken as a bit of quick cutting, a jump forward in time which simply avoids the formalities of an ordinary entrance?

In his interview with Mel Gussow, Pinter expressed satisfaction with this particular effect – 'the woman there, but not there' – and one can't wonder at it. It's a particularly dazzling instance of his skill in keeping the action poised between inner and outer reality. There's a similar filmic quality in the ending of the play. It's all pantomime: stage directions replace dialogue. The characters fall into the positions they've been recalling from their youth: Kate sits on one divan, Anna lies on the other, Deeley walks over, looks at both, 'chooses' Kate, lies in her lap, then after a long silence goes to the armchair and sits slumped in it. The sequence is led into by the sound of his sobbing, otherwise there is no sound heard. It is ended by the lights going on, very bright and sharp, as though a right exposure had finally been achieved; an effect similar to the scene in *L'Année Dernière à Marienbad* when after several faltering attempts a room suddenly snaps into full focus. The effect is of a trauma being acted out in a peculiar mechanical way: there's an alarming sense of emptiness behind it all, as if these incidents are fragments of film pasted together to make something which really isn't a whole.

Another type of filmic effect occurs in *The Homecoming* in the very odd scene where Ruth lies on the floor being made love to by one brother-in-law while the other pokes her with his foot, her father-in-law peers at her face and her husband watches impassively. Can this really be happening? That it's only occurring inside the mind is artfully suggested by the curious lack of connection between what is seen and what is said. The physical acts flow on like a silent film sequence, no one seeming to be aware of anyone speaking, yet Max is speaking all the time and what he's saying is perfectly commonplace:

> MAX: Listen, you think I don't know why you didn't tell me you were married? I know why. You were ashamed. You thought I'd be annoyed because you married a woman beneath you. You should have known me better. I'm broadminded. I'm a broadminded man.

It's as if a pornographic silent film had been dubbed with a sound sequence from a suburban family comedy. Two elements in tension, a brilliant reflection of the state of feeling in which all the characters, except possibly Joey, seem to be trapped.

Pinter's experience of writing for television (in *The Basement* and *Tea Party* especially) can be felt behind effects of this sort. The stage allows for more subtle ambiguities though. In television plays like *Tea Party* we are more obviously committed to a single, distorting point of view, although there is still some delicate shading down from the probable to the fantastic. First we take Disson's view of things as normal, then we become unsure how much of the conspiratorial whispering and giggling he 'sees' is really going on. Finally, though, and well before the end of the play, it's clear that what he sees is a monstrously blown-up version of how things are, like the enormous close-up we get at one point of Wendy's body, when her buttocks fill the screen. There's not much room here for difference of interpretation. *Tea Party* is a very funny play, and as a study in the development of a neurosis it's also gripping and disturbing. But it hasn't quite the pro-vocative ambiguity of plays like *The Homecoming* and *Old Times*. It's when he adapts filmic techniques for the stage that Pinter seems to strike the most delicate balance between the expressed and the un-expressed, the act done and the act dreamed.

At the point where he goes deepest into the mind's interior, especially when it's a mind possessed by guilt and dread, Pinter seems to look quite closely towards Eliot. Their use of ritual[1] is one link. The ritual-istic procession round the birthday cake in *The Family Reunion*, for instance, seems to find a violent echo in *The Birthday Party* when Stanley marches round the table beating the child's drum, 'his face and the drum beat now savage and possessed'. The word 'possessed' points to the strongest and most persistent of these echoes, Pinter's variations

---

[1] J. R. Brown points out that when Pinter wants to show Stanley's 'deeper, inarticulate feelings' he gives him action rather than speech. ('Dialogue in Pinter and others', in *Modern British Dramatists*, 1968.)

on Eliot's 'guardian' motif. Whether accidentally or not, the word itself seems to be recalled in the title of *The Caretaker* (oddly, in its French translation, *Le Gardien*).

Aston, Davies and Mick are all caretakers or guardians of each other and of the house: the idea of being appointed a caretaker is central in the play. It's a role with an aggressive aspect – uppermost in Mick and Davies – and a benevolent one – prevailing in Aston, the double function that Eliot was aiming at in his presentation of Reilly, Julia and Alex in *The Cocktail Party*. Pinter makes the benevolence much more real and believable, though: this, to my mind, is what makes *The Caretaker* still his most touching play.

In *The Birthday Party* the emphasis falls, in Pinter's more usual way, on the aggressiveness of the 'guardian' figures. McCann and Goldberg arrive at the boarding house on Stanley's birthday, uninvited guests like Eliot's Reilly or Lord Claverton's visitors in *The Elder Statesman*: they break him down by relentless inquisition, reducing him to an incoherent wreck. Yet they have come to do him good, or so they say when they cart him off to Monty's for further 'treatment': they have certainly released in full those nervous fears and the sense of nameless guilt that he seems to have been trying to suppress from the start of the play: 'I mean, you wouldn't think, to look at me, really . . . I mean, not really, that I was the sort of bloke to – to cause any trouble, would you?' Pinter brilliantly conveys the suggestion that the inquisitors are unreal beings, a projection of Stanley's obscure dread, without quite destroying the possibility of their being taken as real; this is what makes them so alarming. It's an effect that Eliot was trying for in *The Elder Statesman* by making Gomez and Mrs Carghill stagey, melodramatic figures who couldn't quite be believed in, who almost had to be ghosts emanations from Lord Claverton's guilt-troubled mind.

The illusion wasn't bold enough, though, perhaps because Eliot, hadn't a sharp enough ear for stage idiom. This is what Pinter has, of course, in the highest degree. It's no trouble to him to invent an idiom near enough to life to make for lifelike effect and sufficiently close to parody to raise doubts about it.

Goldberg's Jewish talk could *almost* be appropriate to a play of Wesker's:

> When I was a youngster, of a Friday, I used to go for a walk down the canal with a girl who lived down my road. A beautiful girl. What a voice that bird had! A nightingale, my word of honour. Good? Pure? She wasn't a Sunday school teacher for nothing.

Almost but not quite. Even in small units like this the sense of a careful selection of Jewish elements comes through, and the cumulative effect of his speech is overpoweringly one of caricature, a stage mask of Jewishness.

In coming to these deliberate effects of staginess we come to the heart of Pinter's drama, it seems to me. He uses false voices, phoney performances as a writer like O'Neill uses masks. And for a similar purpose, to convey the terrible sense of non-identity and disconnectedness that almost all his characters, like O'Neill's, suffer from. It's what Eliot's characters suffer from too. This is the ground where he and Pinter meet. But where Eliot mostly relies on imagery to communicate this nightmare, Pinter can act it out. His marvellous ear for idiom and his gift for mimicry allow him to suggest rather than state that all the world's a stage, all people characters endlessly strutting in parts they have created for themselves. One of his characters' most alarming tricks is their habit of mimicking the style they think their opponents aspire to, attacking their right to their part, like one actor upstaging another. This is what Lenny seems to be doing when he puts on an actor's grotesque version of a 'philosopher's' voice to tackle Teddy, the alleged philosopher. 'Do you detect a certain logical incoherence in the central affirmation of Christian theism?', he says, and poor Teddy backs away – 'That question doesn't fall within my province' – revealing himself in that one absurd reply to an absurd question as the man of straw he is, hardly there at all, least of all as a philosopher.

Some critics have taken him as one, though not, certainly, Nigel Dennis, whose account of Pinter's plays in *The New York Times Review of Books* was one that impressed Pinter enough for him to refer to it when he was asked by Mell Gussow[1] if any 'bad things' said by critics had interested him. From memory he quoted Dennis' view that the plays were 'simply acting exercises – for actors. . . . And that was it. There was absolutely nothing else. There was no content whatsoever, merely postures of actors being sad or happy or whatever.' Pinter went on to say that he was fascinated and troubled by this account. I think one can see why. It's so near the truth: there is so much posturing, acting, mimicry, one does begin to wonder, as very much in *Old Times* for instance, if there's anything real behind. I think, though, that this worry is Pinter's too, and that one of the reasons why he is

---

[1] Interview with Pinter, op cit.

generally found so absorbing and haunting, as well as funny, is that he is touching an uneasiness his audience knows from their experience of themselves. He has spoken of his own experience of looking in a mirror and wondering 'Who is that?' It's not a feeling confined to actors, though it's true that thoughts of Pinter having been a professional actor do often thrust into one's mind.

It's in this area of doubt about identity and the truth of feeling that he comes very close to the other English predecessor whom I named earlier on as an important figure in his background – Noel Coward. He doesn't part company with Eliot here, either. It sometimes seems that all roads in the modern English theatre lead back to the Master of *Hay Fever!* Pinter is more thoroughly at home with him than Eliot could be, of course. They have the same inside knowledge of the actor's world and a very similar line in jokes and repartee. Pinter once used the phrase 'the weasel under the cocktail cabinet' when asked what his plays were about. He's since repudiated it, saying – rather amusingly for someone so alert to Freudian slips – that it was a totally accidental remark. It seems no accident, really, though, that it points in the direction of Noel Coward and the Eliot of *The Cocktail Party*. Coward was quick to appreciate Pinter: the 'genuine original' among the new playwrights, he said. It was hardly surprising: there are so many similarities of style and interest. They have the same feeling for streamlined form, the same sharp ear both for lifelike idiom and stage speech, the same love of mimicry and burlesque.

This scene from *Private Lives*, for instance, offers a model that Pinter could obviously use:

> ELYOT: No sense of glamour, no sense of glamour at all.
> AMANDA: It's difficult to feel really glamorous with a crick in the neck.
> ELYOT: Why didn't you say you had a crick in your neck?
> AMANDA (sweetly): It's gone now.
> ELYOT: How convenient. (He lights a cigarette.)
> AMANDA (holding out her hand): I want one please.
> ELYOT (throwing her one): Here.
> AMANDA: Match?
> ELYOT (impatiently): Wait a minute, can't you?
> AMANDA: Chivalrous little love.
> ELYOT (throwing the matches at her): Here.
> AMANDA (coldly): Thank you very much indeed. (There is a silence for a moment.)

The style manages to seem colloquial and natural and at the same time artful and arranged – a performer's style. It's a light-hearted version of Pinter's threatening cocktail chat, this, for instance, between Bill and James in *The Collection*:

> JAMES: ... Here's your vodka.
> BILL: That's very generous of you.
> JAMES: Not at all. Cheers. (They drink.)
> BILL: Cheers.
> JAMES: Eh, come here.
> BILL: What?
> JAMES: I bet you're a wow at parties.
> BILL: Well, it's nice of you to say so, but I wouldn't say I was all that much of a wow.
> JAMES: Go on, I bet you are. (Pause.)
> BILL: You think I'm a wow, do you?
> JAMES: At parties I should think you are.
> BILL: No, I'm not much of a wow really. The bloke I share this house with is, though.
> JAMES: Oh, I met him. Looked a jolly kind of chap.
> BILL: Yes, he's very good at parties. Bit of a conjuror.
> JAMES: What, rabbits?
> BILL: Well, not so much rabbits, no.
> JAMES: No rabbits?
> BILL: No. He doesn't like rabbits, actually. They give him hay fever.

Pinter's characters tend to fall into Coward-like groups: the good actors versus the not so good; those who can project an identity with panache – Goldberg, Lenny, Davies – and those who are ill-defined and unsure – Aston, Teddy, Disson. The wretched Disson, demoralized by the glamorous conjunction of wife, secretary and brother-in-law is in a position remarkably like Ernest's in *Design for Living*, up against the witty triumvirate, Otto, Leo and Gilda. Style is used as a weapon and a facade in much the way that it is by Coward's 'glib, over-articulate and amoral creatures'. Pinter's characters are always pouncing on each others' vocabulary, drawing attention to the implausibility of the identity behind it; Deeley in *Old Times*, for instance, picking on Anna's word, 'gaze':

> ANNA: Ah, those songs. We used to play them, all of them, all the time, late at night, lying on the floor, lovely old things. Sometimes I'd look at her face, but she was quite unaware of my gaze.
> DEELEY: Gaze?
> ANNA: What?
> DEELEY: The word gaze. Don't hear it very often.

He seems to be picking up in sequences like these from hints that Coward lets drop but doesn't follow up himself, the hint given in *Hay Fever*, for instance, when one of the mugs asks naïvely after Judith Bliss has given a big performance: 'Didn't she mean all she said?' – and Sorel says in her casual way, 'No, not really, we none of us ever mean *anything*.' Echoes from this area of Coward's drama have been sounding more and more insistently since they first became apparent in *The Collection* (produced 1961). They're stronger than ever in *Old Times*. It could almost be taken as a re-write of *Blithe Spirit*, Coward's comic piece about a man who calls up the ghost of his first wife – with the aid of the deliciously funny Madame Arcati – and finds himself horribly uncomfortable between the living wife and the dead one who can't be got rid of (the medium is too incompetent). In the end he has two ghosts on his hands, when the first wife kills off the second. The similarities of situation are rather startling and there are some resemblances of detail too: Elvira suggesting to Charles that he might have called her back to talk of 'old times', for instance, and the rather eerie playing of a sentimental tune, 'Always', to help the séance along.

The tunes in *Old Times* – which come to mind at that point – are something rather new for Pinter: along with many pointed allusions to the film of *Odd Man Out*, they seem to indicate a looking out to the audience which might be a move to ease the tightness of the closed form. In his most open play so far, *Silence*, he achieved a rare effect of freedom. To anyone coming to Peter Hall's production in 1969 with strong expectations from the earlier drama, the sense of relief was almost overwhelming: there was this great bare mirror-like stage, with the long shadows cast by the three characters stretching back in an apparently endless series to the back stage distances. Freedom was bought at the price of loneliness in a way, the characters were certainly isolated from each other at the point where they were having their dream or reverie: the soliloquy structure enforced this view. But what came out of the reveries wasn't just loneliness, failure to make contact. That was part of it – sadly for Bates, less so for Rumsey. But there was an experience of shared affection too. A new note of tenderness was struck in the scene when Ellen moved into Rumsey's 'place' and offered to cook for him: their memories of her childhood friendship for him and their adult desires merged in a moment of touching, unforced lyricism.

It looked with *Silence* as though Pinter might be changing direction quite radically: it was rather surprising when he came back so close to

Coward and the centre of the tradition with *Old Times*. But of course to think of the traditional element in that or in any of his plays is to be made all the more aware of his brilliance and audacity as an innovator. At a stroke, it seems, he has lifted English realism out of the novelists' world it developed in during the thirties and into an actor's world. 'Facts first, explanations afterwards' was Madame Arcati's motto. 'Facts – if you can get at them – and no explanations', might be Pinter's. Explicit analysis and explanation disappear, only what can be expressed theatrically and obliquely is allowed in. Realism has acquired a new dimension through the variations he has played on the old forms. What his next variation will be is one of those questions that one most looks forward to having answered.

1. *Texts*
   The Birthday Party, 1959
   The Birthday Party and other plays, 1960. The Room and The Dumb Waiter
   The Caretaker, 1960
   A Slight Ache and other plays, 1961. A Night Out, The Dwarfs and five Revue Sketches ('Trouble in the Works', 'The Black and White', 'Request Stop', 'Last to Go', 'Applicant').
   The Collection and The Lover. 1963. Also contains the story 'The Examination'
   The Homecoming, 1965
   Tea Party and other plays, 1967. 'The Basement and Night School'
   Landscape, 1968
   Mac (On Anew McMaster), 1968.
   Poems, 1968
   Landscape and Silence, 1969. Also contains 'Night'
   Five Screen Plays, 1971
   Old Times, 1971

2. *Critical Writings*
   Esslin, M. *The Peopled Wound*, 1970. With extensive bibliography
   Hayman, R. *Harold Pinter*, 1968. Contemporary Playwrights series
   Hinchcliffe, A. P. *Harold Pinter*, 1967
   Hollis, J. R. *Harold Pinter: the Poetics of Silence*, 1970. Crosscurrents/Modern Critiques
   Sykes, A. *Harold Pinter*, Queensland 1970
   Taylor, J. R. *Harold Pinter*, 1969. Writers and their Work series

VII

Away from Realism

Early Experiments: Shaw, Auden and Isherwood, Sean O'Casey

The move away from realism to more open, freewheeling, mixed forms of drama got under way in the twenties and thirties on the extreme fringe of the professional theatre, among amateur groups, and in outlying theatres like Terence Gray's at Cambridge. The West End theatre kept to its old separation: on the one hand the 'legitimate' drama, on the other the theatre of music hall, musical comedy and the rest. When the twain did meet – in O'Casey's drama, for instance – there was bafflement among the critics. Why could he not keep on writing in the familiar style of *Juno and the Paycock* and *The Plough and the Stars*? This until very recently has been the common cry in O'Casey criticism.

There was some subversion of realism going on inside the convention itself, of course, supremely in the plays of Shaw. His feeling for farce and melodrama came out in increasingly bizarre forms during the period. There are moments in a play like *The Simpleton of the Unexpected Isles* (1935) when one might be in the world of Orton's *What the Butler Saw* or Charles Wood's extravagant epic, '*H*'. In the opening scene, for instance, set in a tropical port somewhere in the British Empire, the disappointed Emigration Office clerk talks out to nobody in particular in classic farce style: 'What am I? An empire builder: that's what I am by nature, Cecil Rhodes: that's me. Why am I a clerk with only two shirts to my back?...' And so on to a final outburst of patriotism: 'Let the whole earth be England: and let Englishmen rule it.' On this note, singing *Rule Britannia*, he shoots himself. 'Dear! dear! dear!', comments the Station Master finding the body, 'What a climate! The fifth this month.'

The restraints of realism have certainly been abandoned here. And so it goes on. The Emigration Officer turns out to be another candidate for suicide. He makes a half-hearted attempt to jump off a cliff and is helped on his way by a kick from an obliging native priest. 'Murderer!' says a young woman bystander when a splash is heard. 'Not at all', the priest assures her: 'The shock will do him good.'

Clearly this is what Shaw means to happen to the audience. It's his old comic shock therapy taking more aggressively physical forms. The Emigration Officer's 'harlequin leap' does do him good. He emerges from his sea dip restored and refreshed: symbolically clad in white robes, he announces that he is 'to all intents and purposes born again'. He has become a native of the Unexpected Isles where as Prola the priestess says, 'Nothing is unbelievable.' In this garden of Eden, ruled over by the imperturbable Pra and Prola, life is a long conversation punctuated by unlikely happenings. Four beautiful 'idols' spring embarrassingly to life when a visiting clergyman kisses one of them: they turn out to be four pert young things with exotic and suggestive names like Maya and Vashti. Later, the sound of trumpets heralds an angel who flies in shaking bullets and shot off his wings and proclaiming the Day of Judgement: those who can't prove they have been worth their salt will simply disappear. The four young people do this instantly; they were only abstractions, never really there at all. Finally the stage is held by Pra and Prola, the life worshippers; defying the stage thunder rolling at them they declare their confidence that 'Life needs us both.'

Various assumptions of realism are upset in scenes like these. The stage illusion is brought into the open; the pretence that the stage isn't really a stage has been dropped. Instead, the idea of the play has become an element in the action, as it is in that other 'super farce', *Too True to be Good* (1932). Comically, the Monster warns the audience at the end of the first act: 'The play is now virtually over; but the characters will discuss it at great length for two acts more.' And at the close, when there is no stage audience left to listen to him, Aubrey, the incorrigible preacher/burglar is still talking – talking out into the vacuum of the stalls, with thick fog gathering round him: 'And meanwhile my gift has possession of me: I must preach and preach and preach, no matter how late the hour and how short the day, no matter whether I have nothing to say. . . .' The curtain comes down on an 'Amen' that nobody joins in.

In the 1965 West End production, this vivid stage picture – the compulsive talker speaking out to a void – came over as a comical and oddly touching image. It had a life of its own, a theatrical force that related ironically and rather sadly to the intellectual force of the ideas the preacher was developing. Shaw's image for himself, it seemed it might be.

It's in effects of this kind – depending on the audience being aware of itself as an audience in the theatre – that his late plays now look so modern. Yet of course he never forgets his readers. It was he, after all, who had brought in the idea of the printed play as something that might be read almost like a novel. It's the reader, not the audience, who gets the benefit of his closing comments on the key contrast of *Too True to be Good* between the incorrigible talker and the woman of action, Mopsy. For the audience, probably, Mopsy has merged with the other characters into the background by the time Aubrey comes to the end of his sermon: that contrast isn't what one carries away from the final scene. The reader, however, is reminded that 'Fine words butter no parsnips' and that the woman of action is Shaw's own favourite.

The pull back to the reader – and to the audience in a 'reading' role – is still strong in the late plays. There are some fine jumps into what looks like a comedy of happenings, freed from the restraints of probability and logic. But the surrealist drive doesn't shatter the old mode. The bizarre and provocative incidents are the flashpoints of conversation, its stimuli, its dynamic illustrations. We always come back to an eminently rational and ordered world where well-educated middle class characters hold calm and purposeful discussions about the nature of things, whether it's Pra and Prola checking on the value of their lives with each other or Aubrey justifying himself in a vacuum.

This piquant Shavian combination – small electric shocks and 'massive conversation pieces', to use Bridie's phrase – has proved a very attractive, though terribly dangerous model for later playwrights. Bridie's own comedy followed a similar pattern: he loved to open with an outrageously improbable event, like the calling up of the devil in a Scottish manse on a wet Sunday[1] and move into a debate on manners and morals, with the devil or equivalent character (an archangel in *Tobias and the Angel*) leading the discussion. There are strong echoes in that situation of the hell scene in *Man and Superman*. And there are many other Shavian echoes in Bridie's comedy.

He thought of himself rather differently, though, as a successor to

---

[1] *Mr Bolfry*, 1944. *Tobias and the Angel*, 1931.

Pinero and Henry Arthur Jones. To him, Shaw's comedy seemed 'in a side street, a little away from the procession of English Drama down the years'.[1] Time has proved him wrong in this. The side street has broadened out into a main thoroughfare, to judge from the number of present-day playwrights who are practising Shaw's 'talk and shock' technique. Fry was the first postwar playwright to pick up the method: his Thomas Mendip in *The Lady's not for Burning* announcing 'The Last Trump / Is timed for twenty-two forty hours precisely', could easily have strayed out of *The Simpleton of the Unexpected Isles*. Osborne has produced interesting variations on the pattern and really most of the playwrights now using the conversational mode of realism try to mix physical and verbal acrobatics in something like Shavian style. Wesker punctuates the long conversations in *Their Very Own and Golden City* with head stands, a character in *The Friends* practises Yoga positions, David Storey's Arnold Middleton turns from talk to standing on his head, and in his latest play, *Jumpers* (1972), Tom Stoppard draws attention to the Shavian mix he is attempting – gymnastics among the professors of philosophy – in his punning title.

Shaw's drama showed how realism could be made freer, turned towards new styles of farce and melodrama, without losing its essentially discursive, analytical character. It doesn't lose that character in his hands. His drama approaches melodrama without ever turning into it. Musical values are important, but chiefly in the patterning and projection of the dialogue. We know that Shaw thought of his casting in operatic terms. 'The four principals should be soprano, alto, tenor, and bass', was the sort of advice he used to give producers. And nonverbal music sometimes gets in, as in the Mozartian strains heralding the Statue's arrival in hell in *Man and Superman*. But that kind of music is kept very much to the background. Some obvious chances for breaking out into song are refused, as for instance in *The Apple Cart* when Amanda tells Magnus and the Cabinet about her way of pulverizing her political opponents by making comic songs against them. It would be natural – and nice – to have an illustration, but we don't get it, only an account. We're given a lot of detail – 'Boo! Hoo! I want Amanda's Teddy Bear to play with' is one of her hit tunes – but not the singing, as we certainly would if she were a character in one of Arden's plays, *The Workhouse Donkey*, for example.

This seems the point where the lines of fundamental difference

---

[1] J. Bridie, in his *Tedious and Brief*, 1944, p 49.

between realism and the alternative tradition are drawn. For Shaw, in the long run, analysis prevails. Other experiments in the twenties and thirties were more radical. There was a great upsurge of interest in the idea of a theatre open to music and dance, where elements from opera, pantomine, music hall, might be mixed in an experience of 'total theatre'. Yeats had already offered a model in his plays for dancers. As early as 1917, Eliot had recognized possibilities in this strange Irish version of Noh, when he saw a performance of *At the Hawk's Well* in Lady Cunard's London drawing room. The line stretching from Yeats through Eliot and O'Casey to Auden and Isherwood is the line of the new age, the counter-revolution.

Yeats had had to create all the production equipment for his dance plays, find dancers, invent a verse-speaking method, inspire musicians and designers – make a whole new theatre out of nothing. Similarly in England, the existing theatre had to be by-passed and altogether different ones conjured up for the new drama. Festival theatres sprang up where Yeatsian experiments with poetry, dance, and music were tried out: Rutland Boughton's music dramas at Glastonbury (one of these, *The Immortal Hour*[1] was a popular success) and Terence Gray's dance dramas at Cambridge. Music and plastic values were to 'speak' as expressively as words. It's hard now to get any idea of how effective these experiments were. 'Total theatre' is a perishable commodity: it was so especially in a period without film or video tape recordings to preserve at least some traces of the experience. But it's clear enough from the texts of Boughton's music dramas and Gray's scenarios that the literary element was the weak link in the chain. Boughton's libretti hardly seem more expressive than the average opera libretto usually is.

The theatre of music and dance needed the poetic imagination to turn it into total theatre. And the poets of the time did become increasingly interested in the physical side of theatre. There are some rather interesting relationships between words and dance in Charles Williams' drama for instance. Not that his words are impressive – he writes a stilted sort of no-language, a mixture of pompous verse and unconvincing colloquialisms. Sometimes, though, he strikes out an arresting line of sensual imagery, often to do with people eating each other (some interesting anticipations of Bond here)[2] and these images

---

[1] First produced at the Old Vic 31 May 1920.
[2] See particularly *The House of the Octopus*, 1945, for some remarkably close foreshadowing of Bond's ideas (though not his methods).

are occasionally picked up and expressed through strong physical movement and dance. The effect could be ludicrous but it could also be genuinely disturbing, one imagines – in the dance scene of *Seed of Adam* (produced 1936), for instance, when a voluptuous negress advances on the Virgin waving a scimitar and threatening to eat her alive – 'She has her own idea of food'.

These are isolated moments. The only solid body of practice in the earlier period to test theories of 'total theatre' against is in the plays of Sean O'Casey and Auden and Isherwood. O'Casey's is the great drama in the new mode, but I want to begin with Auden and Isherwood's, since Auden was the theorist of the movement at its early stage, as well as a leading practitioner.

It was in the year *Sweeney Agonistes* was published – 1926 – that he came out with a great blast against the monstrous inadequacy of the existing theatre.[1] The only traces of theatrical art remaining, he announced, were to be found on the music hall stage. The whole of realistic drama since Chekhov would have to go: later something might be done with puppets. One thinks of Peter Brook in 1961[2] making a similar onslaught on the drama of realism and psycho-analysis as part of a 'nineteenth century materialist process', his plea to scrap it all and start again in the spirit of Artaud, to find 'the new forms, and through the new forms the new architecture and through the new architecture the new rituals of the age that is swirling round us'. Brook has the opportunity to shape a new theatre language within the existing theatre: the tools are all to his hand. For Auden there was no theatre that could begin to understand the language – made up of songs, dance, pantomine, knockabout as well as words – that he imagined in plays like *The Dance of Death*. Like Eliot, he set a much higher value on the actor's bodily skills than the realistic theatre did. Eliot's admiration for the disciplines of the ballet comes to mind when Auden is quoted as saying, 'The basis of acting is acrobatics, dancing, and all forms of physical skill.' Like Yeats, he had to create his own theatre from scratch, which he did (on a smaller scale) when he joined with Rupert Doone and Robert Medley in founding the Group Theatre in 1932.

Before then he had written a strange 'charade', *Paid on Both Sides* (1930), which reminds one of *Sweeney Agonistes* in the violence of its

---

[1] Reported by Isherwood in his *Lions and Shadows*, 1938, p 215.
[2] P. Brook, 'Search for a Hunger', *Encore*, July-Aug 1961.

break with realism, its feeling for spontaneous, popular forms of English drama, especially pantomime and the most primitive form of all, the Mummers' Play. He uses the bold, childlike devices of this drama to communicate obscure psychic impulses and anxieties with what seems to me great subtlety. 'Seems' is the only word to use, because already with this piece – and it is less committed to total theatre techniques than the plays that followed – the difficulty of 'reading' is great. Not that it's too hard to visualize some of the comic/grotesque effects: the Man/Woman, the Mother threatening the Spy with a gigantic feeding bottle – 'Be quiet, or I'll give you a taste of this' – the Doctor curing the Spy of death by drawing an enormous tooth from him. Anyone brought up on English Christmas pantomime, with its Dames played by men, its cardboard nursery-tale sets, is half way to *seeing* all that. That's not the same as feeling it, though. What sort of weight would these elements acquire in the theatre, one wonders. Would figures like the Man/Woman and the Spy function as one imagines they might, both comically and troublingly? Would the broad pantomime effects turn out to be a good surrealist technique for illuminating the cryptic dialogue? The text certainly inspires a strong desire to find out, to experience in the theatre those dream-like moments – when the Man/Woman appears as a prisoner behind barbed wire or when the hero, John, comes together with his 'enemy', the Spy, to plant a tree; a visual gloss, this, on the riddling lines: 'Sharers of the same house / Attendants on the same machine / Rarely a word, in silence understood.'

Without having seen a production, it's harder still to estimate the force *The Dance of Death* (1933) might have on a stage. What would be the impact of the new character – the Dancer – who would come into the play in performance? As a total mute he hardly exists in the text: the stage directions offer only an outline of a Dionysiac figure, attractive and frightening: 'For he has an evil eye as well as a good.' He draws the pleasure-seeking crowds after him in any direction he chooses. While they sunbathe, he steals their clothes and puts them into a basket which is whisked into the wings: when he brings it out again, the clothes have turned into uniforms. The Chorus put them on and move into a new turn, a musical revue of 1916. The Dancer has led them into the middle of a war.

The pierrot war games of *Oh What A Lovely War* don't seem far off here. The whole style of *The Dance of Death* in fact anticipates the improvising, musical style of Joan Littlewood and Theatre Workshop and of John Arden in plays like *The Workhouse Donkey* and *The Royal Pardon*. The boisterous good humour with its sharp edge is similarly turned to satire, the rollicking rhythms are similar, the irreverent handling of history: Marx comes on at the end to the strains of Mendelssohn's Wedding March, to be greeted by the Chorus: 'Oh Mr Marx, you've gathered / All the material facts / You know the economic / Reasons for our acts'.

Light moments sometimes flash a darker side in the seemingly casual way that 'improvised' drama aims at. The 1916 incident is one, and the odd little episode when the girls in the company are told there is no role for them except as scenery. They stand around absurdly representing trees while the young men try out their 'country colony' experiment; it fails, and the girls draw the moral: 'You thought you were escaping from sin / By leaving us out but you left yourselves in.' Swung to tunes like Casey Jones, the moralizing comes over with a music hall type of vigour and zest.

In his feeling for audience participation, Auden again points ahead to writers like Arden. 'Ideally there would be no spectators,' he said,[1] 'In practice every member of the audience should feel like an understudy.' To judge from contemporary accounts, there wasn't much chance of this happening at the Group Theatre; Julian Symons was surely right when he said that Auden's aphorisms were blueprints for dramatic art in a society that did not exist.[2] Perhaps it still doesn't, though the sort of success that Arden and Alan Plater have had with involving provincial audiences might suggest that it's coming nearer. But although there is some strain and selfconsciousness in Auden's attempts to involve the audience – a touch of hostility too, in his portrayal of the complacent Mr and Mrs A., for instance – still, his anxiety to make the attempt brings him closer to present-day writers like Arden than to any of his contemporaries in the thirties theatre.

There is another connection with Arden, a Brechtian one. The way they both use broadly comic, distancing techniques in plays like *The Dog Beneath the Skin* (1935) and *The Happy Haven* (1960) owes something to Brecht, though they have both said that the influence wasn't of the first importance. It can't be missed, though, in certain scenes of *The Dog* – especially the sequences in the Red Light district and the 'eating a girl' episode (identified by Isherwood as a borrowing from

---

[1] In the programme to *The Dance of Death*.
[2] J. Symons, in his *The Thirties*, 1960, p 80.

Mahagonny). Auden was in Berlin in 1928, the year of *The Threepenny Opera*: the Weill rhythms seem to hang about *The Dog*.

And yet Auden and Arden seem much more like each other than either is like Brecht. They are both tremendously English in their theatrical feeling: they look back all the time to the old popular, primitive forms of English drama – mummers' plays, pantomime, melodrama, where 'Brechtian' techniques were used in a very spontaneous, unselfconscious way. Musical comedy, Christmas pantomime, the country house charade, Auden maintained[1] were the 'most living' forms of drama in the period. His first dramatic piece, *Paid on Both Sides*, was a charade, and in *The Dog Beneath the Skin*, written with Isherwood, the models were musical comedy and Christmas pantomime, that marvellous rag bag, where anything from comic pastry-making scenes to trapeze acts can be stitched on to the slender, sentimental story line.

The hero of *The Dog Beneath the Skin*, setting out with his faithful dog to search Europe for the missing heir, has a long line of pantomime Dick Whittingtons with their resourceful cats behind him. The village he starts out from is a pantomime/musical comedy village too, peopled by an overpoweringly wholesome Chorus and a set of highly coloured gentry, suspiciously hearty in the best tradition of pantomime villains.

The touch of fake in all this is good preparation for the revelations of the final scene, when the ruling class come out in their true colours. The fake goes deep: at heart, it seems, they are Fascists, blood brothers to the Ostnian tyrant the hero meets on his travels, who shoots political prisoners in the politest possible way and enquires anxiously of Alan if the ritual is up to English standards.

The pantomime/musical comedy convention gives Auden and Isherwood freedom to look outwards to Hitler's Europe (lightly disguised as Ostnia and Westland) and inwards to Alan's psychological dilemma without losing line and clarity. Dimly we begin to sense obscure connections between the rabid beast at large in Europe and the gentle beast, the dog: 'For he has an evil eye as well as a good.' Broad, comic techniques are skilfully used to distance the harsh material. Their value becomes obvious when one compares *The Dog Beneath the Skin* with the other European play, *On the Frontier* (1938) where a much more solemn approach results in a curiously generalized, featureless

---

[1] Quoted by Ashley Dukes in 'The English Scene', *Theatre Arts* 19, 1935.

allegory[1] about the agony of war. It hasn't anything like the vivid feel of the thirties that comes through the broad caricature effects of *The Dog Beneath the Skin* – the scene of the lunatics saluting a portrait with a loudspeaker-face, the macabre Red light scenes, the Ostnian execution, when the court ladies offer refreshments to the widows the minute the shooting is over and gloat over the handsomest corpses:

> And such strong hands. Why, they're not yet cool!
> Lend me a pair of scissors, dear.
> I want a lock as a souvenir.

A genuine whiff of Nazi Germany comes through some of this 'comedy'.

The same thing is done for England in the brilliant Nineveh Hotel sequences. They're simultaneously jolly and hard, as in the episode of the Diner who is invited to choose a dish from the line of chorus girls and say how he would like her done: 'Will you have her roast, sir, / Or on Japanese toast, sir? / With Sauce Allemagne, sir? / Or stewed in white wine, sir?' The rhythms are light-hearted, but there's a rather nasty jolt into prose when the Diner makes his choice: 'Stewed, I think. But I'll have the finger-nails served separately as a savoury.' Ostnia doesn't seem so far away at such moments. There's another uncomfortable connection in the Destructive Desmond scene, when an innocent art expert is cruelly led on in front of a cabaret audience to value two paintings: one is a Rembrandt, the other worthless. The audience – off stage and on, presumably – is invited to choose which they would like to see destroyed. The on-stage audience chooses the Rembrandt, which Destructive Desmond proceeds to slash gleefully to pieces to the sound of drums and trumpets. What does the off-stage audience do, laugh heartily or not at all, enjoy the vandalism in an uncaring, uninhibited way or enjoy it and feel uncomfortable or disapprove and feel uncomfortable? It's their ability to implicate the audience in prickly situations like these that makes Auden and Isherwood seem so much in the van of the modern movement towards black farce and comedy.

The Dog Beneath the Skin seems to me, as it does to John Fuller, quite the most theatrically exciting of the Auden / Isherwood plays, and the one most deserving revival. I think he is probably right in

---

[1] One ought to keep in mind, however, that the music in the play might help to lift and sharpen the feeling. It is called a 'melodrama', and has songs by Britten which would probably do a good deal to colour the action.

suggesting[1] that the 'lively and eclectic means' it takes to a serious end
have deceived many of its readers into taking it not very seriously.
The Ascent of F6 (1936) generally receives more critical attention and
higher ranking, perhaps partly at any rate because it has more interest
of a traditional kind: there's more to get hold of in the characterization
generally and it has at its heart the full-length character study of
Ransom. This play doesn't call for the same range of skills in its actors:
no dancing or pantomime antics, next to no singing or knockabout.
Most of what there is comes in through the character of Gunn, with
the odd result that he seems in a way the most lifelike of them all.

There's a more pronounced narrative element in *The Ascent of F6*
than in the earlier plays: Ransom's immensely long opening soliloquy
sets the note. But still a characteristically bold, direct theatricality is
called for in certain scenes, the scene, for instance, when Ransom's
domineering mother sits alone on the stage in her high-backed chair,
willing her son up on his mountain top to hear her:

> talking to herself in a hoarse and penetrating whisper, – 'Michael . . .
> Michael darling . . . can you hear me? There, there . . . It's all right . . .
> There's nothing to be frightened about. Mother's with you. Of course
> she won't leave you alone, Michael, never! Wherever you are, whatever
> you're doing, whether you know it or not, she's near you with her love;
> for you belong to her always.'

All those grasping, possessive mothers of the thirties family drama
seem to be epitomized in this uncanny figure. It's a still more uncanny
moment when she comes into the surrealist sequence at the end as
the youthful mother of his memory, taking his head into her lap and
singing him to sleep. He dies quietly, to the sound of her fairy tales:

> And in the castle tower above, / The princess' cheek burns red for your
> love, / You shall be king and queen of the land, / Happy for ever, hand
> in hand.

Sad irony. There is no princess in Ransom's world. The only woman
who seems to exist for him is the Mother.

In the theatre of today, which has seen Peter Brook's *Marat/Sade*
and *A Midsummer Night's Dream* and Joan Littlewood's *Oh What a
Lovely War* there should be a better chance of production for plays
like *The Dog Beneath the Skin* and *The Ascent of F6* which can't be
properly appreciated until they've been given an all-out music hall/

---

[1] J. Fuller, *A Reader's Guide to W. H. Auden*, 1970, p 90.

revue treatment on a musically oriented stage. They certainly deserve
more attention from the professional theatre than they've had up to
now.

For Auden and Isherwood, of course, theatre was a sideline. The
real casualty of the old compartmentalized system was Sean O'Casey,
a major dramatist who found himself without a theatre to practise his
experimental art in. The relative neglect of his later plays must surely
be one of the saddest things in English theatre history. Here were these
marvellously rich and humorous masterpieces, and the theatre didn't
seem capable of responding to them. *Cock-a-Doodle-Dandy* (1949)
wasn't seen in London till ten years after its première at the People's
Theatre, Newcastle; *The Drums of Father Ned* (1960) has never got
beyond the Queen's Theatre, Hornchurch; *The Bishop's Bonfire* (1955)
was six years in getting to London from Dublin and the short plays
collected in the volume *Behind the Green Curtains* (1961) haven't been
seen in London at all. As so often, two theatres – the Royal Court and
the Mermaid – redeemed the general failure. *Cock-a-Doodle-Dandy*
was given at the Court in 1959, and in 1962 the Mermaid staged an
O'Casey Season which included *Purple Dust*. It seems ungrateful to
fault these productions, when it was so good to have them at all, but
in the early sixties the right style for O'Casey's later drama hadn't
been found. It was certainly a difficult style for a theatre tuned to
realism to achieve, for it goes back to the tradition rejected by realism,
the musical style of Boucicault's type of melodrama – melodrama,
that is, with a strong vein of farce. In O'Casey's hand the Boucicault
techniques are turned to a great range of complex effects, from the
savage surrealism of the musical instrument scene in *Red Roses for Me*[1]
to the poetic suggestiveness of the farcical antics in *Cock-a-Doodle-
Dandy*.

Like Auden and Isherwood's, O'Casey's is above all a musical theatre
and a theatre of exuberant physical movement and dance. Scenes and
costumes have an exaggerated, flamboyant quality, like the sunflowers
in *Cock-a-Doodle-Dandy*, 'their blossoms big as shields, the petals
raying out widely and sharply, like rays from an angry sun.' A subdued
production, going for the realism that is always an element in his
drama, is bound to be inadequate. In Act 3 of *Red Roses for Me*, for
instance, it's not enough to give the Liffey scene a discreet sunset glow,

[1] The 1942 version. This scene was omitted from the version printed in *Collected Plays*,
1949–51.

gently softening and romanticizing it, when what O'Casey called for was a bold transformation act, much more in the style of Christmas pantomime or melodrama. The dull, depressing scene – dirty Liffey, 'spongy leaden' Dublin sky, the unemployed men and the women flower sellers in drab dark clothes – all disappear from view, as the widow's poor hovel in pantomime vanishes at the wave of a fairy's wand, to be replaced by an enchanted glade or an Arabian Nights palace.

O'Casey's Dublin poor go through a real Cinderella change. Their black clothes drop away, they stand up heroic figures in green and silver, momentarily lifted to the dignity and passion which Ayamonn had been working to stir in them by his political oratory. He is changed too. The earnest young man struggling to educate himself and to organize his fellow workers in a pathetic fight for a shilling more on their wages, becomes in the strange light falling on him, a mythical creature: only his head is seen 'set in a streak of sunlight, looking like the severed head of Dunn-Bo speaking out of the darkness'. The gods have come in among the company as the fairies come into the panto-mime to work miraculous – but fleeting – transformations. There are other indications besides the reference to the severed head that O'Casey wanted the scene played as a mystery. When the transformation reaches its climax in the 'dignified and joyous dance' performed by Ayamonn and Finoola, the music for it should come from a flute played 'by someone, somewhere'. A mysterious fluty note off-stage is required, one would say, rather than the penny whistle, whipped out of someone's pocket, which is the type of effect – geared to realism rather than magic – generally gone for in productions I have seen.

Of course the strange mixture of farce and sadness, realism and flamboyant stylization that O'Casey calls for in his late plays is a difficult one, especially for actors used to the consistent realistic style. A play like *Cock-a-Doodle-Dandy* has no obvious consistency. Every-thing exists in two seemingly contradictory dimensions. The Cock himself is a figure of broad farce and of poetic mystery. When he goes on the rampage, flapping his green wings and letting out his violent, triumphant crow, he creates a classical kind of farcical con-fusion among the characters who are afraid of him: the Sergeant loses his trousers and the others would too if they didn't hang on to their waistbands: it's all very broad, simple fun. Yet a movement has to be made from this mood to the mysterious quiet that the Cock effects when he is temporarily cast down by the repressive priest: the wind wails sadly, dies away into sombre silence; we are reminded of his Dionysian role as a force in nature, something to be taken seriously. And this is a prelude to two scenes which are very serious, the unpleasant confrontation of Loreleen and the priest, and the return of the dying Julia from Lourdes.

Father Domineer similarly moves in and out of the farcical dimension. He's a comical figure when he's leading his nervous parishioners against the Cock – 'Shoulder to shoulder, an' step together against th' onward rush of paganism!' And then in the next breath he's a real tyrant with the power to hurt. There's a genuinely nasty flavour about the kangaroo court he holds when Loreleen is accused of wanton behaviour by two bullies: he lets them manhandle her and clearly enjoys passing sentence on her. The mood changes again from this unpleasant note to the sadness of Julia's return – uncured – from Lourdes. Here the priest's life-denying spirit is put in yet another and still more sombre perspective.

The delicate shifts of mood involved in sequences of this sort are testing. Still more so, perhaps, are the intermittent breaks from a more homely style to a bold Expressionism. At one moment a character will be seen from an ordinary social viewpoint, as a high-spirited, attractive girl: in the next she comes on with horns sprouting from her forehead and a mocking, cynical expression to match: a visual projection of the pharisaical characters' furtive lustfulness. 'I'd welcome her', says Mahan, 'even if I seen her through th' vision of oul' Shanaar – with horns growin' out of her head!' And pat upon the cue come the horns. A pantomime effect, which is also a serious comment on character.

Effects of the kind I have been describing would have come more naturally to performers in the pantomime/music hall theatre than to the serious actors in the theatre of the first half of this century. In the thirties the odds were against O'Casey's experimental plays getting the kind of performance they needed. Like his admirers now, he was grateful for the productions they did get but as Eileen O'Casey has recorded in her moving biography,[1] he wasn't always happy with them. He knew that the skills these plays called for were more likely to be found in the popular, musical theatre. Like Eliot and Auden, he identified that theatre as the source of the greatest vitality to be found

---

[1] E. O'Casey, *Sean*, 1971.

in the period. Of all the plays he saw when he first came to London, so he said in his autobiography,[1] what stayed in his mind was the chorus from *Rose Marie*: 'the extraordinary beautiful slide and slip, shimmering with colour, of the girls in the chorus of that immensely mortal musical play.' It was deeply appropriate that his masterpiece, *The Silver Tassie*, should have been given its chance on the London stage by someone from the world of *Rose Marie*, that imaginative impresario, C. B. Cochran, 'the greatest supervisor', as O'Casey put it 'of things low and things high in the English theatre'. The title of Cochran's autobiography, *Cock-a-Doodle-Do* (1941) is reflected in *Cock-a-Doodle-Dandy*, a tribute, surely, for this was O'Casey's favourite among his own plays. It was supremely typical that at the time Cochran cast *The Silver Tassie* he was also casting for Noel Coward's operette, *Bitter Sweet* – a happy chance for Eileen O'Casey who managed to get a part in the *Bitter Sweet* chorus. She then had to get permission from Cochran to miss a performance of Coward's piece so as to be at the first night of O'Casey's. An amusing underlining, this, of the connection between the popular/musical theatre of the period and its most revolutionary drama, a drama prophetically created, it might seem, for the theatre that is forming round us now.

Certainly *The Silver Tassie* looked very much at home in the production it was given by the Royal Shakespeare Company at the Aldwych in 1969.[2] The actors had no difficulty with the transitions of style. Touches like the Doctor's little hops and skips and snatches of falsetto song in the hospital scene came over with great naturalness and spontaneity and at the same time lifted the action off the plane of total realism: the right context was formed for the extreme stylization of Act 2. The 'problem' of this act – as it had seemed to Yeats and other early critics – proved to be no problem at all. Shaw was right, after all, when he dismissed the received critical opinion of the time in one pungent sentence: 'A good realistic first act, like *Juno*, an incongruously phantasmic second act, trailing off into a vague and unreal sequel: could anything be wronger?'[3]

The RSC production brought out just what Shaw had noticed in the first act – a 'phantasmo-poetic' quality, a note of hysteria in the football celebrations that is good preparation for the nightmarish

[1] Sean O'Casey, *Rose and Crown*, 1952. In *Autobiographies*, vol 2, 1963, p 261.
[2] 8 Sept 1969.
[3] Letter to O'Casey, 19 June 1928, given in full by D. Krause in *A Self-Portrait of the Artist as a Man*, Dublin 1968, p 28.

9

breakdown effect in the war scene. Conversely, a note of realism was kept alive and warm in the austere Expressionist context of Act 2. Powerful sombre images and sounds dominated the scene: the ruined monastery: the lifesize broken crucifix pointing at the gunwheel where a soldier is 'crucified' for a petty misdemeanour; the rolling cadences of Ezekiel tonelessly chanted by a shell-shocked soldier: 'Son of man, can this exceeding great army become a valley of dry bones?' But poignancy came through the little unexpected outbreaks of natural life, like the game the tired soldiers start up when a football absurdly turns up as a gift in a parcel from home. In the grim setting, this moment of relaxed physical enjoyment came over as an immensely touching thing. When the Staff-Wallah came on, ludicrously strutting, to freeze them back to rigidity with his 'orders regarding gas-masks', it seemed entirely appropriate that he should be represented as a figure of farce – a not quite believable being in some monstrous charade.

In this use of sad farce to control painful material O'Casey struck out a line which was to become one of the main lines of modern drama. Perhaps the Great War could only be fully realized in this way, as a great grim joke, the kind of bad joke it is in the war songs, those haunting expressions of the ordinary soldier's stoicism and irony. The spirit of those songs is strong in the play: the dialogue seems to be always moving in a musical direction.

'Gawd, I'm sleepy', one of the soldiers says. 'Tir'd and lousey', 'Damp and shaking'; the others pick up from him. The sad dreamy note gets dreamier, a stronger musical beat sounds. 'Wen I thinks of 'ome, I thinks of a field of dysies', says one and the others repeat in a dazed, sleepy way, 'Wen 'e thinks of 'ome, 'e thinks of a field of dysies'. A question pushes in, gets more assertive – 'wy'r we 'ere, wy'r we 'ere – that's wot we wants to know?' The answer comes in song, one of those songs laden with associations, that have become part of a common language of feeling: 'We're here because we're here, because we're here, because we're here!' Ironically, it's sung to the tune of Auld Lang Syne.

The impact of these words sung to that tune in that grim setting is something that can't easily be appreciated except in a theatre. To criticize O'Casey's drama on its verbal content alone is to miss one of its most thrilling and poetic dimensions. Who after seeing the Aldwych production of *The Silver Tassie* could ever forget the magnificent close of Act 2? And yet how hard to imagine it fully from the text.

The bitter litany to the gun – 'I believe in God and I believe in thee' – which can seem on the page a rather dubious attempt at literary high-flying came over in the theatre as a deeply satisfying expression of the feeling that had been gathering throughout the scene, a moving prelude to the hellish pantomime that followed, when the gun took over the stage. Alarmingly, the great howitzer wheeled down to threaten the audience at close quarters (a directorial invention that O'Casey would surely have approved) and then into position for the loading and firing sequence, done as O'Casey instructed, in total silence. Flashes of light represented the firing, searchlight beams swept the sky, the men went through the deadly motions like puppets without voices. The Word had failed.

This was a moment of pure theatre that was also a moment of great drama. It made one realize how much O'Casey's poetry needs a stage to express it and raised hopes that the other late plays might at last be given a chance to release the strange poetry – made up of spectacle and music as well as words – that lies in them. The London theatre is catching up with the ideas that O'Casey and Auden and Isherwood and other pioneers were trying out from the twenties to the fifties. Brook's *Midsummer Night's Dream* with its fairies on circus stilts and trapezes might be taken as a symbol of the new openness, the interchange that is starting between the theatre of 'drama' and the theatre of dance and music, comic turns and circus. It is the right climate for the plays I have been speaking of. They helped to form it. Now perhaps they may have a chance to flourish in it.

1. *Texts*
   Auden, W. H.:
   Paid on Both Sides. In Poems, 1930
   The Dance of Death, 1933
   Auden, W. H. and Isherwood, C.:
   The Dog Beneath the Skin, 1935
   The Ascent of F6, 1936
   On the Frontier, 1938

   O'Casey, S.:
   Collected Plays, 1949–51, 4 vols
   The Bishop's Bonfire, 1955
   Five One Act Plays, 1958
   The Drums of Father Ned, 1960
   Behind the Green Curtains: three plays, 1961
   Shaw, G. B. *The Complete Plays*, 1965

2. *Critical Writings*

Ayling, R. (ed) *Sean O'Casey*, 1969. Modern Judgements series

Boughton, R. *A National Music-drama: The Glastonbury Festival.* Proc Musical Assoc 44, 1918

Fuller, J. *A Reader's Guide to W. H. Auden,* 1970

Gray, T. *Dance Drama,* 1926

Hurd, M. *The Glastonbury Festivals: 1914–26. Theatre Notebook* 17, 1963

Isaacs, J. *An Assessment of Twentieth Century Literature,* 1951

Symons, J. *The Thirties,* 1960

VIII

New Forms of Melodrama and Epic Theatre

John Arden, Theatre Workshop (Joan Littlewood), Alan Plater, Charles Wood

An event that must have helped to create a favourable climate for the Royal Shakespeare Company's production of *The Silver Tassie* in 1969 was Joan Littlewood's production in 1963[1] of *Oh What a Lovely War*,[2] with her company, Theatre Workshop. And *Oh What a Lovely War* in its turn derives from *The Silver Tassie*. Songs of the First World War are used for very similar effects of sad irony in this brilliant piece which presents the war as a pierrot show, a sequence of bitterly comic 'turns': – 'We've got songs for you, a few battles and some jokes. I've got the whip to crack in case you don't laugh.' The song Barney sings in *The Silver Tassie* is sung here by wounded soldiers at Waterloo waiting for the transport that hasn't been laid on for them; only the officers are provided for. The men react with humorous stoicism, making rough jokes, teasing the nurses who are fussing over the wounded officers: 'You're wasting your time with him, darling, it's in splints.' Their freedom from self-pity and anger raises pity and anger in us to a high pitch: it gets expression as in O'Casey's play, through a song: 'We're 'ere because we're 'ere, because we're 'ere ...', sung softly at first and then louder and louder till it powerfully releases at least some of the men's feeling – and ours.

Throughout the piece the songs express a sane, truly human reaction to the war; the men's sanity is set in a sharp, black and white contrast

---

[1] Theatre Royal, Stratford, E. 15, 19 March 1963.
[2] By Theatre Workshop, Charles Chilton and the members of the original cast.

119

with the mad abstractness of the generals' and politicians' minds, which is expressed as a form of farce. The abstract experience, one might say, is continually moving towards farce, the human experience towards song, exactly the movement of *The Silver Tassie*. In this scene from Act 2 for instance, on the night before another grim attack, the song the soldiers sing in their trenches records what truly matters – the human suffering and the marvellous spirit that knows and faces it all, and yet can still manage fellow feeling and a flick of bitter humour:

> If you want the old battalion, we know where they are,
> They're hanging on the old barbed wire,
> We've seen them, we've seen them,
> Hanging on the old barbed wire.

Musically, the melancholy, long-drawn-out strain of 'We've seen them' seems to bring the dead men before us as men; the savagely jocular 'Hanging on the old barbed wire' turns them into scarecrows, bits of litter, something non-human that can be joked about – has to be, if the living men are to go out in their turn to face the barbed wire.

Contrasted with this touching expression of sanity and the will to stay sane, is a scene showing Haig as a mad pedant, fussing ludicrously over the most tactful way of phrasing his report on a royal inspection during which the King's horse had a slight mishap: 'The King did clutch the reins too firmly . . . correction . . . the King did clutch the reins rather firmly.'

This bold caricaturist counterpointing is the staple method of the play. From time to time casualty figures and other contemporary evidence are flashed on the newspanel at the back of the stage, a disturbing reminder that the cold facts of the case support the caricature. It's only necessary to speed things up, make some sharp cuts and juxtapositions such as the pierrot convention encourages, for history to turn itself into caricature and reveal – so one feels – an essential truth about the war. We hear the general's voice droning insanely on – 'There must be no squeamishness over losses' – while the men sing their wry, sad songs and on the screen appear the figures 'Allied loss 180,000 men. . . . Gain nil.' As the dreadful evidence accumulates there is an immense, strange relief – as in *The Silver Tassie* – in having the Establishment represented as clowns, in seeing Haig brought on in a pierrot hat to conduct a nightmarish choir of soldiers in gas capes miming burial duties to the jolly sound of 'The bells of hell go ting-a-ling-a-ling, For you but not for me'. The scene places and condemns the whole ethos of the war in a single, grotesque but painfully convincing image.

The use of techniques from music hall and melodrama for handling daunting historical material has been one of the great triumphant discoveries of the postwar English theatre. A new line of freewheeling epic/documentary has been struck out, running from melodramas like *Serjeant Musgrave's Dance* to such recent plays as Charles Wood's '*H*'. The writers in this mode aim at the long perspective that becomes possible only when realism is abandoned and a 'superview' printed over the limited view open to characters struggling in the thick of the historical events. In the documentaries improvised by Peter Cheeseman and his company at Stoke-on-Trent this superview is got by mixing realistic elements, narration and musical commentary. The improvisation is both free and bound; free in the sense that many techniques are open to the actors; bound in the sense that they are confined by their subject matter, the facts of history; Peter Cheeseman's one unbreakable rule, we are told,[1] is that every scene must be based on primary source material; no record of an event, no scene. Authenticity, or 'veracity' (his word), is in a way as much the goal here as in the most painstaking piece of realism. The local subject matter – history of the North Staffordshire Railway in *The Knotty* (1966), federation of the six pottery towns in *Six to One* (1968) – invites 'verification' in realistic terms and the audience is encouraged to make that sort of response by being given so much factual information (spoken often in a dry tone by a commentator reading from documents). There are scenes too in 'true to life' style when these seem appropriate.

But the true to life simulations are liable to shade off at any moment into bold stylization; a Royalist officer shelters behind a tree obviously made out of an old chair leg, the Battle of Marston is represented by seven actors facing each other in a football line-up arrangement, miming encounters by crossing and dipping banners, while a recorded voice speaks an unemotional commentary over them.

And through it all runs music – like the dialogue, authentic, in the sense that genuine folk songs are used (new words if needed are set to the old tunes) – but also, inevitably, functioning as an anti-realistic device, breaking through time and place and changing the atmosphere in subtle ways that are hard to deduce from a text alone. As Peter

---

[1] See 'A Community Theatre-in-the-Round', *Theatre Quarterly* I, 1971.

Cheeseman says, certain scenes could scarcely be imagined at all if one hadn't heard the music. He cites the scene in *The Staffordshire Rebels* (1965) for instance, where what he calls 'walking' music and 'a kind of discursive dance music' were provided by the charming song, 'Till the King Enjoys his Own Again'.

It was only by using music, narration and other non-realistic elements in a highly stylized technique that the company felt able to tackle some of the events they were confronted with: the Battle of Marston, for instance, daunted by sheer size; the casualty figures were as appalling in their way as those for the First World War. The methods of total theatre were in this case a response to the horror of total war.

Our theatre today is bent on making this response. In play after play efforts are being made to treat vast subjects like the wars of 1914 and 1939 as 'whole' events and in the process technique has become extraordinarily free; recorded narration, film sequences, tableaux vivants, song and dance turns, all methods are open; a new concept of theatrical consistency is emerging.

There seems to be a deep need for this long theatrical perspective; it will impose itself at last even if for a time the more limited realistic view is found sufficiently satisfying.

Take, for instance, *Journey's End*, which was for years the play that expressed the First World War for many people. It's still easy to understand this. The horror of trench warfare comes through very strongly[1] in terms of its effect on nerves and personality. We are made to share in the almost unbearable strain the imaginative, highly strung Stanhope suffers, to feel his desolation as his company die around him, his angry pain at losing Osborne, his kindly middle aged mentor, and his rush of pity and feeling for Raleigh, dying at the end a heroic schoolboy's death – 'Could we have a light? It's – it's so frightfully dark and cold.' The idiom is dated but the situation keeps its power to move.

Still one's response nowadays is bound to be qualified. The play's limitations – and the limitations of realism as a method for handling such a subject – can't be shut out. If comparisons are made with *The Silver Tassie* (and it's rather hard not to make them between two

---

[1] As the recent London revival demonstrated. After its success at the Mermaid (18 May 1972) the play moved to the Cambridge Theatre 20 July 1972. A harrowing brutal effect was got through stereo sound; the audience were surrounded by gunfire rather as they were threatened with the howitzer in the 1969 production of *The Silver Tassie*.

plays so close in time,[1]) it is apparent that O'Casey gets an enormous extension of power and interest from his wider perspective.

It's true that to get this perspective he has to dehumanize his officer characters and cut them out from our sympathy. Sherriff's method has the virtue of allowing sympathy to both officers and men (though the men are very inadequately represented by a slightly comic servant). But O'Casey makes so clear what he is doing, establishes the farcical/satirical convention so firmly that we don't feel he is being unfair; the absurdly pompous, affected Establishment figures aren't ever in danger of being taken as full portraits of real men (the way we're tacitly invited to take Sherriff's Private Mason); we can see that they are standing in for the attitudes of mind which help to make wars. And the suffering of the real men who *are* in the play is so great that we have an overwhelming need to try and see outside the suffering, to place and judge it on their behalf, as well as feel it with them.

It's partly the lack of any opportunity to do this that makes *Journey's End* seem now so limited. Faintly a note of satire sounds, as in the scene when the Colonel congratulates Stanhope on the success of the latest raid (in which Osborne was killed) – 'I must go right away and phone the Brigadier. He'll be very pleased about it' – and Stanhope snaps back, 'How awfully nice – if the Brigadier's pleased.' But that's about as far as satire and judgement go. We are confined with the characters in the limits of their pathetically narrow view.

What O'Casey's technique offered was a way of extending the view, making it panoramic, comprehensive (or more nearly so) without sacrificing human interest and feeling. 'Human figures against a world on wallpaper', to use the phrase he picked up from Yeats' hostile criticism of *The Silver Tassie* and applied with pride to the later plays he wrote in similar style.

'A world on wallpaper' might be the motto of the new epic theatre in which some of the most interesting work of the last ten years or so has been done. It is a drama very conscious of its Englishness. Continental influences, Brecht's for instance, tend to be played down by writers in the mode: they prefer to see themselves growing out of the popular English tradition, the old drama of the streets and the halls; they look back to Victorian music hall, melodrama and pantomime and sometimes beyond that again to the conventions of the medieval

---

[1] Both opened at the Apollo Theatre, *Journey's End* 9 Dec 1928 (for one night); *The Silver Tassie* 11 Oct 1929. *Journey's End* opened at the Savoy 21 Jan 1929.

theatre and older forms still, such as the English Mummers' Play. It seems highly characteristic that Alan Plater should record his pleasure, on being asked whether Brecht had influenced his style, at being able to reply 'not so much Brecht as Jimmy James, Norman Evans, Dave Morris and Harry Mooney'.[1] These were performers in the old rumbustious style of English music hall who were still to be seen in Plater's early youth, although that was, as he says, the 'fag end period' of the halls.[2] And it's something of their spirit as well as their technique that he gets into his best known play, written in collaboration with Sid Chaplin and Alex Glasgow, *Close the Coalhouse Door* (1969).

This 'free-wheeling musical based on community experience', to use his own description (which he prefers to 'documentary drama') illustrates well, I think, the value of music hall techniques both for spanning a huge subject and for controlling the writers' passionate feeling about it.

The play is an act of homage to the mining community: the whole heroic and savage history of coal mining is encapsulated in a sequence of party turns at the golden wedding of an old miner. Some of the material is so horrific – eighteen-hour days for six-year-old children, evictions of women and babies from the homes of striking miners – and the local authors' feelings about these things understandably so strong – that the play could easily turn shrill and sentimental. But it's saved from that on the whole by the gay flexibility of its style and the ingenious idea of having everything acted out by this group of tough, jokey Northerners who are always ready to come out with a dour quip against themselves as well as against the coal owners and the experts, the fluctuating 'Them' whom they mimic sardonically in their turns. The quick changes of style keep it taut. One moment we're involved in the present-day scene, following the 'sibling jealousy' between the son who has left the mines for the University and the one who has stayed down the pit, the next we're in the middle of a nineteenth century eviction scene or listening to a string of Prime Ministers making promises and setting up Royal Commissions, all in a broad Tyneside accent:

> THOMAS: ... and come the end of the war and the coal owners come to Lloyd George and they say ...
> GEORDIE: Please can we hev wor coal mines back, please?

---

[1] Alan Plater, Introduction to *Close the Coalhouse Door*, 1969.
[2] A. Plater, 'The Playwright and his People', *Theatre Quarterly* 1, 1971.

THOMAS: And Lloyd George says . . . can ye, hell . . . and then the coal owners say . . .

GEORDIE: What about wor poor bairns running barefoot in South Kensington?

THOMAS: And Lloyd George says, we'll have a Royal Commission . . .

JACKIE (leading Commission): What is it, David lad?

THOMAS: I'd like yes to hev a Royal Commission.

JACKIE: Righto.

(to the audience): So me and twelve other wise men gans down the pub and we talk it over and then we decided. . . .

(to Lloyd George): We think you ought to nationalize the coal mines.

THOMAS: Now hang on a bit, lad. . . . I'm not sure that's what we wanted you to think . . . who've you got on your team?

These scenes contrive to be pleasantly relaxed and funny and uncomfortably near the bone too. *Plus ça change* is the theme running through and binding them together. The Lloyd George turn, the Neville Chamberlain turn (followed by an intermission 'during which we will fight the Second World War') give way to the Whitehall Expert's turn, speciality – finding synonyms (rationalization, diversification, regionalization) for 'closing the pits' and taking the miners back to square one. 'Hadaway to hell', says the old miner. It seems the only reaction, that or a burst of the irreverent song and dance which is a great feature of the play. The songs gather together and release the different feelings raised by the action: militancy in the Union song (coming after the scene celebrating the 1872 Coal Mines Regulations Bill and before the moving sequence called 'The Thin Seam'); derision in the anti-establishment song,

> But there's one thing makes the locals really fall into your lap / Get your picture in the papers with a little cloth cap, / A little cloth cap, a little cloth cap, You'll make a big impression with a little cloth cap.

And in the end the sharp ironic note of the revolution song –

> It couldn't happen here, no, it couldn't happen here.
> We've made a little Eden so it couldn't happen here.

– leading into the melancholy and haunting refrain that opened the play and gave it its name:

> Close the coalhouse door, lad,
> There's blood inside,
> There's bones inside,
> There's bairns inside,
> So stay outside.

Alan Plater attributed the relative failure of this rumbustious piece in London (it had a runaway success in the North) to its being so far from the English theatrical norm. One might wonder whether the difficulty of following the Tyneside accent and local allusions might not have had more to do with it. The theatrical norm is getting closer to his style all the time, and has been, really, ever since the years just after the war when some musical notes were struck in Martin Browne's poets' seasons at the Mercury Theatre by Ronald Duncan and others.

A thoroughgoing musical style didn't really emerge in the postwar theatre, however, until writers like Arden appeared on the scene. So far as form is concerned, he was the great revolutionary among the playwrights of the 1956 burst, the one who made the most sustained and radical break with realism. For him it was a totally outworn convention: 'I think the Ibsen school of playwriting was necessary and valuable in its time, but we need to develop further from it now.'[1] 'Development' meant going back, back beyond Ibsen to nineteenth-century melodrama and earlier popular forms, the 'conventionalized plays of the European Middle Ages', the ritual of the English Mummers' Play. Brecht was in the background too, but not as a model, rather as an encouraging influence, someone who had looked in similar directions from a German point of view.

Like Alan Plater, Arden implies that he didn't need to look outside his English heritage[2] for fertilizing influences. He has a passionate devotion to the English popular tradition, aiming, as a playwright, so he says, to set the life of today 'within the historical and legendary tradition of our culture'.[3] Hardy is among the writers he names as predecessors in that tradition, and this is certainly a name that comes spontaneously to mind when one contemplates plays like *Serjeant Musgrave's Dance* (as well as plays by other writers in the new epic mode such as Charles Wood's '*H*'). Hardy of the ballads and melodramas, Hardy of *The Dynasts* is the spirit brooding over much of this drama, with its grotesquerie, its pathos, its deep feeling for the life of the common people. Arden is close to O'Casey too in his special sympathy with nineteenth-century theatre, especially the melodrama, not so much the melodrama of Boucicault (O'Casey's

---

[1] Interview in *Tulane Drama Review* 11, 1966; rptd in Wager, 1969, p 206.

[2] It is very appropriate that his latest play, *The Island of the Mighty*, written with Margaretta D'Arcy (Aldwych, December 1972), should be described as 'a new treatment of the Arthurian legend as our national myth'.

[3] John Arden, 'Telling a True Tale', in *The Encore Reader*, ed C. Marowitz et al, 1965, p 125.

model) as more primitive, anonymous kinds like the archetypal *Maria Marten and the Red Barn.*

Appropriately, his first play to achieve celebrity, *Serjeant Musgrave's Dance,* had a Victorian setting and a set of characters – redcoats, coal miners, Mayor, Constable and Parson – who could have fitted into the cast lists of a dozen melodramas. He has said himself that he is pleased to think he captured in this play 'a sort of ambiance of English lower-class life in the Victorian period.'[1] The terrible central tableau, – a demented soldier dancing round the gallows where the skeleton of his dead comrade hangs – casts a shadow forward to the grim war tableaux of Charles Wood and backward to those murder and execution scenes that were at the heart of Victorian melodrama. It was from the annals of crime as they were recorded in such places as the 'sensation' ballads that the characteristic plots of these melodramas were drawn. And it was toward a grim final scene of social vengeance that the action often flowed. *Maria Marten and the Red Barn* ends with a gallows scene, the rope round the seducer's neck; in *The Bells* a different sort of villain dies in a nightmare, choking from an imagined rope. Rough justice is done there, but in some plays the gallows threatens the innocent too and is one of the many traps spread for the poor and underprivileged classes; in Douglas Jerrold's *Black Eyed Susan,* for instance, where the sailor hero escapes by a hair's breadth the barbarous rope that dangles at the yard arm for him.

Arden's preoccupation with the gallows as symbol of a rough and doubtful justice relates him to the popular English tradition at a deep level of feeling. He sometimes manages as well to strike something like the note of primitive spontaneity that characterized the old melodrama. Peter Brook indeed singles out the gallows scene in *Serjeant Musgrave's Dance* as an embodiment of the typical process by which 'rough' theatre comes into being: 'Musgrave faces a crowd in a market place on an improvised stage and he attempts to communicate as forcibly as possible his sense of the horror and futility of war. The demonstration that he improvises is like a genuine piece of popular theatre, his props are machine-guns, flags, and a uniformed skeleton that he hauls aloft.'[2]

Arden is responsive as the writers of Victorian melodrama were to strong situations, strong colours, a strong beat. *Serjeant Musgrave's Dance* came to him as a flash of brilliant colour – 'I visualized the stage

---

[1] Interview in Wager, p 198.   [2] P. Brook, *The Empty Space,* pp 70–71.

full of scarlet uniforms and began to get interested from there.'[1]
Ballad colours, ballad rhythms too: his plays often have the look of
ballads expanded to epic size (it is no surprise to learn that he once
hankered after doing an epic film based on Northern ballads and set
on the Northumbrian moors). This strong, highly coloured simplicity
may sometimes be in a rather confused relation with the tortuous,
argumentative vein in his drama, but given that difficulty, it's remarkable how much genuine ballad feeling he does manage to get in. He
uses ballads, sung and spoken, for a variety of effects, often for sardonic,
deflating purposes, as when that awkward character, the Bargee, picks
up Musgrave's obsessive 'We have our duty. A soldier's life is a
soldier's duty' and puts it into more homely perspective:

> The Empire wars are far away
> For duty's sake we sail away
> Me arms and legs is shot away
> And all for the sake of a shilling and a drink.

Or when Mrs Hitchcock, the landlady, menaced by the Parson with
the closure of public houses during the colliers' strike, agrees satirically
that the strike is a bad thing, especially for the coal owning Mayor,
and then breaks out into verse:

> I am a proud coal owner
> And in scarlet here I stand.
> Who shall come or who shall go
> Through all my coal-black land?

Much is implied in the small space of these jingling lines; the Mayor
is reduced to an absurdly pompous, nursery rhyme figure, and yet a
sinister link is made between him and the soldiers (and the blood
that is to be spilt) by that word 'scarlet'. Similarly, a great measure
of the play's essential feeling is concentrated in the ballad Annie comes
out with when she is jokingly asked for her opinion on what soldiers
are good for. 'I'll tell you for what a soldier's good,' she says:

> To march behind his roaring drum,
> Shout to us all: 'Here I come'
> I've killed as many as I could –
> I'm stamping into your fat town
> From the war and to the war
> And every girl can be my whore . . . .

---

[1] John Arden, 'Building the Play' (an interview), *Encore* 32, 1961.

Because we know he'll soon be dead
We strap our arms round the scarlet red
Then send him weeping over the sea

In *Armstrong's Last Goodnight*, Arden comes nearer still to the strange world of Victorian melodrama, where we hardly know (as in *Black Eyed Susan*, for instance) which came first, the ballad or the story it is set in. Echoes of Border ballads drift into the action – *To the hunten ho, cried Johnny Armstrong. And to the hunten he has gaen* – bringing in a note of fatalism, reminding us that the tragic story was settled long ago. And yet it is still being written; the play is really a ballad-making process. Johnny Armstrong's people see him in the same way that he sees himself, as a ballad hero; they stand by ready to turn the events of his life (including some very unsavoury ones like the murder of Johnstone) into heroic song. On an ordinary realistic level of meeting people (Lindsay, for instance) and holding conversations, his congenital speech defect makes him hopelessly incoherent. But like subnormal Annie and the illiterate Bargee in *Serjeant Musgrave's Dance* he gets a great extension of personality and expressive power through the blood-red simplicities of ballad:

> I slew the King's Lieutenant
> And garr'd his troopers flee
> My name is Johnny the Armstrang
> And wha daur meddle wi' me?

Lindsay refuses to meet him on this level. He tries to force him into the world of prose, with its complications and rational perspective:

LINDSAY: Wha daur? David Lindsay daur. King Johnny of Eskdale indeed! King Curlew of the barren fell. . . . Ye are ane inconvenience, I will grant ye. Ye are ane tedious nuisance to the realm. Ye are indeed cause for ane itchy paragraph or twae in some paper of state. But were ye the great man of danger and subversion that ye fain, sir, wad think yourself, can ye credit then the King's Herald wad hae come to your house wi' nae footmen nor horse, nae pikemen nor archers, nae bombardiers nor pioneers – wi' nocht in God's Name but ane demi-priestling writer and sax inches of bent brass bugle! I crave your pardon, Sandy, I had nae intent to disparage ye, but the noise that ye mak on your instrument can scarcely be callit the clangour of warfare.

GILNOCKIE: Armstrang. Mr Armstrang. *Mister* ——

FIRST ARMSTRONG: The Laird has his proper entitlement of style. He's no ashamit to use it, nor yet to hear it usit.

Gilnockie, gif ye please, when ye open your mou to the Laird!
LINDSAY: Gilnockie, gif ye will. He draws his rent frae the local middens,
by all means let us concede him the flattery of their name.

The insult draws Armstrong's men to their feet offering to cut
Lindsay's head off. But the prose view wins. The wild amorous ballad
hero, the heraldic figure, 'emblazonit braid in flesh and blood', in
the Lady's phrase, is trapped and hung up on a gallows, the King's
soldiers tear the clothes off his back and string him up on a tree before
he can finish his song:

> But had I wist ere I cam frae hame
> How thou unkind wadst be to me
> I wad hae keepit the border side
> In spite of all thy men and thee.

Serjeant Musgrave's Dance too, ends on a song with Attercliffe triumphantly declaring that Sparky wasn't the only singer in the barracks
and calling to Musgrave and the rest to listen to his ballad of the blood-
red rose:

> I plucked a blood-red rose-flower down
> And gave it to my dear.
> I set my foot out across the sea
> And she never wept a tear.

This ballad of Attercliffe's moves to a happy ending,

> For the apple holds a seed will grow
> In live and lengthy joy
> To raise a flourishing tree of fruit
> For ever and a day.

It enables him to end on a grim joke: 'They're going to hang us up
a length higher nor most apple trees grow, Serjeant. D'you reckon
we can start an orchard?'

The jokes, the songs, draw the sympathy strongly to the freebooting,
fanatical characters; we probably stop judging the morality of their
actions (the twisted morality of Musgrave preaching pacifism through
the barrel of a gun, Armstrong killing treacherously in the name of
honour) and respond instead to the strange, wild music of their
personalities. This is in the tragic plays. In those weighted rather more
towards comedy sympathy flows in Brechtian fashion, away from the
fanatics to the tricky opportunists, characters like Krank and Butter-
field in *The Waters of Babylon*, who aim to keep alive and comfortable

at any cost: ideas of honour and duty cut no ice with them, and probably not with us either when they're represented as they are in this play by such absurd and deadly beings as the IRA man, Cassidy, and the Polish revolutionary who ends up by killing harmless Krank instead of the Russian VIPs he is supposed to be gunning for.

Butterthwaite and Armstrong in a way represent two opposite poles of temperament. But they can also be seen as facets or moods of the same one – a ballad-making temperament, expansive, impulsive and musical. Armstrong's world is shaped to the form of a Border ballad and *The Workhouse Donkey* is dominated by the grotesque ballad of the outsize, outcast donkey:

> I thanked my benefactors thus
> He-haw he-haw *hee*!

The lines are chanted while Butterthwaite is robbing the Town Hall, flinging pound notes all over the stage in what he intends as a Machiavellian device to divert suspicion but that comes over primarily as a fine burst of Dionysiac ebullience. Their vulgarity and ebullience doesn't protect these characters, though. A melancholy doom hangs about Butterthwaite. The donkey has to go out eventually into the rain and snow. Indeed, when this character first turns up on Arden's stage in *The Waters of Babylon* he brings an aura of failure from the not-yet-written play with him, coming on as a 'miserable, elderly man of shabby genteel appearance', the 'Napoleon of Local Government' in his post-Elba phase ('Your Hundred Days were short, I fear', Krank says to him at the end). His ludicrously ingenious scheme for stealing from the Local Authority by a rigged lottery ends as we can see from the start it must, in comic disaster and triumph for the Policeman, and the scene closes with a ballad of dour survival:

> We're all down in t'cellar – hoyle
> Wi't'muck-slaghts on t'windows.
> We've used all us coyle up
> And we've nowt left but cinders.

Butterthwaite, Krank and their like finally make almost as melancholy an impression as Armstrong and Musgrave, in spite of the different opportunities they're given by the comic mode they partly function in. 'Partly' the crucial word, is crucial in a more general way in discussion of Arden's drama. Part of him seems always to want to give his characters their head, let them loose to function in bold,

simple terms. The other part isn't committed to the single-minded
selectiveness that creates the strong situations of melodrama; situations
such as in the nineteenth century acted magnetically on the literature
of the age, so that not just the drama but more refined and complex
forms like the novel were irresistibly drawn to that humble and
powerful event at the centre of the archetypal melodrama, *Maria
Marten and the Red Barn* – the seduction and murder of the working
class girl by the upper class villain and the terrible movement to
retribution on a public scaffold.

Perhaps no modern playwright could be expected to recreate for
us that deep, primitive simplicity, Arden (ironically, since he loves it
so much) least of all. He wants too much to fill in the detail of his
fables, take us into the complications and the intricate shifts of
sympathy that real life dealings with characters like Butterthwaite and
Musgrave would involve us in. The complications sometimes become
all-engrossing to him if not to us. It's a tendency Arden recognizes as
damaging. 'My principal fault as a writer', he says, 'is to get so
interested in bright ideas that occur to me while I am working on a
play that I forget what the play is supposed to be about. I am always
doing this.'[1] A rather painfully revealing remark, it seems.

He is a little divided, too, in his ideas of how his plays should be
staged. He has expressed his dislike of the proscenium stage: *The
Happy Haven*, he thought, failed when it moved to London from
Bristol because of the changeover to a proscenium setting.[2] But he has
also said that he dislikes theatre in the round: 'I hate looking past the
actors and seeing the audience'. He prefers the audience to have an
'architectural' point of reference, the actors to be slightly set apart,
framed at least to the extent of being on a stage 'with corners'.

Essentially, though, it is closeness (however modified) that he aims
at, a sense of actors and audience all being in the same room, with no
rigid frame between them, a physical relationship reflecting the
emotional one he tries for in many different ways. The use of local
subject matter and settings is one. In *The Workhouse Donkey* all the
material came from local newspapers and Arden's own knowledge
of politics in the Barnsley area: in *Serjeant Musgrave's Dance* and
Armstrong's Last Goodnight the events that inspired the plays (atrocities
in Cyprus and Katanga) were so fully naturalized in North Country

---

[1] Interview in Wager, p 198.
[2] He thought it had a freezing effect: 'The parts of the play that were meant to come
out at the audience completely failed to do so'. Interview in *Encore* 8, 1961.

terms that it would be hard to deduce their place of origin without Arden's comments. In this way he allies himself again with the nineteenth-century melodrama which drew so heavily on local events, especially police court cases. His ideal audience must in a way always be a provincial one, with roots deep in the neighbourhood surrounding the theatre; it's with audiences of that kind that he has had most steady success.[1] One can see too how it would be helpful to him to write as he occasionally does for audiences of children. In his introduction to one of these plays, *The Royal Pardon* (written in collaboration with his wife, Margaretta d'Arcy) he dwells lovingly on the children's freedom from conventional expectations and their capacity to accept the stylization and mixed conventions of this modern Mummers' play.

Just such a simple flexibility and spontaneity is what he is trying to stimulate, it seems, in his adult audiences: if in one way they're to feel at home, in another they're to be jolted into unaccustomed responses, made to stop worrying overmuch about theatrical consistency, learn to take episodes and characters as they come and adapt to the different styles they come in. The means he takes are often the means of the old melodrama. He mixes speech styles much as the Victorians did, moving from prose to verse to song, from racy colloquialisms to stilted rhetoric, from ballads to blank verse jingles. He goes for strong colour and flavour rather than idiomatic persuasiveness, inventing strange phrases and syntax to express the feel of a place or period as he imagines it; 'Babylonish dialect', his phrase for the language in *Armstrong's Last Goodnight* exactly catches his distinctive amalgam of homely, exotic and uncouth elements.

Characters break consistency too by coming out of the action and addressing the audience directly; the Doctor in *The Happy Haven*, for instance, confiding his nasty intentions to the audience – 'Ladies and gentlemen. Twenty-four hours and now I'm going to see if it works' – or Blomax in *The Workhouse Donkey* introducing Wellesley – 'Here I am confronted by the fruits of my loose studenthood. This poor girl without a mother is my own daughter.' Despite his preference for an open stage, he often seems to have a frame of some kind in mind for these effects; in *The Waters of Babylon* it's early Victorian, he says, with sliding flats and drop curtain, the kind that was still in use in provincial pantomime at the time the play was written.

---

[1] In well-established theatres like the Glasgow Citizens' Theatre and in village halls.

Costumes and décor too are usually in the tuppence coloured tradition, often with a slant towards the style of children's book illustrations. The stage of *Armstrong's Last Goodnight* is adorned with toy-like 'mansions', a Castle, a Palace, a Forest; Mr and Miss Balfour in *Friday's Hiding* are described as 'rosy-cheeked, bright-eyed, toytown figures out of a child's picture book of the countryside' (not such a simple effect as it looks, being a device to avoid a cliché treatment of the characters' miserliness); in the so-called autobiographical play, *Squire Jonathan*, costumes and décor are in 'Grimm fairy-tale Gothic' to match the child-like element in the erotic fantasy that is acted out between Jonathan and the Blonde Woman: it involves his stripping her down to her chastity belt and decorating her with jewels.

The companion play to *Squire Jonathan*, *The Bagman* (a radio piece) contains a curious and characteristic image of the playwright's art as Arden sees it. The narrator-hero is sold a bag for ten shillings by a 'dirty old woman, not quite in her right mind' on the strength of her seductive account of the beautiful young woman who might be inside it. What he does find when he finally manages to open it, is something much less immediately attractive, something apparently undreamt of and unlooked for. He can only get at the contents by cutting his way into the bag with a knife, under pressure from the authoritarian rulers of the harsh dream country he wanders into after his encounter with the old woman. When the bag is shaken, out pours a collection of little characters – 'a Soldier in a red coat, and a Policeman, and a Doctor with great spectacles, and a pretty little blonde Popsy . . .' all the characters of the popular, improvising theatre, in fact. The Narrator seems to have no more control over what his characters do than he had over their creation. They simply act for him whenever he opens the bag in front of an audience:

> My little people in a row
> Sit on the stage and watch the show.
> The show they watch is rows and rows
> Of people watching them. Who knows
> Which is more alive than which?

Their life depends entirely on the audience's willing these instantaneous reflections of themselves. When the will is lacking, as it is in the band of armed revolutionaries the Narrator finally comes among, the Narrator and characters are impotent:

Men of war do not require
To see themselves in a truthful mirror
They will snap our wooden joints
And pull out our cotton hair.

To judge from this image, and he rather invites us to by calling
the play autobiographical, Arden sees himself as a writer deep in the
unselfconscious tradition of the street theatres and improvising companies. The plays themselves, I've been suggesting, don't quite give
this impression. One is, rather, conscious of the strong will at work
trying to write itself into that spontaneity, often with a resulting
sense of strain in long soliloquies like Squire Jonathan's, for instance,
or of over-relaxation, as in the almost defiantly uncoordinated scenes
of *The Workhouse Donkey*. The free hand with language can work
against spontaneity; some of his odd lingos fail to persuade on any
level, Colonel Feng's weirdly stilted proposal of marriage to Wellesley
for instance, which as Ronald Hayman says, it's hard to imagine any
actor being able to bring alive.[1]

But if, unsurprisingly, the attempt at the full freedom of unsophistica-
ted modes sometimes leads into difficulties, it leads to great things too.
Such are the moments when, in Arden's words, the poetic issue
crystallizes, the language becomes formal and 'the visual pattern
coalesces into a vital image that is one of the nerve-centres of the
play.'[2] Then we get scenes like Musgrave's dance or the hanging of
Armstrong in the middle of his song; vital images, certainly, and the
kind that stay in the mind in very much the way that the high points
of the best Victorian melodramas do.

Arden's line has proved to be one of the main lines of the new
English drama. Among the writers who have followed him in the
epic mode, one of the most interesting, Charles Wood, has the same
sort of feeling for the nineteenth-century theatre. He too revives the
techniques of melodrama and invents 'Babylonish' dialects: the
Indian dialect in '*H*' goes beyond any of Arden's in weirdness of
syntax and vocabulary. The loose, episodic structure of '*H*' and his
other war epic, *Dingo*, is on a similar line too, but with a crucial
difference. Wood never gives the impression of being unsure where
he is going. He tells us at the start of '*H*' exactly what the direction is:
the play is 'about a march', and we are on the long road leading to

[1] R. Hayman, *John Arden*, 1968, p 48.
[2] John Arden, 'Telling a True Tale', *The Encore Reader*, p 127.

Lucknow. Whatever diversions or distractions are introduced, it is this road we follow to its end, which is also the end of the Indian Mutiny and of General Havelock or '*H*'.

These are Wood's most ambitious plays, though whether they will come to be considered his most characteristic one can't at the moment guess. He is a versatile writer, who also works in a close, microscopic style, as in his claustrophobic play about actors acting off-stage, *Fill the Stage with Happy Hours*, or his current play, *Veterans*, with the Pirandellian recessions of illusion suggested by the sight of John Gielgud playing himself preparing to play a part in a film he had actually played in. War is often – even obsessively – his theme, but his techniques for dealing with it have varied widely from the more or less realistic in *Escort* to the epic style which is what I want to look at now.

It seems clear from his stage directions that he often has the methods of Victorian melodrama in mind, though his interest is not musical so much as visual. What he takes over is that filmic convention (melodrama often seems to have been written for a cinema that didn't exist) which allowed spectacle a crucial role in the play's language. Wood's dynamic treatment of this convention obviously owes a great deal to his experience as a scenic designer and writer for films. '*H*', after all, came out of his research for the film, *The Charge of the Light Brigade*; he was fascinated by the idea of soldiers from the Crimea going on to India to take part in fresh scenes of horror and heroism. One war rolling inexorably into the next, with last year's enemies becoming this year's allies – that dark concept lies behind much of his drama.

The method of '*H*' is indicated in the subtitle, *Monologues at Front of Burning Cities*. Armies of characters are deployed in front of backcloths carrying great crowded pictures of India, one spectacular scene replacing another on a stage which has to be, as he points out, a proscenium, preferably the genuine article rather than a compromise such as the toy theatre used in the production of the play at the National Theatre. The play can't do without its frame or its elaborate *trompe l'oeil* front cloth, made, as he says, of old or soft canvas so that it will hang from a batten with the billowing curve of a sail.

What are the functions of the frame, the front cloth and the other elaborate cloths used throughout the action? 'Paying people have a right to feel safe from bayonets and involvement', Wood says ironically, and then goes on to describe ways of using the front cloth so as to disturb that security – by having bayonets tear through it, men skid from underneath it. The frame finally offers no protection, at least for the front rows, the 'expensive seats and faces' who are most in danger from the bayonets and other kinds of attack, the bombardment with red rose petals, for instance, which represents the broken body of the Jemadar blown from the muzzle of a field gun, one of the savage reprisals taken at the end of the mutiny.

The cloths also serve the traditional nineteenth-century function of providing panoramic views, extending the scene beyond what individual characters might see. British India in 1857 is laid out for us pictorially, partly in 'stills' as classic arrangements of elephants, horses, parasols, the Red Fort, the Grand Trunk Road – and partly in *tableaux vivants* showing key events such as the battle for Cawnpore. The rapid movement of events is demonstrated arrestingly through these cloths. As one episode succeeds another, a litter of old banners accumulates on the stage floor and the *tableau vivant* of Havelock's triumph takes shape out of this 'scenic debris', as Wood calls it: the once splendid display of cloth and silk lies tumbled among the paraphernalia of war (meticulously catalogued as guns, ironhoop gabions, common brushwood gabions and so on). Stage directions which might have come straight out of *The Dynasts* call for a great panorama to be disclosed, with soldiers swarming everywhere, exposed 'as on the palm of a gigantic theatrical hand for inspection as the Triumph of Havelock'.

We go into the delirium of the dying Havelock, an extraordinary sequence where characters relive old front cloth scenes, acting them out as though they were just happening against a pictorial background which places them firmly in history. In a style more familiar to Victorian audiences than ours, the actors pose in the attitudes of well-known pictures. A sentry 'in the portion of the debris called Lucknow' leans on his rifle in classic pose; a vast cloth painted with the scene of the evacuation of Lucknow is pulled over the soldiers and they seek out the historical positions assigned to them, Outram putting out his hand to be shaken in the painted attitude, soldiers crawling into their humble places.

A sense of unstoppable, malign destiny comes through these strange scenes; past and present run together in a bleak epic 'now' in which tenses can no longer be distinguished:

> Was you at The Stand in Dhooly Square?
> What is the position we did / find ourselves in sir?
> Glorious!

Was our position, is, and burned / is the wounded souls in the dhooly /
column desert by the native bearers, / we stand alone against an entire /
army. . . .
Was it not a desperate situation?
It is indeed. . . .
(Act 3 Scene 4 within Scene 1)

This is in a peculiarly literal way a world on wallpaper. And at
many points Wood's technique recalls O'Casey's. The battle of
Cawnpore, for instance, is represented as a totally silent sequence –
men crumpling noiselessly to the ground, silent puffs of flame and
smoke – before the tableau collapses and there is an outbreak of
fearful noises. The generals get some music hall treatment; Havelock
harmonizes with the army, nigger minstrel style, in a rendering of
'Gentle Jesus keep me white'; the sadistic Neill presents himself to
the audience – 'Neill was a very remarkable man' – in a ludicrous
monologue.

These vast, violent and satirical tableaux are interspersed with
smaller, quiet scenes such as the sad one towards the end when Ensign
Mullet and the Havildar meet for the first time since the fatal episode
of the greased cartridges which sparked off the Mutiny:

HAVILDAR: The bugle blown for parley sahib, we wish to carry our dead
and wounded / from the field.
ENSIGN MULLET: You may do that. How is your health Havildar?
HAVILDAR: Well sahib, and the health of you our father?
ENSIGN MULLET: Well.
HAVILDAR: And of the Colonel our father?
ENSIGN MULLET: The Colonel is dead.
HAVILDAR: I am sorry.
You should not have stopped speaking / to us sahib.
ENSIGN MULLET: I never knew what to say.

It's with a similar shift of key that the play ends. The heroic world
dissolves into the personal in a thoroughgoing Victorian scene change.
The Elephant which has loomed up at times of crisis in the pageant
steps forward, stamps on the grave marked 'H', and 'cloths, wood
wings and set pieces slide into position to give us a transformation
scene': the battlefields of the Road are replaced by a quiet park, 'a
beautiful tranquil setting for the epilogue'.

In the gentle scene, a gentle family tableau: Captain Jones Parry
and his wife, with a brown-skinned child, Ayah and Servants. 'It is
the most sacred of places', Captain Jones Parry is saying, 'it is / because

of men like Havelock, bless / the old Governor, that India is the / fine place it is today.' Then the mother speaks to the child:

Timothy, here is where your father
Was shot and died in agony.

This is a remarkably effective change of perspective. Some horrific and comic/horrific scenes are recalled; the rape of Mrs Jones Parry by the Bombardier ('As if in a Dreadful Dream, / I shall never recall anything of this incident'); his wretched death at the hands of an incompetent firing squad. But now we don't see them as elements in epic but from a nearer, homely viewpoint which involves us with the whole action in a new way. Life continues, we see, and something has been salvaged from the heart of the horror: a child for a childless couple, a kind family feeling that has been able to cut across the cruel barriers of race and religion. Paradoxically, the epic gains in stature from the presence in it of these small moments. Wood's earlier epic, *Dingo*, lacks these brighter notes. The style is extremely flexible but the tone is less variable, more consistently dark and grim. Again the scope is vast. The action, Wood says, is set in 'the whole of the Western Desert during the Second World War against the Germans. All of it from a small bit of it.' The compression is got partly in Theatre Workshop style, by reducing the war to a sequence of turns, a 'Tails up and Lick 'em show', conducted from his mobile theatre by a Comic with many faces (from a well-known General's to Churchill's). His jokes are savage:

Brought the house down I did with my 'Man does not live by Bread alone' gag. You like that one . . . it's a lovely story. Always goes down well before a killing match.

And the turns are ghoulish, the ventriloquist's act, for instance, with the doll's voice coming out of the charred corpse of Chalky whom we heard at the beginning of the play screaming as he burns to death in a tank. In the second part, the prison camp scenes are played out in a boxing ring: always the visual imagery presses forward the idea of the war as a brutal game organized for profit and somebody's pleasure. Cross cuttings and aggressive anachronisms force us, as in 'H', into the epic 'now'. Escapers in the prison camp talk with knowledge from the future – 'He's not well for escaping – and I get terrible claustro-phobia in tunnels and wooden horses.' The wailing heard at the end as the soldiers queue to see Belsen and Buchenwald turns into the crying of Dingo's wife:

she won't stop crying and she will go out of her mind and be put in a
hospital forever,
which she did,
which is where she is today in 1967 . . . .

and that merges with the piping cry of Tanky coming out of the
darkness – 'He killed me.'

The play builds up to a dizzying impression of all wars rolling into
one war. Wood seems to be creating a new convention of visual
fluidity to get this and the similar effects in '*H*' – perhaps working
rather far ahead of his audience if we're to judge from the box office
failure of '*H*' at the National Theatre.[1]

Whether he will succeed in familiarizing his convention is still
very much a question. He is certainly, like all the playwrights I've
been discussing in this chapter, very conscious of his audience and
aims at a dynamic relationship with them, though perhaps a rather
hostile one (such as the stage directions in '*H*' suggest).

The wish to involve the audience in very direct, even physical
ways, is an outstanding feature of the new epic/documentary drama.
Along with it goes the idea of the play as a malleable, fluid thing,
changing shape under pressures from the audience. Some playwrights
working in the mode take a special delight in this concept of adapta-
bility. Alan Plater says in his introduction to *Close the Coalhouse Door*
(1969) that there can be no such thing as a definitive text; the play
changed and should change from one production to another.

Peter Brook deplores the 'fixing' that nightly repetition imposed
on *US*, the Royal Shakespeare Company's group-happening-
collaborative spectacle on the Vietnam war: ideally, he says,[2] it should
have played for one performance only. The improvised, rough
theatre craves freer acting conditions, a more casual 'lunchtime' type
of relationship with its audience. The idea of the medieval street
theatre seems always there in the background. Joan Littlewood, presiding genius of this scene, works for 'fun palace' environments where
drama can grow naturally as the collaborative activity she so passion-
ately thinks it should be. Arden imagines a play running on for anything from six to thirteen hours, with the audience free to drop in for
any item that takes their fancy. Companies have been formed to take
drama into the streets, the Guerilla Theatre at Keele University, for

---

[1] For Kenneth Tynan's comments on this, see the interview with him in *Theatre
Quarterly* 1, 1971.   [2] P. Brook, *The Empty Space*, p 23.

instance, who aim to 'bring something to the people where they are' and find themselves most at home when they are performing 'as part of a continuous show with morris dancers and a pop group'.[1] The concept of drama as a continuous show is taken still further by the company called Cosmic Circus. They have a vision of a travelling, environmental theatre that will absorb its material and its pattern of meaning from the places it touches. They talk of[2] a circus-like journey in Caravans from Glastonbury to St Michael's Mount, a 'month-long processional theatre' ending with an alchemical wedding on the hills by Marazion, with performances at key places on the route of an 'epic show', incorporating geographical features of the actual journey, the 'wilderness' of Dartmoor and the Harlers, for instance, into traumatic areas of the hero's mental journey.

Whether plans as ambitious as this can be brought off, whether one can expect to see interesting plays emerge from such wide open, improvised situations, are questions one can't even begin to answer yet. But we're bound to feel hopeful, I think, if only because so much of value has already been given us by artists sympathetic to the concept of popular, open theatre. There are plenty of hazards attending this concept – Peter Brook's word 'rough' is an apposite one – but when it takes shape as an *Oh What a Lovely War* or a *Serjeant Musgrave's Dance* roughness comes to seem a most desirable virtue.

1. *Texts*
   Arden, J.:
   Serjeant Musgrave's Dance, 1960
   Live Like Pigs. In *New English Dramatists* 3, 1961. Rptd in *Three Plays*, 1964
   The Happy Haven. In *New English Dramatists* 4, 1962. Rptd in *Three Plays*, 1964. (With Margaretta D'Arcy)
   The Business of Good Government, 1963. (With Margaretta D'Arcy)
   The Waters of Babylon, In *Three Plays*, 1964
   The Workhouse Donkey, 1964
   Ars Longa, Vita Brevis. In *Eight Plays* ed. M. S. Fellows, 1965. (With Margaretta D'Arcy)
   Ironhand. Adapted from Goethe's *Goetz von Berlichingen*, 1965
   Armstrong's Last Goodnight, 1965
   Soldier, Soldier and other Plays, 1967

---

[1] An account of these and other street theatre activities in the Stoke area is given by Jim Lagden in an article, 'Theatre in the Market Place', *Theatre Quarterly* 1, 1971.

[2] An account of this programme, planned for September 1972, is given under the title, 'Welfare State', in *Time Out* 118, 1972.

The Royal Pardon, 1967. (With Margaretta D'Arcy)
The Hero Rises Up, 1969. (With Margaretta D'Arcy)
The Bagman: Squire Jonathan, 1971
Wood, C.:
Cockade. In *New English Dramatists* 8, 1965
Fill the Stage with Happy Hours. In *New English Dramatists* 11, 1967
Dingo, 1969
'*H*', *or Monologues at Front of Burning Cities*, 1970

2. *Critical Writings*
Hayman, R. *John Arden*, 1968. Contemporary Playwrights series
Taylor, J. R.:
Anger and After, 1969 rev
The Second Wave, 1971

IX

Forms of Freedom and Mystery: Beneath the Subtext

Beckett, Joe Orton, Peter Barnes, Heathcote Williams

Another expression of the opening out impulse in today's theatre is the movement towards farce and strange new forms which could best be described, perhaps, as 'mysteries'. These are the plays I want to discuss now. They fall naturally together, I think, for they all, in their different ways, are concerned with the irrational and the primitive, with ecstatic or demonic states of being, with the kind of communication that goes on beneath the subtext.

Much of the dramatic experiment in this area, as in the epic theatre, is bound up with the actors' search for a new theatrical language. But here, where Peter Brook is the presiding genius, a similar vocabulary produces very different effects. Improvisation, acrobatics, stylistic flexibility are still the favoured means but they are directed towards the exotic and mysterious rather than the local and familiar: Artaud and Grotowski replace Jimmy James and Marie Lloyd as exemplars.

When Peter Brook, with Charles Marowitz, launched his Theatre of Cruelty programme in 1964 as a 'public session of work-in-progress', he explained that phrase of Artaud's in an illuminating way. Cruelty, he pointed out, didn't mean 'blood' or 'the cruelty we can exercise upon each other by hacking at each other's bodies'. It meant 'the much more terrible and necessary cruelty which things can exercise against us. We are not free. And the sky can still fall on our heads. And the theatre has been created to teach us that first of all.'[1]

---

[1] Peter Brook, Programme of Royal Shakespeare Experimental Group in Theatre of Cruelty (LAMDA Theatre 12 Jan 1964).

This is a Beckettian-sounding vision. All those images swim into mind, the woman sinking into the earth, the man gazing through a telescope out of the high tower window to see if the world is still there. Beckett has been a key figure for Brook. In his deeply intuitive book, *The Empty Space*, he takes the plays as a crucial illustration of what he calls 'holy theatre', linking them with the theatre of Grotowski which also, he says, 'has a sacred aim . . . is a vehicle, a means for self-study, self-exploration; a possibility of salvation'.[1] He hasn't produced Beckett's own plays so much as exposed others', notably Shakespeare's, to the Beckettian light to trace new shadows from them: *King Lear* in the light of *Endgame*.

In this looking back to Shakespeare, Brook touches hands with the exponents of epic theatre. He has been immensely responsive to new work, to Artaud, to Grotowski, to Weiss, but these influences have not turned him away from the English inheritance. On the contrary, Artaud has sent him back to the Elizabethans where he has found, he says, a theatre waiting which is just the kind dreamed of in *The Theatre and its Double*; in Artaud's words a 'seraphim's' theatre with an 'agonizing magic relationship to reality and danger', a theatre of 'fiery, magnetic imagery' which seeks to release the 'magic freedom of daydreams' through a language in which the non-verbal, musical, physical elements are as vital as the words; a theatre of ecstasy which doesn't aim at analysis or explanations but in a direct, intuitive way expresses 'transcendental cosmic preoccupations.'[2]

Artaud's special vocabulary, as Brook points out, was very much of his period and place: voluptuous and rhetorical, with a heavy emphasis on shrieks, groans, whippings and breast beatings – a style that would normally be uncongenial to the English temperament, though the Grand Guignol element in it has begun to turn up in a rather curious way in some of our recent drama. Brook had one of his greatest successes with Shakespeare's nearest-to-Grand Guignol play, *Titus Andronicus*, played straight for horror, but in recent work he has put more emphasis on 'play' elements, in his sensationally successful production of *A Midsummer Night's Dream*, especially. Shakespeare's Artaud-like point – 'Methinks I see these things with parted eye, Where everything seems double' – is driven home in an unequivocal, physically aggressive way. The actors stand round to watch scenes they're not playing in, the magic is a man-made affair of circus stilts

---

[1] P. Brook, *The Empty Space*, p 59.
[2] Antonin Artaud, *The Theatre and its Double*, 1970 (tr V. Corti), p 68.

and trapezes, at once unusually accessible and (unless we happen to be circus performers) formidably remote. Perhaps in such a sophisticated performing context the amateur players, Bottom and company, more or less fell out of the play (looking for a Joan Littlewood world?). But the eroticism and irony so commonly concealed in more traditional productions was brilliantly communicated.

It is this sort of vision, exuberantly free and releasing and yet, in Brook's phrase, 'locked to the dark side of the spectrum' that is becoming potent in our theatre now. For Brook himself the vision is associated with a hunger for ritual. He finds the lines laid out for him in plays from other traditions – Seneca's *Oedipus*, the Weiss *Marat-Sade* – and in his productions of these as well as of Shakespeare he tries many devices – the hypnotic silence around the golden phallus in *Oedipus*, the descent of Titania and company into the auditorium at the end of *A Midsummer Night's Dream* – to embrace his audience, draw them into the ritual, a dark one in *Oedipus*, dazzlingly white, witty and mocking in *A Midsummer Night's Dream*.

Modern English models have been slow to appear, however. There has been a crop of 'cruel' plays which have worked the Grand Guignol vein in the Artaud concept and occasionally one which sounds a deeper note, David Rudkin's *Afore Night Come*, for instance, a play about ritual killing in a Midlands orchard which Brook has singled out for praise and James Roose-Evans has linked with Martha Graham's dance drama, *Ardent Song* (seen in London in 1954), as illustrations of 'the dark poetry of perversion'.[1] But mostly the plays in this vein have been frigid rather than poetic exercises in perversion, more likely to depress and confine the mind than send it spinning into another dimension – the goal Artaud aimed at. Too often the play element in the ritual – the dressing up of the sacrificial victim in *The King*[2], for instance – comes over as the type associated with earnest amateur actors. One begins to long for a fuller professionalism in the performance, more virtuosity, including the ability to make the jokes real before turning them sour.

It's just these qualities that distinguish the most important drama so far produced in this region of mysterious darkness, the drama of Beckett. The most serious is also among the funniest, a paradox which can be taken as the deepest meaning of his plays. They are funny in a heart-warming way unknown to Grand Guignol and yet his situations

---

[1] J. Roose-Evans, *Experimental Theatre*, 1971, p 115.
[2] Stewart Conn, 1970.

often have the black, threatening look of the genre; blind Hamm shut up in a bare room with crippled Clov, 'bottling' his dying parents in their dustbins; Pozzo dragging Lucky by the rope, one of them going blind, the other dumb; the child pushed out of the train in *All That Fall*. Beckett himself has used a word about *Endgame* which brings out this Grand Guignol element: 'It depends upon the power of the text to claw.'

Discussion of Beckett always turns on paradoxes of this kind. His plays have been seen as – and in a way have to be – a dead end, the dead end of realism, the final bottle-neck, the cerebral tradition parodying itself in a last desperately cerebral gesture. No movement, no music, no bodies to speak of, only heads sticking out of earth and urns, and droning voices. But here comes in the strangest paradox, for these plays have been one of the great freeing influences on modern theatre, have moved it away from the well-worn tracks to the unknown ones it is venturing on now.

His plays can be produced anywhere, from an elegant little proscenium theatre like the Criterion where *Waiting for Godot* had its celebrated London run,[1] to a prison auditorium or a circus round, and always they seem to open up the scene, give the audience a sense of being pushed out into a totally new dimension. They remind us, as Kenneth Tynan put it, how much the drama can do without and still exist. Motive, plot complications, dénouements drop away, along with the scenery, and we're left with a bareness that is alarming but also exhilarating: it gives the same kind of freedom as the austere concentration of Japanese Noh plays. Perhaps the most crucial of his innovations for the English theatre has been his break with motive and character analysis. He has demonstrated very decisively that characters can draw fascinated attention without being wrapped in a psychological envelope such as the Ibsen/Chekhov drama provides. Events on his stage are too deeply mysterious for ordinary questions about motivation to come up, or the kind of probing into past history that is so much a part of the other tradition. Estragon and Vladimir, Winnie and Willie have no past: we don't even want to know such things as how they came to meet or what sort of separate lives they once led; they can't be imagined outside their situations, waiting for Godot, getting through a day in the ground: 'The earth is very tight today'. The past only gets in as present, supremely in *Play* where the trio in

---

[1] After opening at the Arts Theatre 3 Aug 1955.

Alan Howard as Oberon and Robert Lloyd as Puck in the Royal Shakespeare Company's production of A Midsummer Night's Dream, *directed by Peter Brook, at the Aldwych Theatre.*
                    Photograph: Morris Newcombe

PLATE 9

Estelle Kohler as Gwenhwyvar and Richard Pasco as Medraut in the Royal Shakespeare Company's production of The Island of the Mighty *by John Arden and Margaretta D'Arcy at the Aldwych Theatre.*

Photograph: Reg Wilson

PLATE 10

*John McEnery and Robert Lang in the National Theatre's produc-
tion of Charles Wood's* H *at the Old Vic.*

Photograph: Dominic

PLATE II

Elvi Hale as Nell, Sidney Bromley as Nagg, Patrick Magee as Hamm, and Jack MacGowran as Clov in Samuel Beckett's Endgame *at the Théâtre des Champs Elysées.*

PLATE 12

the urns have nothing to do but run through the sequence of the traumatic experience they seem to have got stuck in. For them it's an oppressive process, but for the audience this experience of being compelled to live so rigorously in the present – all distractions and low-power pressures cut out – is wonderfully freeing as well as rather terrifying.

We're freed from so many things in Beckett's drama – from the tyranny of the commonplace, from exposition (it's left to the critics to provide that), and analysis, from the muddiness of ordinary experience. The action forces a peculiarly concentrated attention, but like Estragon and Vladimir we're not sure how it is we are being held:

> ESTRAGON (his mouth full, vacuously): We're not tied?
> VLADIMIR: I don't hear a word you're saying.
> ESTRAGON (chews, swallows): I'm asking you if we're tied.
> VLADIMIR: Tied?
> ESTRAGON: Ti-ed.
> VLADIMIR: How do you mean tied?
> ESTRAGON: Down.
> VLADIMIR: But to whom? By whom?
> ESTRAGON: To your man.
> VLADIMIR: To Godot? Tied to Godot? What an idea. No question of it.
> (Pause.) For the moment.

The insouciance of Beckett's characters is one of their most attractive qualities. It's exhilarating to see them in such desperate situations playing so confidently with the idea of being in a play – 'I'm warming up for my last soliloquy'; 'What is there to keep me here? The dialogue' – but it's disturbing too, in the way of Chaplinesque clowns who keep hold of their hats and sticks, and bob up irrepressibly with pained smiles while cars crash all round them, trains come off rails, people fall off precipices.

It would be hard to overestimate Beckett's importance as the opener of the door to this disturbing freedom. English audiences seem able to respond to the darkness in his drama, its Artaud-like, Strindbergian aspects, because of the farce; it gives a special kind of reassurance, is almost, one might say a guarantee of sanity and a very impressive one in circumstances that would be appalling and comfortless taken in cold blood. Farce has certainly come into its own again in the post-Beckett theatre. It has been taken out of its Victorian box, where it was laid away in the era of conversational realism, and set going in some startlingly new directions.

11

Victorian notes still sound quite strongly in the plays of Joe Orton, the most accomplished and witty of present-day practitioners in the genre. His tragic death when his powers were just maturing was a great loss to the English theatre. Partly it's his preoccupation with clergymen and policemen that links him with his Victorian predecessors. These are both types of more ancient lineage certainly, but a nineteenth century odour of sanctity does seem to hang about the clergymen. One hears the echoes of fruity voices – Wilde's Canon Chasuble (My metaphor was drawn from bees), Pinero's sporting Dean (What dreadful wave threatens to engulf the Deanery?) – behind the bland tones of the manic clergymen in *Funeral Games*. There's a note of Lewis Carroll too:

> What shape is your hot water bottle?
> I haven't got one.
> Too proud. Mine takes the form of a cross. There's piety for you.

But the macabre vision of the hot water bottle cross pulls one up short: this is certainly a new twist to the family likeness, an unlooked for, formidable regrouping of the genes.

I suppose it is this power of his to shock and offend susceptibilities that first comes to mind when Orton is named. He goes in such a head-on way for taboos and sacred areas of all kinds. One of Winston Churchill's missing parts turns up in a cigar box (double take here, it *is* a cigar); psychiatrists compete madly to certify each other; clergymen murder their erring wives to demonstrate to their flock their soundness on the seventh commandment; a son takes over his mother's coffin to hide stolen goods in and ends up playing horrific funeral games with the corpse, spilling false eyes and teeth all over the stage. 'Your sense of detachment is terrifying, lad', says the Inspector, 'Most people would at least flinch upon seeing their mother's eyes and teeth handed around like nuts at Christmas.' Orton's characters don't, but his audience presumably do: if they don't, the farce hasn't really served its purpose; the worst fears, the most nightmarish anxieties haven't been given the airing he offers. As in nightmares, ideas keep turning into their opposites on his stage. It's always the clergyman who is the lecherous killer, the policeman – who starts off seeming a solid Dr Watson figure (You must have realized by now, sir, that I am not from the Water Board) – who turns out to be the most adept in corruption.

It's rather curious to find this dream subversiveness sometimes taken

by critics firmly towards social commentary,[1] a spur to social conscience rather than as one might have thought, a diabolical sort of
holiday from it. There are topical allusions in the plays, certainly, but
they seem to function on the whole in a traditional way of farce as
antidote; like Alice's little bottle marked 'Drink me' they change the
perspective alarmingly, might even turn out to be poison, but the
final effect is wonderfully freeing. 'Health is the primary duty of life',
said Wilde's Lady Bracknell. Orton's farces seem to be playing that
game, working out dark fantasies in extravagant comic terms that
both express and exorcize them.

He is arrestingly original in his ability to push the dark elements
so much to the fore without losing that sense of health. Some of the
risks he takes do almost but not quite shatter the convention. In
Funeral Games, for instance, there's a disturbing moment when Tessa,
bound to a chair, is being threatened by the two mad clergymen
and it seems that after all murder might be a real possibility just when
we've got used to thinking of it as an abstract affair of macabre comic
props like the hand chopped off at the wrist (it turns out not to be real)
and bad taste jokes about dead bodies – 'She's under a ton of smoke-
less. I got it at the reduced summer rate.' And his handling of the
comic nemesis is worrying, too. One thinks of Wilde's saying – 'Life
is so terribly deficient in form. The catastrophes happen in the wrong
way and to the wrong people.' Farce normally corrects that deficiency
with a very strict nemesis. On Orton's stage, though, the most harmless characters tend to have the worst time sometimes right to the end.
It's certainly disturbing when *Loot* ends with the corrupt policeman
joining forces with the thieves (one of whom is supposedly a multiple
murderer), while McLeavy who knows nothing whatever about what
has been going on is dragged off shouting 'I'm innocent! I'm innocent!'
and the others look ahead to the 'accidental' death in prison that will
tie everything up for them.

It's a daring departure from the farcical norm to leave us suspended
in the dream, on the other side of the looking glass: the effect is
unsettling. But although the incidents aren't reassuring the tone and
the gargantuan exaggerations are: Truscott saying carelessly 'Oh,
anything will do' when he's asked what he'll charge McLeavy with,

---

[1] John Lahr, for instance draws some precise social morals, comparing Inspector
Truscott with Spiro Agnew and Doctor Rance with the Nixon administration in his
interesting article, 'Artist of the Outrageous', reprinted from *Evergreen Review* as introduction to *What the Butler Saw* (New York 1969).

Fay making everything cosy for Hal – 'We'll bury your father with your mother. That will be nice for him, won't it?', and McLeavy himself, absurdly lamenting as he's led off, 'Oh, what a terrible thing to happen to a man who's been kissed by the Pope'.

Orton's skill in keeping his situations delicately balanced between real life and fantasy, daylight and dream can be seen developing steadily, it seems to me,[1] between his first play, *Entertaining Mr Sloane* and the posthumous *What the Butler Saw*. *Entertaining Mr Sloane* is cast on more Pinteresque lines than the later plays: its terms are too human, the mechanism is too slow, to let us take the characters as figures of farce, and yet the central events, the brutal mishandling of the old man and the sexual blackmail that follows, are presented with a kind of unyielding comic aplomb that undercuts human responses and raises worrying doubts about the playwright's own sympathies. It's hard to avoid ordinary human uneasiness about Mr Sloane's attack on Kemp: there's too strong a feeling of real pain and fear in it to allow the detachment Orton seems to invite with his tough jokes and his cool handling of the manslaughter (as it proves to be).

In *Loot* the cool convention is much more firmly established. 'It's a theme which less skilfully handled could've given offence', Truscott says to Fay, complimenting her on the direct, simple style of her murder confession. Style does have this sort of vital function in the play, not to prevent offence exactly, but to keep feeling in its place. There is still a good deal of physical brutality: Truscott getting Hal on the floor and kicking him isn't a pleasant sight. But it's kept at a careful distance, partly by being taken so fast, partly by the jauntiness of the dialogue at the receiving end of the violence. Whereas old Kemp lets out realistic cries of pain and calls for his son – 'I want Ed' – Hal comes back with repartee:

> TRUSCOTT: Under any other political system I'd have you on the floor in tears.
> HAL: You've got me on the floor in tears.

So long as the victims can keep their end up with this sort of stoical calm we can keep up our detachment too. It's rather harder in a way where the corpse is concerned – no chance for repartee there – but Orton finds other means; he stresses the artificial elements – the glass

---

[1] For one of Orton's critics, J. R. Taylor, the reverse is true. He finds *Loot* less satisfactory than *Entertaining Mr Sloane* 'because the balance has shifted slightly in the direction of farce', *The Second Wave*, 1971, p 131.

eyes of the wrong colour, for instance – until the corpse finally comes
to seem very little different from the dressmaker's dummy that is
substituted for it at one point in the frantic game of hunt the treasure
it is caught up in.

The technique is assured in *Loot* but there are rough notes in the
play that keep it more earthbound than Orton's last full-length work,
What the Butler Saw. Here his control of his anarchic material reaches
its high point. There's a blend of steel and airiness about it that brings
Wilde irresistibly to mind, remarkably really, considering how outrageously physical in vulgar picture postcard style Orton's farce is,
how much closer in some ways to the Aldwych tradition or to French
sex farce than to the ethereally refined version Wilde arrived at in
The Importance of Being Earnest.

Trousers come off with grotesque regularity in *What the Butler
Saw*: half the characters are half naked most of the time. The command,
'Undress and lie on the couch' rings maniacally through the action;
starting as a simple (if unorthodox) start of a seduction and ending
as a hysterically funny and desperate expression of the total bafflement
about sexual identity that finally enwraps the characters.

And yet despite the picture postcard grossness, a demure note is
beautifully kept up:

> Two young people / one mad and one sexually insatiable / both naked, are
> roaming this house. At all costs we must prevent a collision.

The content belongs to Orton's world but the style wouldn't be
out of place in Wilde's; it's rather how Canon Chasuble might put
it, one feels, if he were to run out of metaphor.

There are other similarities with *The Importance of Being Earnest*:
the plots are in fact strikingly close at crucial points.[1] Wilde's plot
turns on the double identity of Jack and Algernon and the emergence
of Jack's other self 'Ernest' as the mythical being whom practically
everyone in the play is pursuing or trying to be. Orton works out a
vastly more complicated version of this identity theme in *What the
Butler Saw*. We begin with a single self, a simple secretary, Geraldine
Barclay, who sets things going when she applies for a post as secretary
in Dr Prentice's psychiatric clinic. Out of his abortive attempt to
seduce her (which she never appears to understand) comes the struggle

---

[1] In an interview in *Transatlantic Review* 24, Orton spoke of his admiration for Wilde
and his wish to write a play as good as *The Importance of Being Earnest*.

to hide her from his wife and the wild game of hide and seek in which Geraldine Barclay begins to break up into a number of different selves.

Geraldine palpitates nakedly on stage while Miss Barclay, the missing secretary is hunted by the psychiatrist's wife, the rival psychiatrist and a policeman. Geraldine – frantically on the lookout for clothes to put on – takes shelter in the identity of Nick Beckett, the pageboy, and then under pressure of the chase creates an alter ego for him too, Gerald Barclay, his imaginary brother. So two mythical free floating beings take shape for the 'real' characters to go in and out of. As Wilde's Algernon steals the identity of Ernest, so Nick and Geraldine steal each other's secondary identities. She vanishes into a shape with cropped hair and boy's clothes, he into a woman's dress, blonde wig and 'low cultured voice' to match. Getting rid of the alter ego, as in Wilde's play, proves more difficult than creating it: an attempt to kill off the surplus personalities leads into monstrous new growths, till Dr Prentice – desperately trying to get rid of women's shoes in flower vases and drugged bodies in the garden – comes to be seen as 'a transvestite, fetishist bi-sexual murderer'.

Again as in Wilde's play, the crowning joke comes at the end when the invented identities turn out to be after all, the true ones. There really are twin selves, a Geraldine and Gerald, who were conceived in the linen cupboard at the Station Hotel, that off stage dream area – equivalent to the handbag in *The Importance of Being Earnest* – associated with sexual orgies, illegitimacy, the pleasure principle unrestrained. Here Mrs Prentice pursues Platonic dreams – 'I went to the linen cupboard . . . hoping to find a chambermaid' – and enjoys fantasies of being sexually assaulted, fantasies in which objects like handbags have a strangely prominent place – 'When I repulsed him he attempted to rape me. I fought him off but not before he'd stolen my handbag and several articles of clothing.'

The final recognition scene introduces new dark notes into these adventures. Mrs Prentice's claim to have been assaulted by Nick and Dr Prentice's attempt to seduce Geraldine become rather disturbing when Nick and Geraldine are revealed as their lost twin children, fruit of a 'real' rape in the linen cupboard. Not that there's any danger of our seeing it in real life terms – who could take the linen cupboard seriously! – but the fantasies are peculiarly vivid: we do see Geraldine up on the couch and throwing her clothes out from behind the curtain. In a way, the loathly Dr Rance is proved right:

If you are this child's father my book can be written in good faith – she *is* the victim of an incestuous assault!

Rance, however is the great warning against our taking the events too literally. He is the epitome of literalness and earnestness and quite the maddest character in the play, never further from the truth than when he's congratulating himself on having found the right answers. He is certainly right when he tells Prentice,

You can't be a rationalist in an irrational world. It isn't rational.

But he is the one who creates the unreason. Nothing is real to him till it's been turned into a theory. He can't really see facts at all: when people press them on him, he converts them at lightning speed into monstrous theses, as when Geraldine, weary of her boy disguise, says, 'I can't go on, doctor!.... I'm not a boy! I'm a girl!' and he snaps it up, 'Excellent. A confession at last. He wishes to believe he's a girl in order to minimize the feelings of guilt he experiences after homosexual inter-course.' Or when Prentice recklessly ventures a joke about white golliwogs – 'She's making white golliwogs for sale in colour pre-judice trouble-spots' – only to have it drawn into the humourless Rance analysis – 'What was the object in creating these nightmare creatures?... The man's a second Frankenstein.'

Earnestness is the root vice of the play: all the other ills are seen branching out from it, above all the determination to categorize and label and pin people down that afflicts characters in this play as it does, though in so much more mild and decorous forms, in *The Importance of Being Earnest*. The comparison with Wilde can hardly be avoided – even his title would be appropriate to Orton's play, the resemblances of plot and theme are so striking. It wouldn't be so true to the tone, however. Orton's title, *What the Butler Saw*, exactly catches the saucy and slightly menacing notes, its bold, highly coloured quality.

The features of his style which are indicated by this splendidly right title are also the features which relate Orton to the modern movement in the English theatre and make him one of the chief in-fluences in it. Farce is, as Eric Bentley says, the most direct of forms, but even within the convention Orton's is remarkable for the direct-ness of its impact. Comparisons with Wilde – or Pinero, or for that matter Sardou and the French farceurs – bring out how much more thoroughly and ruthlessly Orton involves us in the confusion of his characters. We are made dizzy like them by the bewildering sexual

double bluffs, are scarcely sure at some points whether we're confronted with a girl dressed as a boy who is being taken for a boy who
thinks himself a girl – or vice versa.

There's one such disorientating moment when Rance says to Nick
in his girl's disguise, – 'Suppose I made an indecent suggestion to you?
If you agreed something might occur which, by and large, would be
regarded as natural. If, on the other hand, I approached this child –
(He smiles at Geraldine) – my action could result only in a gross
violation of the order of things.' We surely begin to lose our hold
on what *is* the natural order of things at this point, an effect Orton is
evidently aiming at – he made this point explicitly in speaking of
Entertaining Mr Sloane: 'What I wanted to do was break down all the
sexual compartments people have.'[1]

We experience too, I think, – and this is very unexpected and
surprising – a faint sense of poignancy as the chase works up to its
desperate climax. No break with the farcical convention is involved
in this. Rance is ludicrously wrong as usual when he lectures Dr
Prentice on his supposed bisexual tendencies: 'There are two sexes.
The unpalatable truth must be faced. Your attempts at a merger can
end only in disaster.' And yet his phrases catch the note of real desire
that can occasionally be sensed behind the fantastic distortions, a real
longing for the alluring, hermaphroditic wraith that has been created
out of the hopeless confusion between Gerald and Geraldine.

This double effect is an impressive indication of Orton's maturing
virtuosity. It rises so naturally out of the comic confusion, which
depends on the action being taken at a dazzlingly fast speed. Speed is
always the essence of farce but Orton's is the supersonic variety. He
spends no time at all on preliminaries but goes straight to business
with the directness of Dr Prentice setting about his seduction of
Geraldine. One sometimes wonders, indeed, if the mechanism isn't
too fast, too loaded with repartee and fantastic turns of invention for
slow, waking brains to take in. Orton seems to be aware of this danger;
he deals with it by offering moments of rest, pauses for recapitulation
and getting bearings. One such occurs towards the end when Dr
Prentice, Geraldine and Nick are left alone together while Rance,
convinced now that they are all mad, goes off in search of tranquillizers.

GERALDINE (with a sob): Twice declared insane in one day! And they said
 I'd be working for a cheerful, well-spoken crowd. (She blows her nose.)

---

[1] Interview, op cit.

NICK: Why is he wearing my uniform?

PRENTICE: He isn't a boy. He's a girl.

GERALDINE: Why is she wearing my shoes?

PRENTICE: She isn't a girl. She's a boy. (Pouring whisky.) Oh, if I live to be ninety, I'll never again attempt sexual intercourse.

NICK: If we changed clothes, sir, we could get things back to normal.

PRENTICE: We'd then have to account for the disappearance of my secretary and the page-boy.

GERALDINE: But they don't exist!

PRENTICE: When people who don't exist disappear the account of their departure must be convincing.

Sanity momentarily returns here, or at any rate the nearest thing one can get to it in this situation of mad unreason. As Prentice says, 'I've been too long among the mad to know what sanity is.' But for a moment we're on relatively solid ground, we get a glimpse of a normal perspective before the chase starts off again and we hurtle on to the gorgeous confrontation between the two psychiatrists, one brandishing a gun, the other a strait jacket – 'I'm going to certify you.' 'No, I am going to certify you' – and the breathtaking climax when Prentice presses the alarm and chaos breaks out all over – a siren wails, grilles come down over the doors, the light goes out. For an unnerving instant we share the characters' panic: 'An overloading of the circuit! We're trapped!' The thought of being shut up in Dr Prentice's clinic for ever—or even for another five minutes – is enough to cause a shiver or two: the strait jacket and the padded cell have a rather horrid reality, after all.

Happily, Orton is able to get us right out of the dream in this play. A ladder descends, Sergeant Match appears as *deus ex machina*, a Bacchanalian bisexual god in a leopard-spotted dress torn from one shoulder and streaming with blood. 'We're approaching what our racier novelists term "the climax" ', says Rance in the ebullient spirit induced by the discovery that *all* his theories have been proved right and his thesis is well set for a runaway success ('Double incest is even more likely to produce a best-seller than murder'). The characters scamper through the remaining 'explanations' and then 'bleeding, drugged and drunk, climb the rope ladder into the blazing light'.

'Let us put our clothes on and face the world.' What resilience, and what a tonic experience to share in it! It seems especially poignant that Orton should have died as he did before this most freeing of his plays was produced, fallen into the brutal reality it lifts us so triumphantly out of. He manages in his farce to give us both a great id-releasing experience and a reassuring demonstration of the power of wit to control it: it's certainly reassuring to have all the mad earnestness of *What the Butler Saw* taken up into gaiety. Already it's clear (as I suggested in speaking of the realistic drama) that his drama has been a very influential model and it seems likely that he will continue to exert considerable influence through the playwrights who have assimilated elements of his style.

One of these, to judge from his baroque comedy, *The Ruling Class* (1969)[1] is Peter Barnes, a playwright who takes farce in curious new directions, mixing it with melodrama in a most unlikely and distinctive style. His affinity with Orton comes out in his leaning to Victorian matter and manner (*The Importance of Being Earnest* is very much in the background of his play too) and in his way of handling similarly sensational material – sex murders, bizarre complexes – in a similarly cool, deadpan style.

> DR HERDER: His lordship is a paranoid-schizophrenic.
> SIR CHARLES: But he's a *Gurney*.
> DR HERDER: Then he's a paranoid-schizophrenic Gurney who believes he's God.
> SIR CHARLES: But we've always been Church of England.

We're in the dry, farce world here all right and this tone is never quite dropped, even in the second half of the play when melodrama becomes the dominant mode. It's full scale melodrama, with music, songs, extended soliloquies and grotesque transformation scenes in thorough Victorian style. The Victorian world, in fact, takes over the stage, as the hero's lurid sex fantasies are acted out in a setting representing the London of Jack the Ripper: old street cries are heard, the gory headlines – Murder and Mutilation in Whitechapel! – are shouted; the modern victim merges with her Victorian counterpart, the prostitute, Mary Ann Nichols.

Barnes seems to be fascinated by the Jack the Ripper tale. He has done an English adaptation of Wedekind's Lulu plays[2] in which also the Ripper appears at the end as a lordly upper-class character, a folk-lore belief that fits in well with the concept of the aristocratic Gurneys in *The Ruling Class*. The play explores the relation between their

---

[1] Nottingham Playhouse 6 Nov 1968; Piccadilly Theatre, London 26 Feb 1969.
[2] A conflation of *Erdgeist* and *Die Büchse der Pandora*. Produced as *Lulu* at Nottingham Playhouse 7 Oct 1970; Royal Court Theatre 8 Dec 1970.

repressive morality – 'the Hangman holds society together' is their motto – and their furtive sex life and shows it as a breeding ground for mania. It's done partly in grotesque farcical terms, as in the prologue when the 13th Earl, the Judge, accidentally hangs himself during a sado-masochistic rite involving a homemade gallows, or in the sotto voce guerilla warfare conducted against the family by the jauntily malevolent butler:

> A lot yer don't know about Daniel Tucker. Just old faithful Tucker. Give doggy boney. Just 'ere for comic relief. Know who I really am? . . . Alexei Kronstadt. Number 243. Anarchist – Trotskyist – Communist – Revolutionary. I'm a cell! All these years I've been working for the Revolution, spitting in the hot soup, peeing on the Wedgwood dinner plates.

The farcical note is kept up in the portrayal of the 14th Earl, the schizophrenic at the centre of the play. There is almost always something ludicrous about him, from his first entry – he comes on in a monk's habit calling himself Jesus Christ – to the final scenes where he drags his way across the stage in the persona of a Victorian actor playing Richard III ('Deform'd, unfinished, sent before me time').

The elements of caricature in the characterization allow Barnes to relate the painful private material to the broad social comedy, make it in fact the centre of the satire. It's in their attitude to the 14th Earl's madness that his family place themselves most decisively. He is cured, in their eyes, when his hippy Jesus self is replaced by his Victorian self, Jack, a decorously costumed, tight-buttoned character who campaigns fanatically on behalf of sexual propriety – and capital punishment – 'They're undermining the foundations of our society with their adultery and fornication' – while underneath he is degenerating rapidly into a Jack the Ripper.

The farce takes on an increasingly manic note as the hysteria rises in the buried self, but it keeps its comic exuberance until very late in the action. There are entertaining scenes: when the Earl convinces the Master of Lunacy that he's cured of his delusions, for instance and the two go into a 'barber-shop duet', singing the Eton boating song, or when he wins round the visiting Conservative ladies, who were scandalized by his earlier talk of love, with his new prudishness: – 'Tucker, why are those table legs uncovered? Stark naked wooden legs in mixed company – it's not decent.' Dark notes invade without quite destroying the comic zest. It's not until the very end that the farce darkens to the same shade as the melodrama (in which Claire is killed) and the grotesque no longer makes us laugh. The Earl in his Richard III persona stumping into the House of Lords and making his 'Bring back hanging' speech to tiers of mouldering dummies – with Claire's blood on his hands – is not a sight to raise laughter, however wry.

Barnes is wonderfully skilful at keeping up this distant, satirical view of the madness while at the same time giving us a closer view which invites more complex emotional responses. In the first part of the play the sympathy is quite intricately divided. Up to a point, we can hardly avoid seeing the 14th Earl with his relations' eyes. Can a man be anything but a certifiable lunatic who gets up from time to time on a crucifix, and invites his family to address their prayers to him – 'You are talking directly to God. . . . For I am the Creator and Ruler of the Universe, Khoda, the One Supreme Being . . .'?

And yet, of course, we can catch, as they can't, the Blakean notes in the madness: 'a great brush dipped in light swept across the sky. And I saw the distinction, diversity, variety, all clearly rolled up into the unity of Universal Love.' Then again, he is a much more sympathetic character than his greedy relations, who are squalidly plotting to get the family inheritance into their hands. In his openness, his capacity for enthusiasm and affection, he is in a way far more sane than they are. They are certainly emotional cripples as Claire says, in the scene when she tries to seduce him – 'Poor Jack. You didn't know how impossible it was for our sort to feel.'

So long as he is Jesus Christ we find ourselves wanting him – and his kind of sensibility – to triumph. A plot is hatched to marry him to his uncle's mistress, for the sake of getting an heir (he can then be certified and got rid of). All that stands in the way is his conviction that he is already married – to the Lady of the Camelias, Marguerite Gautier. His cousin sets out to deal with the delusion:

> DINSDALE (gesturing with the book): But I've shown you it's in here. *The Lady of the Camelias* by Alexandre Dumas. *Camille*. The opera by Verdi, *La Traviata*. Same woman. A figure of romance.
> EARL OF GURNEY: My dear chap, you prove my point ipso facto, a divine figure of romance.

The madman certainly comes off best here, and gradually he draws us further into sympathy with his point of view, till we come, I think, almost to entertain a hope that he might be able to 'prove' the existence of another dimension, his world of light and love, as the relations contemptuously invite him to do: 'Show us a miracle. . . . A miracle like the making of loaves and fishes.' He tries to lift a table 'by the power of love': when nothing happens, Claire taunts him – 'There's no miracle. No wife. She doesn't exist. She's fiction. . . . Not real.' Then Barnes springs a virtuoso surprise. To the sound of the Drinking Song from *La Traviata*, the Lady of the Camelias appears picked out in spotlight carrying a camelia: the stage is blacked out on the Earl's rapturous cry 'Marguerite!'

Once the shock is over, it's obvious enough that the Lady with the Camelias is Charles' mistress, Grace, and it's all part of the plot to cheat him into marriage. But for a moment – and this is very much the result of the stage convention being so free and flexible – anything seems possible. It could be that we are being drawn right into the Earl's mind, seeing with his eyes (as we do later on in the expressionistic scenes of the 'cure' and the murder). Or even, one might wonder for a split second, if this is a revelation, a sign that faith can work miracles, that music and the divine figures of romance *are* the real world.

Some of these impressions carry over into the later scenes and remain with us even after the Jack self takes over and sex becomes a dark demonic thing. 'We were more loving when you were batty', Grace says to him sadly at the end. It's his ability to capture sad notes like these, as well as caustic and disturbing ones, that makes Barnes' satire so distinctive. The murder of Claire comes over partly as a caricature of the perverted morality of the ruling class, but it is also painful in a personal way. And it's sad as well as horrific – because there *was* a happy time in their marriage – when Grace becomes Jack the Ripper's second victim: her scream ends the play. The flexibility of technique that allows for this flexibility of mood is a striking achievement. Barnes has succeeded in doing what it had almost begun to seem couldn't be done; he has naturalized Expressionist techniques – the techniques of Strindberg and Wedekind – in a theatre which has been peculiarly resistant to them. For one critic, Harold Hobson, *The Ruling Class* was another high-water mark in the history of the postwar theatre: he ranked it along with *Look Back in Anger*, *Waiting for Godot* and *The Birthday Party* as the sort of experience that opens up doors in the mind, an 'explosive blaze of an entirely new talent of a very high order'.[1]

---

[1] Harold Hobson, Introduction to *The Ruling Class*, 1969.

One of the strangest scenes in the play is the Expressionist sequence of the Earl's 'cure'. His psychiatrist applies violent shock therapy, confronting him with another madman who believes himself God: his is the Old Testament kind, vengeful and authoritarian, a 'braw God fer bashing bairns' heads on rocks, a God for strong stomachs'. The idea is that one God will drive out the other and this is what happens. Under pressure from the mad McKyle – and from the plot (Dr Herder reveals the conspiracy to certify him once his wife gives birth to the heir she is in labour with) – the Earl breaks down. He has an epileptic fit on stage, represented partly in realistic terms (saliva, writhings) and partly in a ludicrous and macabre Expressionist vision of a monster eight foot high – covered with black facial hair and dressed in the height of Victorian aristocratic fashion – who leaps in through the French windows, seizes the victim and shakes him unconscious. When he comes round, he is answering to the name of Jack and his tormented Victorian phase has begun.

An extraordinary aspect of the scene is the use made in it of a peculiar electricity motif. McKyle thinks of himself as a kind of great power house: he is a higher voltage man than the Earl, he says: electricity streams from his fingers and eyeballs; the booster converter in his forehead turns everything he eats and drinks into watts and kilowatts; his power is so great that he has to earth himself before turning his full current against the other God. He is the High Voltage Messiah, the Electric Christ, the AC/DC God, who has flown in from outer space, to visit earth, the 'privy o' the Cosmos'. The Earl picks up the imagery and develops it in a terrifyingly personal way. 'You're trying to split my mind with his tongue', he shouts at Herder: later, after the murder he taunts the troubled doctor with the success of his 'adjustment': 'You trepanned me, opened my brain, telephoned the truth direct into my skull as it were!'

These violent ideas and images lead straight into a play still stranger than *The Ruling Class* – Heathcote Williams' *AC/DC*, a profoundly original piece of *avant-garde* theatre, a play with such virulent power that one feels it must make a significant impact on the modern tradition, even though it may be hard to imagine it ever being regularly played outside small experimental theatres like the Royal Court's Theatre Upstairs, where it was first performed and has since been twice revived.[1] This is the most substantial, virtuoso per-

[1] First produced at the Theatre Upstairs at the Royal Court Theatre 14 May 1970. Revived there Oct 1971 and Oct 1972.

formance in ritualism and cruelty we've yet had, the first play, perhaps, that it seems natural, even necessary, to describe in terms of
Artaud's 'seraphim's theatre'.

It's a play about people picking up from each other, so it seems
appropriate to begin at the point where it looks to be picking up from
The Ruling Class.[1] In *AD/DC* not one but all the characters direct
'currents' at each other and battle for psychic power; they enact
strange rituals to get direct mental contact, telephone messages straight
into the skull, in Peter Barnes' phrase, 'send ESP telegrams', in
Williams'. 'You are who you eat' is, as Williams says, a key phrase for
the characters. Here too a character has an epileptic fit on stage; here
the trepanning image of *The Ruling Class* is acted out as a gruesome
climax to a prolonged ritual.

The electrical idea informs the whole action. The stage is set up as
a machine environment: in the first part (*AC*) the characters are
introduced to us playing the machines – Photomaton, pin machines –
in an amusement arcade; in the second (*DC*) they are in a room dominated by banks of video screens. Ultra-violet lights flash, bulbs explode,
the video screens give off a steady hum that mounts to a crescendo
during the cataclysmic breakdown – or break out – of the trepanning
scene.

It's rather hard to give proper weight to this bizarre visual and aural
interest in reading the play; on the page it makes such an overpowering
impression of words, words, words. They pour out in copious and
aggressive floods, the image of 'flushing the mind' that recurs in the
dialogue – Where's the toilet in my brain? How do I flush it? – seems
peculiarly appropriate. Streams of ideas, images, jargon, technicalities
flow together, electrical and biochemical languages run into each
other: a horrific impression builds up of man as a soft machine,
receiving a driving energy in mysterious ways he is struggling to
understand:

PEROWNE: At one point I was trying to . . . I don't know . . . trying to
find, you see, some kind of Unified Field Theory of facial movements,

---

[1] Although as the electrical metaphors are so much more an integral part of *AC/DC*
one would have expected the derivation to be the other way round. Heathcote Williams'
play was available in manuscript some years before it was published. He tells me that
he began writing it in 1965 and there were twelve or thirteen drafts. An important source
for the play was M. Rokeah's *The Three Christs of Ypsilanti* (1964). Heathcote Williams
points out that Rokeah also uses the phrase 'hollow out' and takes electricity as a metaphor
for (or measure of) human interaction. (Letter of October 1972.)

eye contact patterns, speech intonations . . . so on . . . I mean, every-
thing's interconnected, you know. If you drop a bottle of tomato ketchup
in Tokyo, ultimately it affects the red gases on Jupiter.
SADIE: Hey, have you got into Ectohormones yet?
PEROWNE: No. What are they?
SADIE: There's this Biochemical Effluvia that's comin out of us the whole
time. Pheromone trails, Hexanol transmitters and receptors. Ectohormonal
BEAMS, and they may be the TRUE PLOT.

It's interesting that Pinter, with his strong views on the dramatic
function of obscene language, should pick out Heathcote Williams
as one of the most promising of the younger English playwrights.[1]
It's a tribute, surely, to Williams' power to force acceptance of his
own terms; certainly nothing could be further from Pinter's 'dark,
secret language of the underworld' than the obscenity of this play.
Four-letter words are used in a violently monotonous rhythm that is
insidious and disturbing, there is such a strong sense of occult purpose, of language as an element in a monstrous ritual of purification,
exorcism and transcendence.

Fashionable hippy elements are so pronounced in this ritual, and the
thought-flow so wild, so full of random-sounding observations that
one begins by wondering if the piece is coming out of some sort of
uncontrolled drug trance. But it soon becomes clear that the trance is
the characters' and that the playwright's control is very tight, down
to the elaborate ordering of the typography[2] to suggest distinctions
(admittedly not easy to read) among the speaking elements.

'Elements' seems a more appropriate word than characters, but this
isn't a matter that can be lightly settled. Who is really there, is in
fact one of the burning questions of the play. Is Perowne the only
flesh and blood character, and are the others projections from his
mind? The first personalities we meet – Gary, Melody and Sadie –
certainly seem quite distinct from him, a tangle of identities on their
own, taking snaps of themselves inside the Photomaton and trying
to fuse the images, get 'a real deep communal brain buzz'. From these
three the personality of Sadie emerges, separate and dominant – 'I
wanna go solo' – and soon after the other two drop out of the action

---

[1] In the interview he gave in the *New York Times*.
Williams' first play, *The Local Stigmatic* was produced in a double bill with Pinter's
The Dwarfs at the Traverse Theatre on 1 March 1966.
[2] Williams' original idea, so Irving Wardle says in his introduction to the text of
AC/DC published in *Gambit* 18, was to have hollow letters and fill in with colour accord-
ing to the characters' influence on each other.

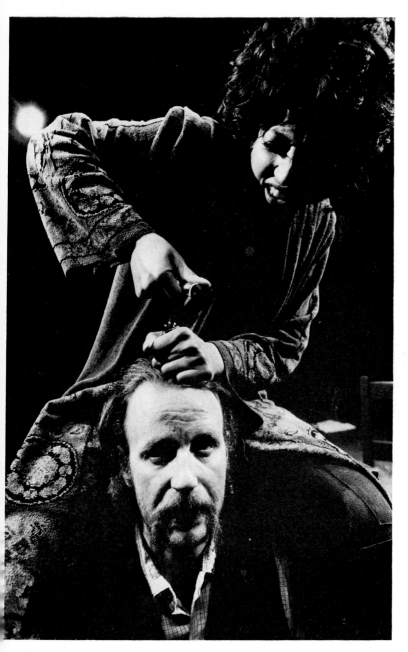

Sheila Scott Williamson as Sadie and Victor Henry as Perowne in Heathcote Williams' AC/DC at the Royal Court Theatre.

Photograph: John Haynes

PLATE 13

Deborah Norton as Melody and Tony Shear as Gary in Heathcote
Williams' AC/DC *at the Royal Court Theatre.*

Photograph: John Haynes

PLATE 14

Marianne Faithfull and Peter Eyre in Edward Bond's Early Morning *at the Royal Court Theatre.*

Photograph: Douglas Jeffrey

PLATE 15

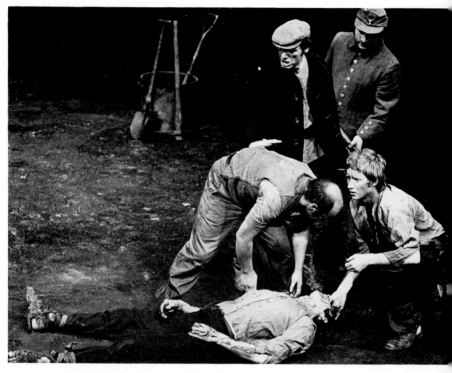

Geoffrey Hinsliff, Matthew Guinness, Struan Rodger, Ron Pember ('dead') and Bob Hoskins in Act 1, Scene 1, of Edward Bond's Lear at the Royal Court Theatre.

Photograph: John Haynes

PLATE 16

altogether: they weren't real minds, after all, only a hippy imitation; finally they are shown up as totally conventional – Mr and Mrs Jones.

Once Perowne appears, however, more or less in conjunction with Maurice – he is brooding over the energy he's wasted on a pin table Maurice is repairing ('Centralized Data Storage. That's all it needs') – he becomes the pivot of a Perowne/Maurice/Sadie combination and we move steadily deeper into the obsessions and intuitions of this three-headed monster. Perowne is pulled first towards one, then to another (the bisexual reference in the title becomes meaningful here) till in the closing sequence Sadie takes over completely. 'He ran you flat, didn't he?' she says about Maurice when he is finally driven from the scene.

Perowne is the 'overloaded circuit' the others try to relieve by a variety of extraordinary rituals; incantations, acts of sympathetic magic, exorcisms. Maurice specializes in obliterating old tracks, playing over painful mental sequences, blotting out words with words, to give Perowne 'clean breaks'. He does some virtuoso turns in this vein – great narratives recalling traumatic experiences in which it's hard to distinguish lived-through events from fantasies. Lines from what could be a real encounter with a psychiatrist, for instance – 'You talk too much about electricity' – merge with baroque images of Maurice stealing electricity from the psychiatrist, reducing him to a paranoiac state, leaving him crawling on the floor. A picture builds up of a man receiving different kinds of treatment for his mental disorder; hypnosis in one sequence, electrical shock treatment in another.

Maurice himself, like the other characters, tries to take it beyond the clinical. Intimations of mystical experience creep in, strikingly in the hypnosis sequence when he acts out stages of recall under hypnosis in terms of reincarnation: he feels himself entering a violent 'former' experience in the Spanish Civil War and comes out of it understanding, so he says, the nature of the scar left on his 'supra-physical self'.

A similar double pattern develops in Sadie's area of the play. She specializes in exorcising 'media freaks', the bogies who so oddly haunt all three personalities. In the DC part, when the current gets stronger, there seems no way of escaping the oppressive impact of the images that stare from the walls – about two thousand photos, arranged like sheets of stamps, the stage directions say – and appear with a menacing, throbbing effect on the ubiquitous video screens.

Sadie finds ways, though: she strips photos from the walls, rubs them together to neutralize them – 'Mia Farrow – rubbing you dry as a witch's tit! John Wayne – never gonna be able to lay your grade be sex energy on me again!' In the final scene when she hollows out Maurice, a roll of photos enters into the exorcism in a peculiarly obscene way.

In the dark light of these episodes one begins to understand the motivation in Williams' early one act play, *The Local Stigmatic*, and appreciate the skill that makes one feel there is a genuine impulse behind its freakishly unexplained action, the carving up by two thugs of a seemingly harmless film star; that it isn't just a fashionable exercise in pointless violence.

'He is one of those people you follow', Ray tells Graham when he points out the victim in the bar. What the philosophy behind this obsession is we never see in *The Local Stigmatic*; we only feel the intensity of the hatred. *AC/DC* supplies an explanation – but not one that is very easy to understand. In a way the hatred becomes more baffling when its grounds are exposed. All that virulence directed against commonplace television personalities, news readers, over-publicized film stars; poor Mia Farrow, John Wayne, Elizabeth Taylor, do they really deserve the devastating treatment they get! 'Unbalanced' goes on seeming the word for the characters' attitudes as the explanation develops. Up to a point their obsessive feelings about the media have to be seen simply as a feature of the distressing schizophrenic condition that is being examined through them.

But as for all the other phenomena in the play, a mystical explanation is offered too. 'I sometimes think', says Perowne 'what those . . . those people have (Gesture towards the wall of photos) is a sort of astral body on the cheap. Mmn? And perhaps that accounts for the sense of cosmic irritation that other people have.' And – 'It's no accident that film stars are called stars, you know. They use up the magnetic field to the same extent as any asteroid.' Sadie picks up this idea and develops it into a rococo fantasy about the psychic capitalism practised by different celebrities:

> THINK of all that energy that went into the Beatle-machine. THINK if you'd had a Cosmic Energy Transformer when they first surfaced in Hamburg 1960.
> . . .
> I mean: REAL BRAIN TO BRAIN CONTACT, instead of just exhausting the energy needed for that by selling the same Fake Chauvinistic Sex Bonds (chanting) Ooo – oo OO OO Love Me Do I Love You. . . .)

Strangely – and here Williams' control over his barbaric material is very impressive – the characters have enough eloquence to make their views seem, if not exactly reasonable, disturbingly persuasive at times. We are brought – protesting, perhaps – to see from their point of view, it's this that prevents us from taking the action solely as allegory.

Allegorical interpretation can hardly be avoided, of course. It's almost necessary to see it at least in part as a gigantic allegory of the physiological structures and movements inside a human head (in the tradition represented by Evreinov's *Theatre of the Soul*). Clearly the machines can be taken as representing different mental processes – memory, imagination and so on – and the various attempts that are made to correct malfunctioning as a kind of inner struggle, the mind in labour with itself. Sometimes the inner events are represented symbolically – Maurice mending a stripped-down machine, for instance – sometimes they express themselves in violent physical actions like the epileptic fit that frightens even Sadie, the witch.

But Maurice and Sadie have too much distinctive life of their own to be written down simply as symbols of opposing principles in the mind. They seem to have that function, male/female, negative/positive, and at times they fuse into the group mind which Williams says he was concerned to explore in the play,[1] but they also give an impression of being separate beings with separate areas of experience (Sadie reveals at the end, for instance, that she has already experienced the operation Perowne is about to undergo) and they have real, changing, complex relationships with one another.

By the time the trepanning scene is reached the action has been widely opened up to different interpretations. The mystical note has become much stronger. Sadie promises Perowne not just relief from his afflictions, his 'overloaded' state but a positive ecstasy, a totally new kind of non-verbal communication with non-human sources of power, a direct line through to the 'unfrequented frequency' which seems to have been her goal from the start. The physiological and electrical imagery takes on a more overtly religious cast. Sadie tells Perowne that the trepanning operation will restore the Third Eye; she speaks of a lost paradise:

There really was a Lost Paradise dig? When the Deva Eye, the eye of

---

[1] See interview with Williams in *Gambit* 19 (for this and other comments of his mentioned here).

Shiva was open, in the days of the Cyclopean root race . . . and then man
fell into matter, and the Third Eye atrophied, leaving just the pineal gland
as witness. A Lost Paradise of Lost Brain Blood Volume. Lost again when
your fissures and fontanelles closed up at three. Lost again when your
cranial sutures ossified. Lost when you stood vertical. More and more
horrible adrenalin, the more upright you stood.'

After the trepanning, Perowne loses the power of ordinary speech:
he gropes for words – 'Above the . . . Above the . . .' and finally can
only express himself with a scream and a flood of non-human sounds,
represented in the text by hieroglyphs. From one point of view – and
no doubt it remains the dominant one – this gruesome climax is a way
of showing the conventional brain surgery which has been threatening
from the beginning of the play. From another, though, it is the climax
to an elaborate sexual ritual out of which the female principle has
emerged triumphant; what he is experiencing is an orgasm in the
brain, Sadie tells Perowne. And rising out of this and offering itself as
the deep underlying interpretation is a religious view of the ending as
the culmination of an esoteric rite in which Sadie is both suppliant –
'Lay it out for me', she begs Perowne when the psychic power starts
coming through – and the high priestess who brings the initiate into the
god's presence.

Heathcote Williams' skill in keeping all these interpretations open
and in drawing so many virtuoso effects from his esoteric material
makes one well understand Pinter's praise of him and the awards the
play collected in the year it came out.[1] He is one of those who seem
bound to leave his own mark (a fearsome one decidedly) on whatever
he touches.

In its prophetic intensity and savage rhetoric, *AC/DC* is a vastly
different play from the baroque comedy of Peter Barnes I began by
comparing it with. In mood and style it is at the opposite pole from
Orton's witty farces and Beckett's austere and delicate mystery plays.
And yet it is in its way a mystery play too and has crucial elements in
common with the plays I have been discussing, as they all have with
each other. All the playwrights I have been considering in this chapter
have great virtuosity of technique which they apply to the task of
looking into the depths of the psyche, confronting and exploring madness and its relation to ecstasy and enlightenment. Under pressure from
this drive they have opened out dramatic form in some remarkable

---

[1] In 1970 it was awarded the *Evening Standard* drama award and the George Devine
award.

ways, paradoxically through structures that are often nightmarishly constricting and claustrophobic. What next, is a question that in this area one is almost afraid to ask; perhaps that is why a 'seraphim's' theatre is a theatre we need to experience.

1. *Texts*

Beckett, S. B. (English Texts):
Waiting for Godot, New York 1954, London 1956, 1965 rev
All that Fall, 1957
Endgame, 1958. Also *Act without Words*
Krapp's Last Tape, 1959. Also *Embers*
Happy Days, New York 1961, London 1962
Play, 1964. Also *Cascando, Words and Music*
Come and Go, 1967
Eh Joe, 1967. Also *Act without Words* 2; Film
Joe Orton:
Entertaining Mr Sloane. In *New English Dramatists* 8, 1965
Loot, 1968
Crimes of Passion, 1967. *The Ruffian on the Stair; The Erpingham Camp*
What the Butler Saw, 1969
Funeral Games; The Good and Faithful Servant, 1970
Heathcote Williams:
The Local Stigmatic. In *Traverse Plays*, 1966
AC/DC, 1971

2. *Critical Writings*

R. Cohn (ed) *Casebook on Waiting for Godot*, New York, 1967
B. G. Chevigny (ed) *Twentieth Century Interpretations of Endgame*, Englewood Cliffs. N.J., 1969
Taylor, J. R. In his *The Second Wave*, 1960
Reid, A. *All I can manage, more than I could*. Dublin, 1968. Beckett's plays
Gambit nos 18 and 19. Special Double Issue on Heathcote Williams

X

Edward Bond

Bond's is the most thrilling and powerful of the new talents that have emerged in the English theatre during the last decade. He provides the most massive demonstration that a new theatre is forming round us, a theatre of acting out rather than analysis, a colloquial theatre that is also visionary and poetic. He constructs his plays poetically, around images: *Lear*, he says,[1] grew out of the image of the Gravedigger's Boy, and others have begun from phrases or sentences 'which seem to have some sort of curious atmosphere about them that one wants to explore and open up.' One such – 'I throw my mask into the sea' – was haunting him at the time that he said these things: it had come into his mind unbidden; he knew his next play must develop from it, without yet having seen quite how.

Bond is also a very conscious moralist and has much in common with the writers in epic mode I mentioned earlier, especially with Charles Wood. There is a similar fascination with Victorian subjects, a similar feeling for big, episodic forms and for broad, pantomime techniques. Linguistically, however, he stands apart. His isn't a Babylonish dialect but something much more convincing, that can sound natural even in the act of defining some darkly fantastic, gargantuan event like the cannibalism in *Early Morning* or the ritualistic blinding of Lear.

His language has a peculiarly flat, deadpan quality and a rather unexpected range. It can be wonderfully comical and winning: Florence Nightingale, for instance, wandering into Windsor Great

---

[1] In an interview, 'Drama and the Dialectics of Violence', in *Theatre Quarterly* 2, 1972. In his letter to me of 24 Oct 1972, however, Bond adds, 'There were several images. And it also grew from the inescapable emotional-intellectual problem of how you change a society. This is Lear's problem, just as it is Len's in *Saved*.'

Park to join the royal picnic, murmuring, 'Queen Victoria raped me. I never expected that to happen', or Gladstone, talking to Prince Arthur, 'Allow me t'introduce meself. I'm William Ewart Gladstone. You're wanted for war crimes', to which the answer is, 'Don't touch me. I've got Porton Plague'. In scenes like the last one, Bond gets the same sort of time blur that Wood aims at but with much less sense of strain. His style is always open to this sort of knockabout but he can move easily into plain statement with a kind of highly charged simplicity about it, as when Prince Albert explains the conspiracy against Victoria, 'Your mother's the first danger. We must stop her before she causes the wrong revolution. She should have been a prison governess. She's afraid of people. She thinks they're evil, she doesn't understand their energy. She suppresses it.' And he can produce rhetoric of some grandeur when the feeling requires it; in the scene, for instance when Arthur talks to the self that has died: 'I'm a limited person. I can't face another hungry child, a man with one leg, a running woman, an empty house. I don't go near rivers when the bridges are burned. They look like the bones of charred hippopotamuses.' Or Lear looking awestruck at the dead body of Fontanelle under the doctor's knife: 'She sleeps inside like a lion and a lamb and a child. The things are so beautiful. I am astonished. I have never seen anything so beautiful. If I had known she was so beautiful . . . Her body was made by the hand of a child, so sure and nothing unclean . . . If I had known this beauty and patience and care, how I would have loved her.'

It's the relation between this austere rhetoric and the coarse, gritty ground it grows out of that gives Bond's language so much of its special flavour. In his earliest plays the groundwork is almost everything. *The Pope's Wedding* might even be mistaken for a plain piece of faithful realism with its slow moving, day-to-day action and its choked dialect exchanges among the inarticulate teenagers who are its characters. Wesker doesn't seem too far off in scenes like this one between Scopey and the old hermit, Alen, for whom he and his wife have accepted a curious responsibility.

SCOPEY: In the war they reckon yoo was flashin' secrets a the jerries with a Woolworth's torch. Yoo couldn't even light a cigarette.
ALEN: Tobacco an' drink are Satan's whores.
SCOPEY: Yoo owd nut! I thought yoo 'ad them papers for keepin'. All yoo want 'em for's t' stare outside. Yoo owd fake!
ALEN: No.
SCOPEY: All day!

ALEN: Don't row at me!

SCOPEY: Don't yoo? Yoo're at that crack all day! Starin' out! It all goos on outside an' yoo just watch!

ALEN: I ont said I –

SCOPEY: Yoo're a fake! There's nothin' in this bloody shop!

ALEN: My little jobs –

SCOPEY: Jobs! Starin' out! Talk t' yourself. I 'eard! What for?

ALEN: No.

SCOPEY: What about? What yoo talk about? Nothin'!

ALEN: No. No.

SCOPEY: What about?

ALEN: Not my –

SCOPEY: Let's 'ear yoo! Goo on – talk! Drivel!

ALEN: Stop!

SCOPEY: Talk!

ALEN: She lied to –

SCOPEY: Liar!

ALEN: I sing sometime.

SCOPEY: Sing?

ALEN: Sometime.

SCOPEY: All right –

ALEN: No.

SCOPEY: Sing! What sort a singing? What sort a songs?

ALEN: Hymns.

SCOPEY: Sing a hymn.

ALEN: No.

SCOPEY: Sing it mate! Sing it. By chriss I'll rip this junk shop up if yoo don't sing!

But the sense of some terrible incident looming up gives this close, dry accumulation of detail a peculiar, un-Wesker-like force. There is a feeling of mystery. The questions Scopey presses on Alen are torment-ing; they may seem sadistic. But they are tormented too. We feel the frustration – partly caused by inarticulacy – of a mind groping to understand why things are as they are. Eventually something explodes and he murders the old man.

The handling of the murder is very distinctive. It happens between scenes: we're told nothing about it until the very end and yet we seem to be deeply involved in it from the moment Scopey is discovered sitting alone, seven or eight unopened tins of food on the table, listening in a long-held silence to the ribald insults and sounds of stones thrown by the gang outside the hut, receiving them, as it were. Somehow, it seems, he has deliberately put himself into Alen's place, is experiencing for him. Finally, still sitting in the same place, now with five hundred tins on the table, he tells Pat how he killed him, never why. The lack of any attempt at explanation makes a strange effect here. Partly, I think, it seems a little arbitrary and unsatisfactory – the technique is more tentative than in later plays – but partly too the bareness, the inarticulacy, the withholding of meaning creates a mysterious sense of meaning; a poetic dimension starts to take shape.

These are unexpected notes in a play which like all Bond has so far written asks in a way simply to be taken as moral fable. Moral passion is certainly a great driving force behind his writing. He is very close in some ways to the moralist playwrights in the Shavian tradition, to Osborne and even to Shaw himself. He has written moral fables (*Black Mass, Passion*) for specific occasions of social protest and in all his plays characters are apt to moralize and talk in parables. Like Shaw, he uses prefaces and pamphlets to drive home prophetic warnings, calling on us to turn from our violent ways before Judgement falls (in a mushroom cloud):

> 'I write about violence as naturally as Jane Austen wrote about manners. Violence shapes and obsesses our society, and if we do not stop being violent we have no future. People who do not want writers to write about violence want to stop them writing about us and our time. It would be immoral not to write about violence.'[1]

For Bond, like Shaw, unjust social arrangements are a root cause of the evils we suffer from: 'People with unjust social privileges have an obvious emotional interest in social morality'; 'Social morality is a form of suicide'. Even the style often has as here, a touch of Shavian aphorism and paradox. And he allies himself with Shaw by continually drawing attention to the social optimism of his plays; *Saved* is 'almost irresponsibly optimistic', and *Early Morning* is 'easily the most optimistic of my plays'. People *can* be changed, there *is* free will. In both plays, as also in *Lear* (much less equivocally than in *King Lear*) the movement is towards redemption. *Saved* ends with restorative acts: Len mends a chair, a great proof of his resilience in that grim context, as Bond remarks, and the outline of a family group dimly appears. *Early Morning* ends – grotesquely and beautifully – with the resurrection of the suffering character, Prince Arthur, the one who chose to be consumed rather than join in consuming his fellows. And

---

[1] Preface to *Lear*.

Lear dies in the act of working to undo the wall, symbol of all that he
ought not to have done.

To speak of the images through which Bond expresses his passion is
at once to feel his great distance from Shaw, however. Emotionally, he
is closer to Osborne and in fact there are some rather striking affinities
between them. Both put an un-Shavian emphasis on suffering, are
taken up with characters who have unusual capacity for feeling the
pain of others. Their phrases and ideas could often be interchangeable.
Osborne speaks of the pain of being alive and Bond talks in an
Osborne-like way of 'the mental shallowness and emotional glibness'
of 'well adjusted' people who succeed in avoiding despair at the cruelty
of life. 'I can't forgive God', Bond says. 'Are we not too poor to afford
God?' asks one of Osborne's characters. 'Lessons in feeling', Osborne's
phrase for his own plays, would be equally appropriate to Bond's.

There are similarities too in their feeling for metaphor. Osborne
believes in the responsiveness of English audiences to violent and poetic
metaphors and this is what he tries to give them. But here a gulf begins
to open up as wide as the gulf between Osborne and Shaw. In fact the
line from Shaw through Osborne to Bond could almost be taken as the
characteristic movement towards a more violent, more poetic theatre
which has been developing during the period. On Bond's stage metaphors are acted out in a stunningly direct way. His imagination for
'incidents' is one of the most impressive things in his art. He wants a
metaphor for what society does when it is 'heavy with aggression' and
he finds it in the horrific incident of some youths stoning a baby in its
pram for no reason that any one of them could possibly give. He looks
for a way of suggesting inner deadness – the feeling expressed by
Osborne's Archie – 'I'm dead behind the eyes, I'm dead, just like the
whole inert, shoddy lot out there' – and gets it in the form of a monstrous heaven where dead people picnic on each others' bones and
congratulate themselves on feeling no more pain.

Early Morning represents a great leap forward in technique. The
focus is sharper than in *Saved*, where the stoning incident is rather too
overwhelming, thrusting itself forward as a rather too believable and
very particular event. No danger of that happening, one would think,
in a play which renders the Victorian scene in such fantastic terms as
Early Morning. It's a strange dream we're in, where Victoria rampages
like the prison governess Prince Albert says she ought to have been,
enjoying in her spare moments an affair with Florence Nightingale
disguised as John Brown (a hilariously funny episode, this); where

Disraeli and Gladstone are almost indistinguishable power-mad gang-sters and at the centre is a mythical character, Prince Arthur, who drags round with him his Siamese twin attachment even after it has died and turned to a skeleton.

The danger here, one might suppose, would be of our refusing to take the action in real terms at all or possibly of our trying to turn it into a rather rigid allegory. In fact for some of the first audiences (in-cluding, presumably, the Lord Chamberlain, who banned the play) it came over in astonishingly real terms as a tremendous libel on eminent Victorians. This seems a great testimony to Bond's skill in clothing his fantasies with flesh. His ability to keep so many lines open, juggle with so many different sorts of reality is what makes *Early Morning* such a startling achievement, coming after one-level plays like *The Pope's Wedding* and *Saved*.

As we watch the play we will surely be reading the symbolism and probably interpreting images like the Siamese twin very much as Bond does – it's the 'acceptable, socialized version' of Prince Arthur he says. And yet although the parabolic element is strong, the sense of it all somehow *really* happening is wonderfully preserved. We recognize ordinary human feelings, commonplace situations behind the fantastic forms and this can be both very funny and very disturbing. The trial for murder of Len and Joyce is a lively instance. Patiently they explain how they came to kill this man, how natural it all was: there they were in the cinema queue waiting to see 'Policeman in Black Nylons', with Len getting hungrier all the time, and more irritated:

LEN: We'd bin stood there 'ours, and me guts starts t' rumble. 'Owever, I don't let on. But then she 'as t' say 'I ain arf pecky'.

JOYCE: Thass yer sense a consideration, ain it! I'd 'eard your gut.

LEN: I 'ad an empty gut many times, girl. That don't mean I'm on the danger list. But when you starts rabbitin' about bein' pecky I ——

JOYCE: Now don't blame me, love.

LEN: Truth ain' blame, love.

JOYCE: Then wass all this she says for? Anyway the 'ole queue turned round for a good look! . . .

LEN: Look, we're stood outside the State for 'Buried Alive on 'Ampstead 'Eath' – right? – me gut rumbles and there's this sly bleeder stood up front with 'is 'ead in 'is paper – right? – so I grabs 'is ears, jerks 'im back by the 'ead, she karati-chops 'im cross the front of 'is throat with the use of 'er 'andbag, and down 'e goes like a sack with a 'ole both ends – right? – an she starts stabbin' 'im with 'er stilletos, in twist out, like they show yer in the army, though she ain' bin in but with 'er it comes natural, an 'e says 'Ere, thass my place', an then 'e don't say no more, juss bubbles like a nipper, and I take this 'andy man-'ole cover out the gutter an drops it on 'is 'ead – right? – an the queue moves up one.

So of course they had to make a meal of him, politely shared with the queue – 'Yer can't nosh and not offer round, can yer?' 'Who cut him up?' says Victoria, practically. No doubt about this being a dream, but the lineaments of the real show through it sharp and clear: the irritation, the hunger, the pressure of the queue situation (overcrowding is one of Bond's nightmares). The scene offers a lead in to the equally macabre but more adroitly rationalized killings in the political area where Disraeli and Gladstone function; they are engaged in a deadly tug-of-war which is eventually expressed – in characteristic Bond style – as literally that, a marvellous image to draw the first 'earthly' part of the play to its close – Arthur and Victoria lining up their sides on the edge of Beachy Head, pulling on the rope to shouts of 'To the future! The dawn! Freedom! Justice!' and all crashing to their death, one side over the cliff top as Victoria's men artfully leave go of the rope, the rest going down with the cliff fall.

The move from this into the concentration camp heaven of the second part is brilliantly done. A new ghostliness comes in, rather a stunning distinction to bring off in a context already so fantastic. We are drawn into Arthur's panic as he realizes that he hasn't after all shaken off the violent creatures who seemed to destroy themselves in the tug-of-war, that he and they still have a strange kind of life. What kind of life it is Bond indicates with great precision. The broken dummies who represent the dead, the dumb ghosts in black cowls who rise up, 'joined together like a row of paper cut-out men': these are clearly elements in an altogether inner landscape, a landscape which repeats in a hysterical and obsessive way dominant features of past experience. We get a sense of looking through the mirror into the monstrous meaning of things.

The seemingly total absence of freedom is a terrifying aspect of this mirror world. One of the worst moments in the play is the rising up of the Siamese twin who had been gradually shrinking to nothing, 'a skull and a few bones, like a ragged epaulette, on Arthur's shoulder'. Now he is back to where he was at the start; the scene ends with him fastening himself again to Arthur, who is just sufficiently conscious to groan, 'No. No. No. No. No.'

On this Lear-like note (there are many signs of *Lear* forming in this play) 'heaven' begins. Bond provides an explanation for it in the preface to *Lear* where he talks of people getting fixed in mental patterns: 'It is as if they had created in themselves a desolate, inhospitable landscape in which they had to live out their emotional and spiritual lives. ... By calling the unjust world good they recreate it in themselves and are condemned to live in it.' It's easy enough to imagine this idea taking shape in a dramatic allegory but who other than Bond could have imagined it in such a grotesque and haunting shape as the heaven of *Early Morning*? The relation between his prefaces and the action of his plays is always clear, but there are such fantastic leaps of imagination between one process and the other that the plays seem to exist in a dimension entirely their own.

In heaven, Queen Victoria, Disraeli and the rest, are joined at a deep level with Len and Joyce. 'Eat or be eaten' is the rule they have agreed to live by: the cannibalism of the queue episode has become the universal way of life. Bond gets an enormous extension of control in this play by the surrealistic pantomime techniques he uses (significantly, good effects can be got by directorial inventions like having Joyce played as a pantomime dame by a male actor in drag).[1] These techniques from a children's entertainment – as English pantomime now is – are a deeply appropriate means of expressing a vision which has so much of a child's directness in it. This horrific, funny and upsetting world in which 'angry, gleeful ghosts' chase each other for their next meal is like a world of Blake's crossed with Lewis Carroll's, a child's view of a baffling and terrifying grown-up life. When Queen Victoria rushes on shouting that it's time for yet another trial – 'But you're very late – we were here long ago. Let's start the Trial straight away!' – one almost expects to see the White Rabbit pop up nervously, apologizing for being late, or Victoria turning into the Red Queen bellowing, 'Off with his head!'

Heads do come off very easily in *Early Morning*. Arthur loses his, or rather, one should say, his head loses the rest of him. He becomes a talking head, in fact, for part of the time grotesquely concealed under Florence Nightingale's skirts, in her effort to save him from being totally eaten. This scene shows Bond's art at its most brilliant and subtle: there are astoundingly delicate shifts of mood in it. He invites us to enjoy the ludicrous aspects – Florence whipping the head in and out of her skirts, Queen Victoria stalking the stage, complaining 'You don't just lose a head'. And yet – against all possible expectation, in defiance

---

[1] As in a recent production by the Apollo Society, St Catherine's College, at the Oxford Playhouse.

of all known dramatic laws almost – a poignant love scene gently comes into being, a painful, tender eroticism develops.

'There are black lines round your eyes and your mouth. Your skin looks like cloth', she says to the dummy head she is holding in her hand. We laugh, perhaps, but it's a different laughter from the unfeeling kind Victoria sets up whenever she talks about the head. A sense of human sadness comes through the grotesquerie; it is a bitter separation of two people who might have been able to love each other. Still stranger, there is too a sense of human achievement; in this context it *is* an achievement to feel, however faintly, stirrings of love and desire. We understand what the voice of Arthur means when it says to her, 'I'm like a fire in the sea or the sun underground. I'm alive.' When he begs her to kiss him, we don't laugh; we might even feel inclined to wish that she could and would. If she actually did, of course there could be trouble: it's a measure of Bond's control that he steers so carefully clear of unintended laughs at sensitive points like these. Florence is just hesitatingly raising the head to her mouth when Victoria's voice is heard, still clamouring, 'You don't just lose a head' and the spell is broken, 'normality' returns. Similarly the resurrection of Arthur at the end is kept well within the pantomime mode though it creates in production an extraordinarily touching and serious effect. As they all sit round his coffin enjoying their gruesome picnic, the lid comes off and Arthur steps out, unseen by any one, even Florence who is crying for him. The play ends as he rises into the air and hangs suspended over them while they obliviously get on with their eating and Victoria complacently reflects, 'There's no dirt in heaven. There's only peace and happiness, law and order, consent and co-operation. My life's work has borne fruit. It's settled.' Against all the odds, the dominant effect produced by this extraordinary tableau was relief and a curious lightening of the spirit. We want Victoria's words contradicted and it's very satisfactory when they are – in a fantastic way by Arthur's apotheosis, in a human way by Florence's tears.

Early Morning occasionally threatens to become repetitive. But the rush of invention in it is enormously exhilarating. In the next play, *Narrow Road to the Deep North*, similar techniques are applied with more austerity: perhaps the Japanese element – it is set in Japan 'about the seventeenth, eighteenth or nineteenth centuries' – disciplined the Gothic exuberance of *Early Morning*. The control is impressive (though one rather misses the wild zest of the earlier play) and certainly needed, for the atrocities here – the slaughter of the five children, Kiro's self-

disembowelling – could easily become oppressive; they are more
'real', more easily imagined happening than the events of *Early
Morning*. It's a painfully believable moment, for instance, when
Georgina tries to save the children from the soldiers, calling them to
their prayers as though nothing threatened: 'It's nothing, children.
The men are playing. On your knees. Eyes shut. Hands together.'
But the horror is kept well in control by sharp distancing techniques,
Noh-like devices such as the identical, paper cut-out look of the five
children – their bodies were represented by Japanese rag dolls – and the
absolute silence of the ritualistic disembowelling sequence. Attention
isn't allowed to settle on physical torment but is directed to what the
play is really about, different attempts to deal with the horror of life –
by acquiring power or by withdrawing like Basho in search of enlightenment. *Narrow Road to the Deep North* is a particularly difficult[1]
play to appreciate without aid of production partly because the style
is so especially dry and laconic and so much of the effect depends on
these very austere visual stylizations.

   This ability of his to create compelling and deeply meaningful stage
pictures is an enormous help to Bond in his latest and richest play so far,
Lear. For a start it makes it easier for him to cut free of Shakespeare.
Bond's scene is so much his own that it immediately takes our full
attention; we drop the comparing and measuring we must surely have
started out with (it would be hard to come to a play called *Lear*
leaving Shakespeare quite behind). There's a strange dream-like in-
consistency in the costumes: Lear and his daughters in flowing robes
(Fontanelle a dreadful schoolgirl with hair in bunches); the guards and
soldiers in modern uniform with guns and hints of concentration
camp equipment. A common-place business-like episode is taking
place, it seems. Lear is behaving like a works supervisor, or, as Bill
Gaskill suggested,[2] he and his daughters are like the Royal Family visiting a shipyard, carrying umbrellas. He enquires into the trouble holding up the building of the off-stage wall; a man has been accidentally
killed by someone dropping an axe. Suddenly the action lurches into
nightmare. Lear calls the act sabotage, sentences the offender to death,
not for manslaughter but for holding up the work; when his daughters

---

[1] For Jane Howell, actress and producer of Bond's plays, *Narrow Road to the Deep North*
was 'one of the easiest plays, easy and most difficult, because it's very simple and therefore
very difficult and when you get it, it's very easy'. See discussion with Bond in *Gambit* 17.
[2] This and other comments on the Court production are recorded in Production
Casebook no 5 (Lear). *Theatre Quarterly* 2, 1972.

object and countermand the order to the firing squad he takes a gun and shoots the man himself. As Bodice and Fontanelle express it, he has gone mad.

So the wall imposes itself from the first moment as a dark shadow over the action, the central symbol, and this at once takes us away from the familiar Shakespearean ambience and lures us to think in Bond's terms. We remain constantly aware of it but don't see it until the last scene when a tremendous physical shock is got by having it suddenly appear, filling the whole stage – horizontally, as Bond wanted it – looking like a cross between the Pyramids and the Great Wall of China;[1] a great earthy monster threatening us as well as the characters. The effect brings home the terrible, sad irony of people in the play continuing to see this dreadful wall as their defence and protection. 'Pull it down', says Lear at the end. 'We'd be attacked by our enemies', says Cordelia. After all she has suffered because of the wall she still believes that good will be served by maintaining it.

The inconsistencies, or anachronisms, I first spoke of run through the action and are a vital part of the technique;[2] 'desperate facts' Bond calls them. 'They are for the horrible moments in a dream when you know it's a dream but can't help being afraid.' Obvious signposts to time and place go; place names, topical allusions; even some of the Shakespearean place marks are taken out. Lear and Cordelia remain, but the rest change name in a way that usually points to something primitive or fundamental about them. The Gravedigger's Boy, like his Shakespearean counterpart, the Fool, has no name; the Duke of Cornwall becomes the Duke of North, a curiously unfinished sound suggesting the undeveloped being he is; Regan's new name, Fontanelle, makes a similar effect by its worrying association with a tender, incomplete and easily damaged part of the human body.

It would be possible to take *Early Morning* as essentially a satire on Victorian history, though the kaleidoscopic technique includes plenty of pointers to our time, lines like Arthur's: 'Don't touch me. I've got Porton Plague.' That mistake couldn't be made about *Lear*. The action is kept astoundingly open, with lines leading back to antiquity (the Wall, the Sophoclean scenes at the end) to Tolstoy, to Shakespeare, and insistently and sadly to our own time.

If we can never for a moment forget that it's our time, this is very largely because of the idiom: the slang, the rough colloquialisms and

[1] An early earthwork was how they saw it at the Court.
[2] Which the cast at the Court found a major problem.

above all the humour. The sombre incidents are continually being
checked and measured against humour; the tragic flights lead into
roughly down-to-earth passages, as in the first prison scene when we
move straight from Lear's communion with his ghosts – 'The animal
will slip out of its cage, and lie in the fields, and run by the river, and
groom itself in the sun, and sleep in its hole from night to morning' –
into a brisk guard-changing inspection routine in a gruff Fred Karno
style, the new guard playing stooge, forgetting to check under the
mattress and the old hand putting him right:

SOLDIER H: Watch careful and take it all in.
SOLDIER I: Corp.
SOLDIER H: Under the sack an' in the corners. . . . Can yer remember it?
Five times a day. Yer skip the personal.
SOLDIER I: Corp.

Even the cruelty is in a way humanized by the humour. The
elements are very skilfully balanced. 'Yer wan' 'im done in a fancy
way?' the soldier given the job of disabling Warrington asks Bodice.
'Fancy' turns out to be a very nasty word indeed; the victim who has
already had his tongue cut out is finished off by having his ears punc-
tured by Bodice's knitting needles. But the word gets its laugh, as
other bits of humorous understatement do that accompany the horrific
events. Laughter is our way into the horror, our interim response to
behaviour that seems to defeat understanding and reason. Fontanelle,
for instance jumping about the stage with glee while Warrington is
being tortured, squealing like a schoolgirl: 'Throw him up and drop
him. I want to hear him drop. . . . I've always wanted to sit on a man's
lungs. Let me. Give me his lungs.' We laugh again when the soldier is
thrown into total confusion by Bodice suddenly switching round and
ordering him to beg for the victim's life. 'Is? (Aside) What a pair!
O spare 'im, mum.'

There's a kind of relief in it this time – at being allowed to feel
human again. And yet it doesn't obliterate the effect of the incidents:
these, as Bond says, always 'speak for him'. The Grand Guignol
distances, but not so as to let us forget that what Bond is showing us
has been 'real' in our time; this is really a much cleaned up version of
the obscene events that took place in the Nazi concentration camps.

It's by that route that Bond came to Shakespeare; not that he set out
to measure himself against him, but that in these areas of feeling all
lines run to that point. He has said that he wanted to rewrite *King*

Lear 'so that we now have to use the play for ourselves, for our society, for our time, for our problems . . .'[1] and also that he needed to clear Lear out of his path before he could move on to his next thing, a very interesting statement that makes one more than ever curious about what that next work will be.

It's a measure of Bond's power that he can impose his own vision and his own terms on the great, formidable material and take us away from Shakespeare in the act of using him. And it's a measure of his subtlety that he can risk venturing as close as he occasionally does to the Shakespearean version, most audaciously perhaps, in the scene of the autopsy. Here he takes up[2] the Shakespearean metaphor – 'Then let them anatomize Regan; see what breeds about her heart. Is there any cause in nature that makes these hard hearts?' and characteristically projects it in a fantastic incident. The body of Fontanelle is placed on a table in the prison camp for the doctor – who is also a prisoner – to 'anatomize'. He does it in cool scientific terms, appropriate to the subject but hideous in the context with the dead woman's father standing by. The horror of the scene when Lear put his hands into Fontanelle and drew out her entrails is about as far in the direction of Grand Guignol as Bond has gone. It was a 'big gesture', as Bill Gaskill put it and obviously a risky one: it could so easily have been either ludicrous, or overpoweringly offensive. But it worked. There was no laughter of the wrong kind and indeed, unlike earlier episodes in the vein of horror, this one drew no laughter at all. We were too deep in feeling, too affected by the solemn and complex movement of events. Lear looking down at Fontanelle, gasping out incoherent questions, was felt to be moving into a new dimension of the spirit, where the doctor, who can't get beyond the incoherence, has no hope of following:

> LEAR: Who was she?
> FOURTH PRISONER: Your daughter.
> LEAR: Did I have a daughter?
> FOURTH PRISONER: Yes, it's on her chart. That's her stomach and the liver underneath. I'm just making a few incisions to satisfy the authorities.
> LEAR: Is that my daughter . . . ? (Points.) That's . . . ?
> FOURTH PRISONER: The stomach.
> LEAR (points): That?

---

[1] Discussion in *Gambit* 17.

[2] Bond says (in the letter quoted earlier) that he didn't consciously have Shakespeare's lines in mind at this point. He was thinking, rather, of Rembrandt's autopsies.

FOURTH PRISONER: The lungs. You can see how she died. The bullet
track goes through the lady's lungs.

LEAR: But where is the ... She was cruel and angry and hard ...

FOURTH PRISONER (points): The womb.

LEAR: So much blood and bits and pieces packed in with all that care.
Where is the ... where ... ?

FOURTH PRISONER: What is the question?

LEAR: Where is the beast? The blood is as still as a lake. Where ... ?
Where ... ?

FOURTH PRISONER (to *Soldier O*): What's the man asking? (No response.)

The echoes of Shakespeare called up here enriched without undermining – a remarkable achievement. It was as though at this level of
suffering and imagination all Lears must inevitably echo and pick up
from each other's words.

Some of Bond's divergences from the Shakespearean model make
his play seem the more pessimistic of the two. He calls himself a pes-
simist by experience and an optimist by nature (another of his Shavian-
sounding phrases) and it is the pessimism of experience that forces him
to see Cordelia – not in his play Lear's natural daughter – as doomed to
go the same way as the 'wicked' daughters, once she starts to use force
to combat them. This is the great central theme of the play, the idea of
violence as a vicious circle of chain reactions; the chain gang of
prisoners, where tyrants end up shackled to their victims, Fontanelle
fastened on to Lear, is the fierce visual image that expresses it. Bond
can't believe that Shakespeare's Cordelia would have been able to go on
using her power justly if she had kept it. His own Cordelia begins as a
sympathetic, affectionate character who contrasts favourably with
Lear's true daughters in her willingness to support her husband's
charitable acts.[1] But when their violence destroys her happiness and she
reacts by taking up arms she goes to meet them and becomes like them.
It is almost the bitterest irony of the play that she – not the 'bad'
daughters – is the one who causes Lear's blinding. This is indeed the
pessimism of experience. (It was also another feature of the play situation
that the Royal Court company found particularly difficult to deal
with.)

In his handling of the blinding, however, Bond's optimism asserts
itself. The change he makes here – transferring Gloucester's blindness
to Lear – allows him to push the Shakespearean action to the Sophoclean

---

[1] She doesn't initiate them and Bond points out that she never actually likes Lear, a
subtle point that was delicately but firmly made in the Court production.

end he has designed for it. Blindness becomes an unequivocal symbol of insight. Just before he was mutilated, Lear had prophesied – 'I must become a child, hungry and stripped and shivering in blood. I must open my eyes and see!' This is what happens. Slowly, clumsily, he gropes towards first an Oedipean and then a full Tiresias-like vision, which releases him in the end from the circle of destruction. Tolstoyan notes begin to sound. We move back to the idyllic pastoral scene, where Lear was sheltered by Cordelia and the Gravedigger's Boy back to the well, the Russian-looking[1] house and its associations with charity, fruitfulness and simple contentment.

Dark associations hang about this landscape still. The violence that happened here was in a way the most disturbing in the whole play, involving as it did characters we were allowed to get closer to in ordinary human terms. The fantastic Grand Guignol note was missing from the killing of the Gravedigger's Boy and the terrible rape of his pregnant wife, although Bond takes care – this is important for the mysterious effect of the ghostly scene at the close – to fix the horror in our memories with a theatrically flamboyant sound, the frantic squealing of the pigs, mixing in a ghastly way with the woman's screams.

It is these traumatic memories which are exorcised by blind Lear. Like Oedipus at Colonus, he becomes a sacred figure, both receiving and extending care, and attracting pilgrims to the place where he is. We are right out of Shakespeare and into Sophocles in the scene where the blind old man leaning on his stick relates to a devout chorus of villagers the parable of the bird in the cage; 'just as the bird had the man's voice, the man now had the bird's pain'. Our faith in Bond's optimism at this point is kept up, I think, by the reminders of human frailty behind the rhetorical eloquence; shortly after this magisterial passage, Lear is shown irritated and bewildered when Cordelia's men come to arrest the deserters who are sheltering with him: 'What have I been telling you? There's nothing to learn here! I'm a fool!' And later, in the scene of confrontation with Cordelia, Bond isn't afraid to give her a strong and up to a point convincing case: we are able to appreciate – and possibly even to some extent share – her feeling that it is Lear not she, who is being unreasonable: 'a stupid old man is speaking against her when she has changed society', as Bill Gaskill imagined her thinking. What tells against her are not Lear's arguments but his state – his blindness (inflicted in Cordelia's name as a political necessity)

---

[1] An effect aimed at and well brought out in the Court production.

and his mature generosity of spirit that makes him stronger than her, an unstoppable voice, 'untouchable', as Bond puts it, like Tolstoy. It's because of this complexity, this recognition of shades of light and darkness in human character that Bond is able to bring off so triumphantly – as it seemed to me he did in the Court production – the stunningly simple, parabolic ending (obviously fraught with theatrical hazards) when Lear in his Tolstoyan tunic crawls up the wall to dig it up with a peasant's spade and is shot and dies there.

Although it seemed to me this worked as Bond intended and one was able to accept the heroic gesture because of all that had gone before, there were moments in the humanly optimistic parts of the play where the didactic intention seemed rather too pushed, and one sometimes became uncomfortably aware of a flat, thematic quality in the characterization (of Thomas and Susan, for instance).

As so often with Bond, it's in the most grotesque areas of the play that his technique is seen at its most boldly inventive and – strange paradox – the mystery of human feeling is given most delicate expression. In this area the Fool or Ghost is a key figure; finally his relationship with Lear comes to seem the most interesting in the play.

Around him the action is kept exquisitely balanced between moral fable and mystery. From the start there is a fairy-tale quality about him; he is a man without a name, the Gravedigger's Boy who puts dead bodies into the ground and draws them up from deep wells. After his own death, when he reappears as the Ghost, a bizarre visual poetry begins to operate very strongly. It's pathetic and terrifying to see the gentle Boy dwindling and wasting until he has become one of the walking Auschwitz skeletons who haunt Bond's stage: at the end he is hardly more than a death's head, with a face 'like a seashell', Bond says, and eyes full of terror. Only Lear sees him and clearly in a way he represents something in Lear, something which has to die before he can find his true strength. This happens when he is able to tell Thomas and Susan that he has been 'lucky' in their affection, a totally new concept of good fortune for this passionate and violent man, and that his phase of withdrawal is over: 'Now I have only one more wish – to live till I'm much older and become as cunning as the fox, who knows how to live. Then I could teach you.' Then the old black memories well up again; the frenzied sound of pigs' squealing is heard and the Ghost stumbles in, covered with blood, to die finally and leave Lear free.

But although he has to be seen partly as an inner thing, he is also rather frighteningly separate and independent. He often seems cut off from Lear's mind, as when they are in their first prison together and Lear begins to develop his vision of the animal in the cage: 'There's an animal in a cage, I must let it out or the earth will be destroyed.' 'What animal is it?', says the Boy, 'I've never seen it.' And sometimes a sinister, even diabolical note creeps in. 'Ghosts are always nasty and corrupt', Bond says, and this is the impression we get when, for instance, the Ghost says to Lear after the blinding, – 'I can stay with you now you need me', or still worse, when the illusory peace of the Tolstoyan idyll is threatened again by the soldiers and he gives Lear dreadful advice: 'That's the world you have to learn to live in. Learn it! Let me poison the well.' This last scene came over in the Court production as one of the most unexpected and disturbing moments in the play, the moment when, in Shakespearean terms, the Fool turned into Edmund.

And yet the Ghost is pathetic and childlike too, Lear's 'boy' whom he comforts and who comforts him. And he has too – it's such distinctions that deepen one's trust in Bond – a separate existence which he never quite loses as the husband of Cordelia, an identity which is movingly recalled in his final scene.

Some of these different aspects are brought out in two scenes which seem to me to show Bond's art at its most thrilling and poetic. In the first, the prison scene (Act 2, Scene 2), the childlike aspect is dominant. The Ghost offers to call up Lear's children. He whistles softly and on come Bodice and Fontanelle, looking like the women who had sat in judgement on their father in the previous scene but talking and behaving like the children they once were. That whistling summons was a breathtaking moment in the Court production. It seemed to take us into the uncanny world of some ancient ballad; the mood was remote and dreamy and yet the childish memories they acted out were so concrete and vivid: Bodice neglected by her father, trying to struggle into her mother's dress; Fontanelle terrified by the sound of the death bell.

FONTANELLE: Do my hair. . . . Father comes home today.
BODICE: I must put on my dress.
FONTANELLE: O you dress so quickly! Do my hair. (Bodice attends to her hair.)
LEAR: My daughters!
BODICE: They're burying soldiers in the churchyard. Father's brought the coffins on carts. The palls are covered with snow. Look, one of the horses is licking its hoof.

FONTANELLE: This morning I lay in bed and watched the wind pulling the curtains. Pull, pull, pull. . . . Now I can hear that terrible bell.

LEAR: Fontanelle, you're such a little girl. (He sits on the stone shelf.) Sit here.

FONTANELLE: No.

LEAR: On my knees. (He sits her on his knees.) Such a little girl.

BODICE (listening): Father! I must get dressed! I must get dressed! (She struggles frantically into her dress.)

LEAR: That's better.

FONTANELLE: Listen to the bell and the wind.

LEAR: (wets his finger and holds it in the air): Which way is it blowing? (Bodice gets into the dress and comes down to him. He points at her.) Take it off!

BODICE: No.

LEAR: Take it off. Your mother's dress!

BODICE: She's dead! She gave it to me!

LEAR (pointing): Take it off!

BODICE: No!

LEAR: Yes, or you will always wear it! (He pulls her to him.) Bodice! My poor child, you might as well have worn her shroud.

This sad tableau – father and three frightened children – was one of the most memorable in the play: it recalled, as so much in Bond's work does, the visionary scenes of Blake: Job and his daughters were in the background here. The sense of Lear arriving, too late, at partial understanding, made it very poignant. 'Lear didn't have to destroy his daughters' innocence' Bond says, 'He does so only because he doesn't understand his situation. When he does understand he leaves Thomas and Susan unharmed.'

That is all painfully comprehensible in ordinary human terms. Other aspects of his relation with the Fool take us into more mysterious territory. Here, Bond suggests, Lear had no choice. 'I think he had to destroy the innocent boy. Some things were lost to us long ago as a species but we all seem to have to live through part of the act of losing them'. In the final meeting of Lear and Cordelia I think we do feel that some deep, primeval event is taking place. It's such a long time since the Ghost looked human, he is so nearly a walking death's head, a medieval Death, that we inevitably interpret what happens to him in symbolic terms. And we have too this strong, uneasy impression of the diabolical rising up in him. So when he collapses, I suppose our predominant feeling is relief:

GHOST: The pigs! I'm torn! They gored me! Help me, help me! I'll die!

LEAR (holds him): I can't!

GHOST: Lear! Hold me!

LEAR: No, too late! It's far too late! You were killed long ago! You must die! I love you, I'll always remember you, but I can't help you. Die, for your own sake die.

GHOST: O Lear, I am dead!

The Ghost's head falls back. It is dead. It drops at Lear's feet. The calls and pig squeals stop.

LEAR: I see my life, a black tree by a pool. The branches are covered with tears. The tears are shining with light. The wind blows the tears in the sky. And my tears fall down on me.

It's an extraordinarily complex form of relief, I think. Partly it's on behalf of Lear; now at last he can be free of this being who exudes terror and darkness. Partly it's relief at our own escape – it may even be as Bond suggests, that we have been imaginatively involved through the Boy in some ancient trauma of the race; at any rate we must have felt him a heavy and painful weight on our imagination. And mixed with all this is pity and relief for the Ghost himself. 'Die, for your own sake die!' we say with Lear.

The symbolism is immensely powerful here and yet Bond finds room for small, human, one might almost say Chekhovian, touches: Lear asking Cordelia, 'You've been to the house? Did it upset you?'; the Ghost pathetically urging Lear, 'Tell her I'm here. Make her talk about me'. Such scenes make very clear what one means by speaking of Bond's art as poetic. It is a true dramatic poetry of structure and dynamic imagery in which brilliantly imagined visual elements play an essential part.

It seems appropriate to end my discussion of recent drama on this high note of audacious innovation by a playwright who seems almost certain to be foremost among the shapers of the modern English tradition.

1. *Texts*
   Saved, 1966
   Early Morning, 1968
   Narrow Road to the Deep North, 1968
   Passion. In *Plays and Players*, June 1971
   The Pope's Wedding, 1971. Also contains Sharpeville Sequence
   Lear, 1972

2. *Interviews with Bond*
   In: *Gambit* no 17

Theatre Quarterly 2, 1972. Also in this issue of *Theatre Quarterly*, production
   Casebook no 5: *Lear*

General Critical Studies of the Period
Armstrong, W. A. (ed) *Experimental Drama*, 1963
Brook, P. *The Empty Space*, 1968
Brown, J. R. and B. Harris (eds) *Contemporary Theatre*, 1962
Brown, J. R. (ed) *Modern British Dramatists.* Twentieth Century Views, 1968
Cole, T. (ed) *Playwrights on Playwriting*, 1960
Esslin, M. *The Theatre of the Absurd*, 1961
Findlater, R. *Banned!* 1967

Kitchin, L.:
Mid-Century Drama, 1960
Drama in the Sixties, 1966
Marowitz, C. et al (eds) *The Encore Reader*, 1965
Marowitz, C. and S. Trussler (eds) *Theatre at Work*, 1967

Taylor, J. R.:
Anger and After, 1969 rev.
The Rise and Fall of the Well Made Play, 1967
The Second Wave; British Drama for the Seventies, 1971
Tynan, K. *Curtains*, 1961

Wager, W. (ed):
The Playwrights Speak, 1969
Twentieth Century. 169, 1961. Theatre issue
Tulane Drama Review. 11, 1966. (T34) British Theatre issue
Waterhouse, K. and W. Hall (eds) *Writers' Theatre*, 1967.

Reference
Who's Who in the Theatre. Fifteenth Edn, 1972
Wilson, S. *The Theatre in the Fifties.* Lib Assoc, 1963.

Theatres

Unless otherwise stated, theatres referred to in the text are situated in London. Addresses for the most important of those mentioned are given below:

Aldwych	Aldwych, WC2
Old Vic	Waterloo Road, SE1
(Young Vic at The Cut, SE1)	
Mermaid	Puddle Dock, Blackfriars, EC4
Round House	Chalk Farm Road, NW1
Royal Court	Sloane Square, SW1
(Theatre Upstairs in same building)	
Stratford Theatre Royal	Salway Road, E15

The National Theatre is being built on the South Bank, downstream of Waterloo Bridge, opposite Somerset House.

Index

Index